安藤忠雄の建築 1

Tadao

TADAO ANDO 1 Houses & Housing

First published in Japan on March 30, 2007
Fifth published on July 30, 2019

TOTO Publishing (TOTO LTD.)

TOTO Nogizaka Bldg., 2F, 1-24-3
Minami-Aoyama, Minato-ku, Tokyo 107-0062, Japan
[Sales] Telephone : +81-3-3402-7138
Facsimile : +81-3-3402-7187
[Editorial] Telephone : +81-3-3497-1010
URL:https://jp.toto.com/publishing

Author : Tadao Ando
Publisher : Takeshi Ito
Book Designer: Tetsuya Ohta
Printing Direction : Noboru Takayanagi
Printer : Tokyo Inshokan Printing Co., LTD.

ISBN978-4-88706-277-1

Ando 1

Houses & Housing

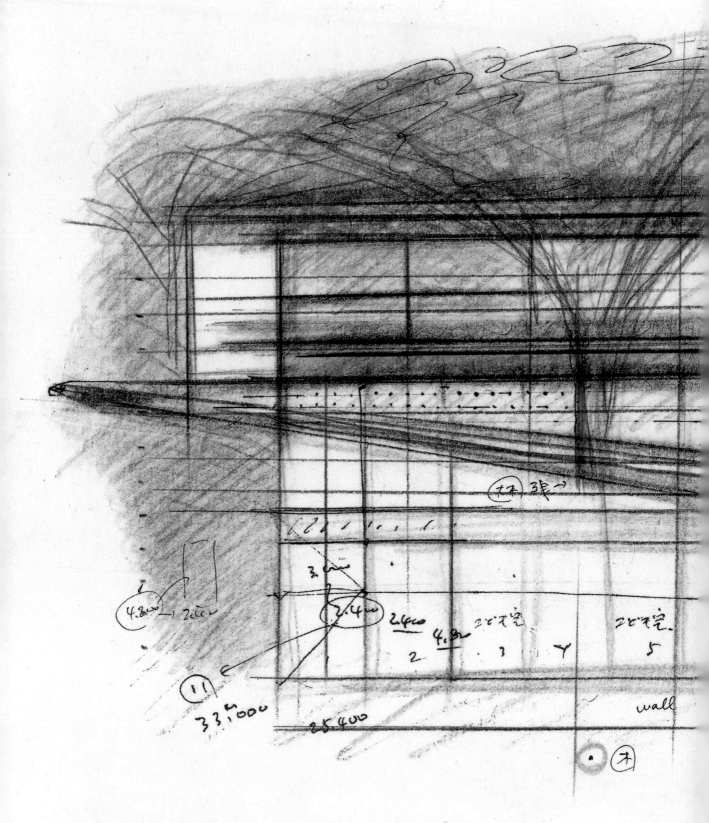

Koshino House

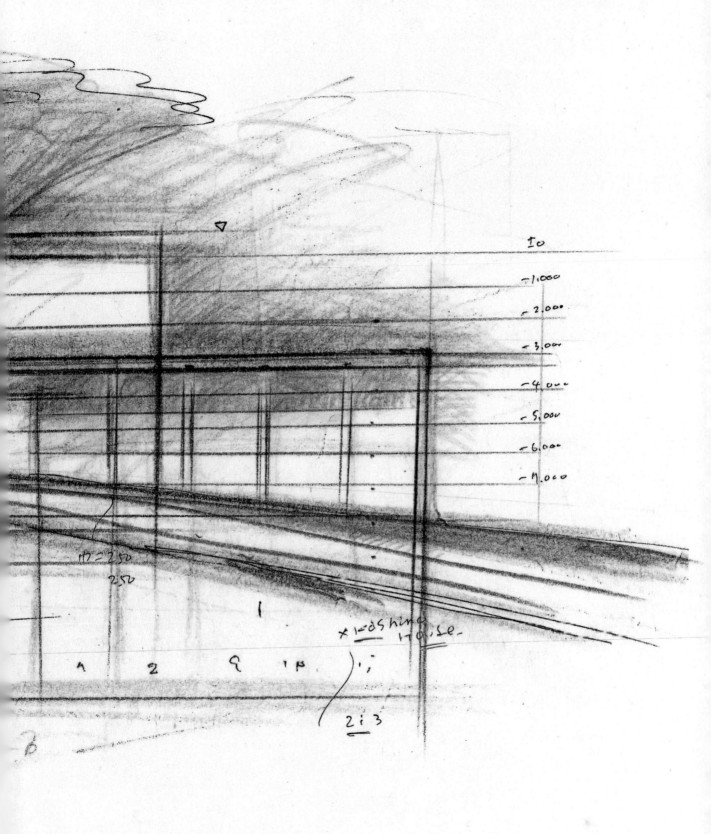

Rokko Housing

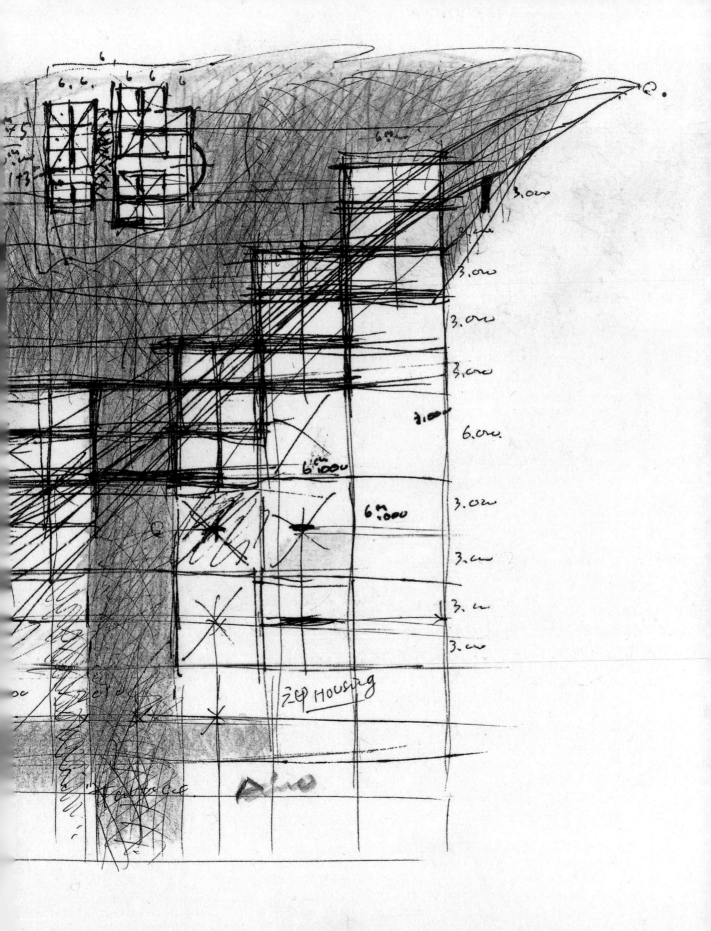

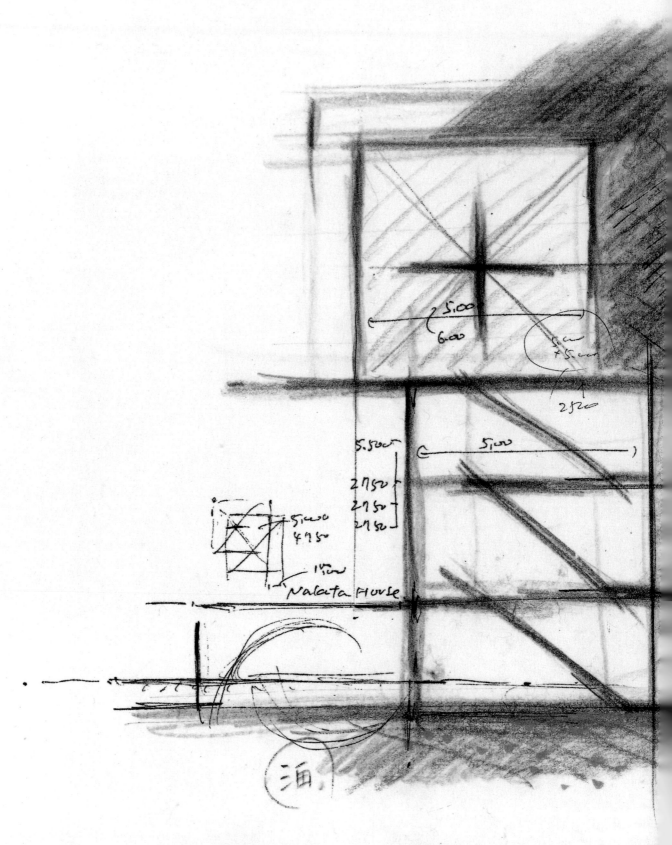

4×4 House

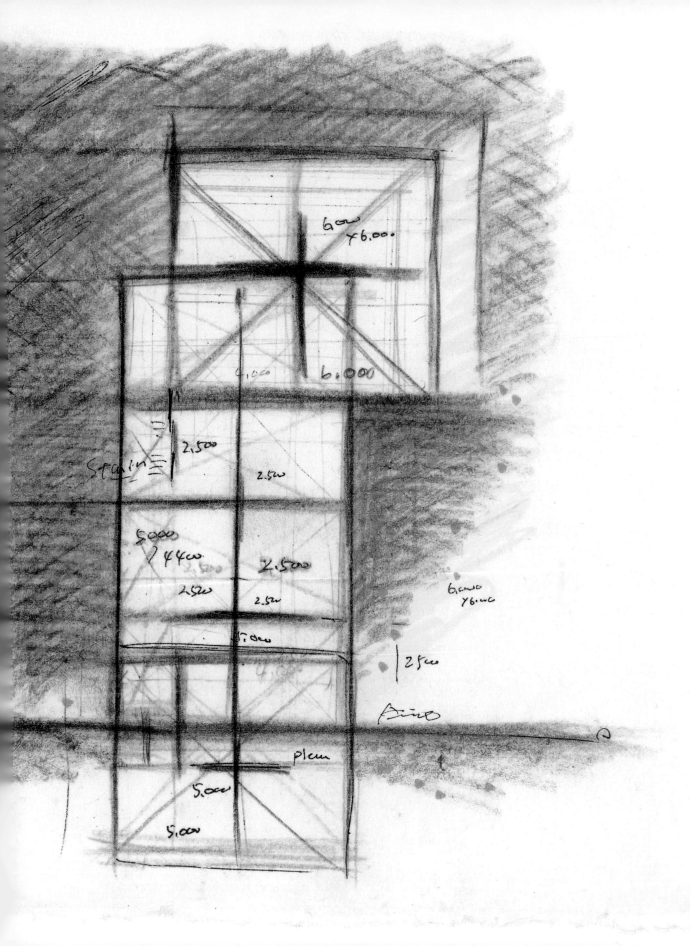

Tadao Ando 1 Houses & Housing

目次
Contents

見えない家

Invisible House

1999-2004

イタリア トレヴィゾ——Treviso, Italy

イタリア、トレヴィゾ郊外の豊かな自然環境の中に計画された独立住宅である。敷地、配置計画ともにわれわれの判断に委ねられ、かなり自由度の高い条件での仕事であった。唯一クライアントが要望として掲げたのは、周辺道路はもとより、敷地周縁部からの視線をも遮断する完全なるプライバシーの確保だった。その控えめな希望に最大限応えながら、大地と切り離されることなく、周辺環境と常に呼応し合うような住まいのあり方を考え、イメージとして得たのが、地中に半ば埋もれた＜見えない家＞であった。そのイメージのもと、広さ32,000m²に及ぶ敷地の中での配置が決定された。

　地中に埋もれる＜見えない建築＞において、問われるのは表層的なかたちの問題ではなく、より本質的な空間の是非である。ここでは、構成の見えない内に、日々予想を裏切る多様な空間体験が展開するような、地中の迷宮空間を目指した。

　平面的には、7.2mグリッドを基本とした単純な方形平面である。その厳格な枠組みの中で、床レベルの変化、内外空間を反転させるさまざまなタイプの中庭空間、頭上に切り込まれたスカイライトといった、光を主題とする建築的操作が、変化に富んだ空間のシークエンスをつくり出す。移ろう光の表情を建築空間に最大限取り込むために、構成、ディテールは徹底して恣意性を排除した、簡明な形式、秩序を意図した。

　＜見えない家＞の存在を、外部に対し発信するのは、玄関アプローチと屋外テラスをもつ書斎として地上に現れる、連続する1対のボックスのみである。その周囲を幾重にも囲うように、土地の樹木が植えられている。樹木の生長とともに、自然の城塞のような雰囲気が、この場所に与えられればと思う。

A detached dwelling planned amid the rich natural environment on the outskirts of Treviso, Italy. With both site planning and layout planning entrusted to our hands, the project allowed great flexibility and freedom. The only request presented by the client was the total protection of privacy, from adjacent streets as well as from the perimeter of the site. I have explored about an image of a house connected to mother earth and responding to the surrounding environment, in keeping at maximum with this modest wish, and have come up with the idea of an 'invisible house' half buried underground. From this, I have worked on the layout of this 32,000m² site.

The question raised upon an 'invisible building' buried in the earth is not about superficial forms, but a more fundamental space. What I have aimed here was a labyrinthine space under ground, filled with diverse spatial experiences unexpected in daily life, within an invisible structure.

Its floor plan is rectangular and plain, based on 7.2m grids. Inside this rigid framework is a spatial sequence full of variety, realized through architectural manipulations focusing on natural light, such as the skylight cut open above the head, various types of inner courts that invert internal and external spaces, and change of floor levels. In order to introduce the changing expressions of natural light to the architectural space, arbitrariness was completely excluded from the composition and details, with focus placed on simple form and succinct order.

The presence of this 'invisible house' is only transmitted to the outside world through the continuum of a box that shows itself over ground as the study, integrating the entrance approach and the outdoor terrace. Layers of trees native of the land are planted along the perimeter. I hope that as the trees grow, the place would affect a natural, rampart-like atmosphere.

イメージスケッチ。地形の中に幾何学の片鱗が
見え隠れする建築のイメージが描かれている。

Image sketch. An architectural image of
discontinuous glimpses of the geometry is
depicted in the topography.

エントランスから見る外観。イタリア、トレヴィゾ郊外の広大な敷地の中に建つ。
Looking at the exterior from the entrance. It is built on a vast site in the suburbs of Treviso, Italy.

Site plan   1:5,000

南側から見る外観。周囲の緑の成長にともなって
「見えない家」のコンセプトがより強化されていく。

Looking at the facade from the south.
The concept of an "invisible house" will be further
strengthened as the surrounding greenery matures.

Section 1:500

左頁：スリット状のトップライトにより、強い軸性が表現
されたエントランスロビー。右頁：ダイニングルームに
面して設けられた2層分の深さをもつ中庭。

Left page: The entrance lobby expresses a
strong axiality due to the slit-shaped skylights.
Right page: The courtyard established adjacent
to the dining room has a two-story depth.

地下1階メインベッドルームより南東を見る。
Looking southeast from the main bedroom on the first basement level.

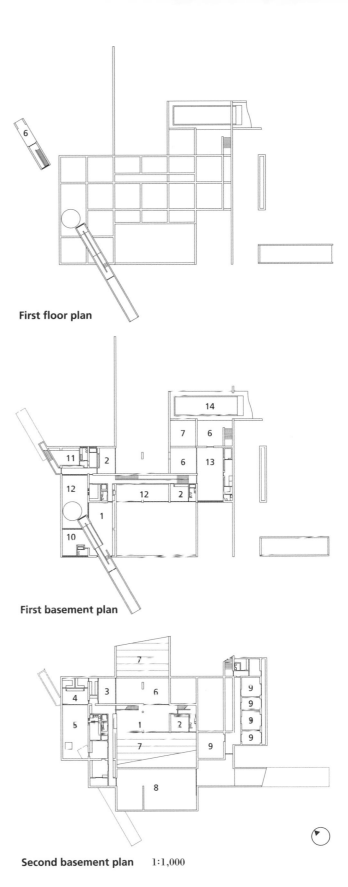

First floor plan

First basement plan

1 living room	8 parking
2 bedroom	9 mechanical
3 kitchen	10 guest room
4 dining room	11 cloak
5 court	12 void
6 terrace	13 gym
7 planting	14 pool

Second basement plan   1:1,000

地階のテラスへなだらかに続く傾斜した庭。　The garden gently slopes toward the ground level terrace.

テラスよりリビングルームを見る。 Looking at the living room from the terrace.

地下2階リビングルーム。天井高さ6mの吹き抜け空
間。プライバシーを確保しながら、サンクンコートに面
したガラス面から充分な光を採り込んでいる。

The living room on the second basement level, a space with a
6m-high ceiling. While ensuring privacy, sufficient light is brought
in through the glazed wall facing the sunken court.

この家の中心に配されたリビングルームは、南西面・北東面ともに緑の斜面に大きく開かれている。

The living room placed in the center of the house is wide open to green slopes on the southwest side and the northeast side.

左：プール越しに見たテラス。
右：グリッドの構成の中に組み込まれたプール。

Left: The terrace seen across the pool.
Right: The pool is integrated with the compositional grid.

敷地はシカゴの都心近い、閑静な住宅地に位置する。ここでは、南北に細長い敷地に沿って自然と交歓しながら展開する、伸びやかな居住空間の創出を目標にした。

建物は南北に配された2つの棟をデッキとスロープで結んだ構成による。南端の40ft（約12m）角平面3層のヴォリュームには、クライアント家族のためのプライベートスペースを納め、北端の40ft×20ftの2層のヴォリュームには建物のエントランス、ゲストルームなどのパブリックスペースをあてる。2棟の間には、この2棟を貫いて南北それぞれの延長でコートを形どる壁を軸に、2階レベルで幅20ftのデッキテラスを架け渡す。残りの幅20ftの西側の部分は水庭とし、その水庭に面するテラス下のスペースを、住まいの中心となるリビングルームとする。水庭とテラスとは、スロープによってつながれ、回遊性の高い半屋外の緩衝領域を形成する。それぞれの棟は外部には閉じて、内側のこの緩衝領域に向かって開かれた表情を向ける。

厳格な幾何学的構成の中で、ふいに登場し北棟の一部を円弧状にかきとる壁は、既存のポプラの樹をそのままのかたちで残すために設けられたものだ。この住宅が、われわれがアメリカで手がけた初めての建築となった。

シカゴの住宅

House in Chicago

1992-97

アメリカ合衆国 シカゴ —— Chicago, U. S. A.

The site is located in a quiet residential district close to the center of Chicago. Along this long, narrow north-south oriented site, the objective was to produce a comfortable residential space while developing an interaction with the natural environment.

The building is organized as two wings aligned on a north-south axis, connected by a terrace and a ramp. Private spaces for the client's family are accommodated in the three-story, 40ft-square (about 12m) volume to the south, while public spaces such as the building entrance and the guest rooms are contained within the 40ft by 20ft two-storied volume to the north.

Between these two wings, a 20ft-wide terrace is placed along the axis of a wall that defines the court, extending through the north and south areas. The remaining 20ft width to the west has been turned into a water garden. The space below the terrace facing this water garden is the living room, the focus of the dwelling. The water garden and terrace are connected by a ramp, forming a semi-outdoor buffer zone of circulation space. Both parts are closed to the exterior but on the inner side they have an expression of openness toward the buffer area.

Within this strict geometrical composition, the arc-shaped wall that interrupts part of the north wing was established in order to preserve an existing poplar tree. This house was our first building in the United States.

配置のスタディ。敷地いっぱいに離れて配された2つの
ヴォリュームを「つなげる」ことでつくられた住宅。

Study of the site layout. A house made from two
separate volumes, placed to fill the entire width
of the site then "linked."

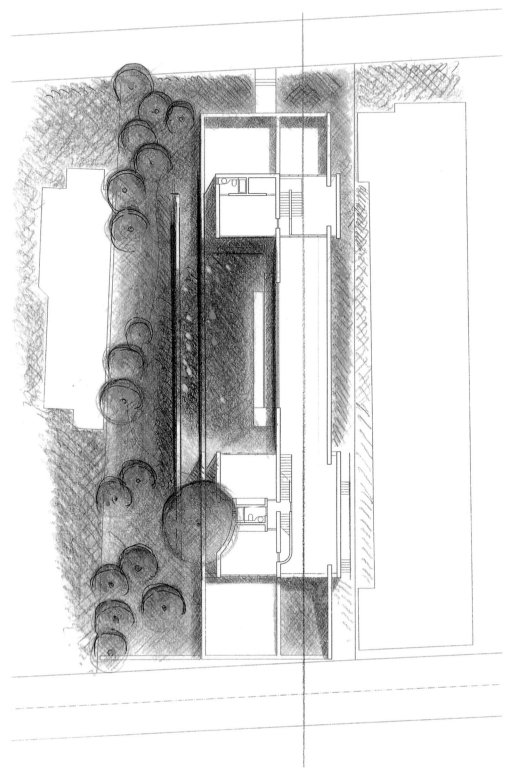

西側の水面越しに建物を見る。建物と周囲を緩やかに仕
切る、コンクリートの門型フレーム。

Looking at the building across the water surface
to the west. A gate-shaped concrete frame gently
divides the building from its surroundings.

水面に浮かぶスロープ。リビングとコートをつなぐ、住居内の散策路。
A ramp floats on the water surface. This is a stroll path within the residence
that connects the living room to the court.

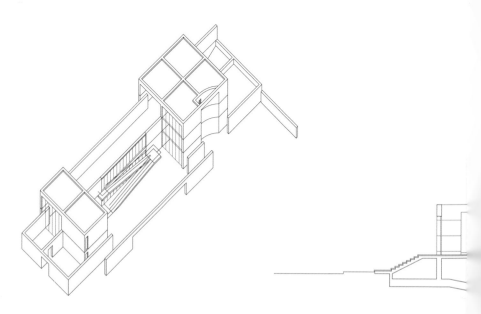

Axonometric

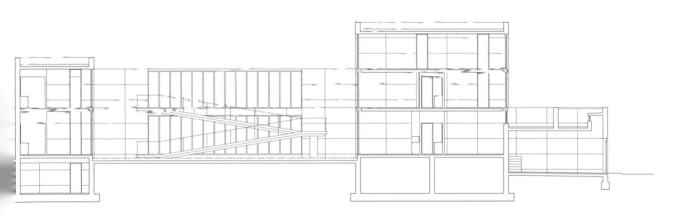

Section   1:300

壁に囲まれたコートに面する2層吹き抜けのエントランスホール。

The double-height entry hall faces a court enclosed by a wall.

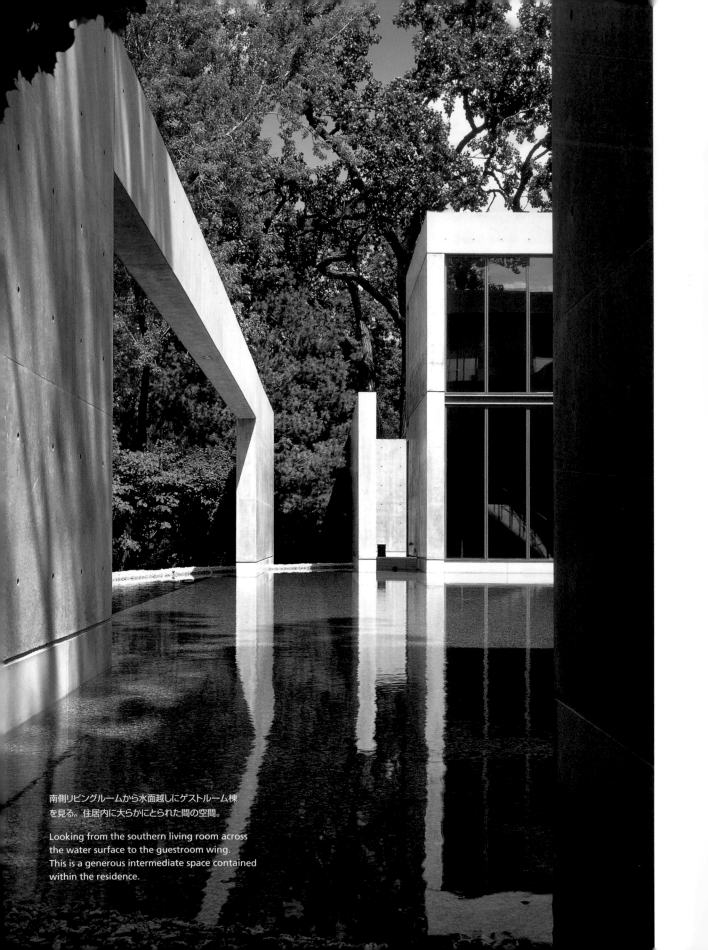

南側リビングルームから水面越しにゲストルーム棟
を見る。住居内に大らかにとられた間の空間。

Looking from the southern living room across
the water surface to the guestroom wing.
This is a generous intermediate space contained
within the residence.

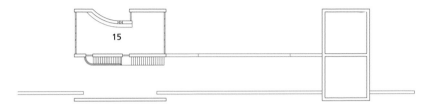

Third floor plan

1 entrance
2 living room
3 dining room
4 kitchen
5 library
6 bedroom
7 garage
8 court
9 guest room
10 entrance court
11 pool
12 void
13 terrace
14 studio
15 atelier
16 mechanical
17 gym
18 utility room

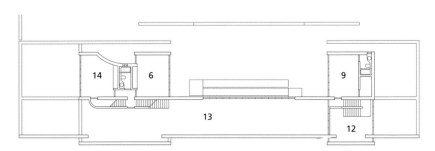

Second floor plan

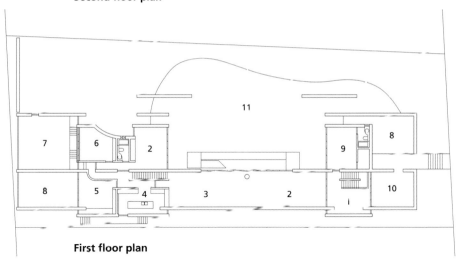

First floor plan

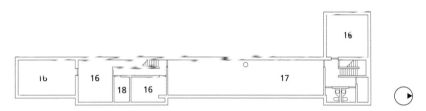

Basement floor plan   1:500

リビングから水面を見る。スロープ、水面、門形のフレームと二重、三重のフィルターを介し、周辺環境と連続する。

Looking at the water surface from the living room. It is connected with the surrounding environment through the double and triple filters of the slope, the water surface, and the gate-shaped frame.

敷地はニューヨークのマンハッタン。1920年代に建てられた様式主義の高層ビルに、住居及びゲストハウスとして使用するペントハウスを増築する計画である。新旧の混在の中から絶えず新しい刺激を生み出していくニューヨークという都市の住まいとして、われわれが提案したのは様式的な高層ビルに、鉄・ガラス・コンクリートという現代を象徴する材料を用いた現代建築が直截的に衝突するイメージである。

　ペントハウスは、建物の最上階にガラスの皮膜で覆われたコンクリートの箱として、宙に浮くように載る。屋上には、水を張り、その水庭の向こうにマンハッタンの摩天楼群が浮かび上がる。ダイナミックな都市の借景だ。

　さらに最上階より5層分ほど下がった位置にも、同素材、同形態の箱を、シンメトリーをなす高層ビルとは角度を振って貫入させ、空中の住まいの存在、そこに住みつく居住者の意思を強く外部に発信する。都市の風景を文字通り突き刺さすかのように挿入されるこのささやかな建築が、欲望の都市マンハッタンに新たな刺激をもたらすことを期待している。

マンハッタンのペントハウス

Penthouse in Manhattan

1996-
アメリカ合衆国 ニューヨーク —— New York, U.S.A.

The site is in Manhattan, New York. The project comprises a penthouse addition that will serve as a residence and a guesthouse for a high-rise building constructed in a 1920s style. As a dwelling in a city like New York, which ceaselessly generates new stimuli from the mixture of old and new, we proposed an image of direct collision between this style of high-rise building and a contemporary architecture that adopts steel, glass, and concrete as materials symbolic of the modern era.

A concrete box wrapped with a glass membrane placed on the topmost floor, the penthouse appears to float in the air. There is a stretch of water on the rooftop, and the skyscrapers of Manhattan rise from the surface of this water garden. This is a dynamic urban "borrowed scenery."

Another box, of identical form and materials, has been placed five floors below the topmost level, as if penetrating the symmetrical building at an angle; the presence of a dwelling in the air sends a strong message to the outside of the intentions of the residents. I hope this modest architecture, inserted as if literally stabbing the urban scenery, will bring a new stimulus to the city of desire that is Manhattan.

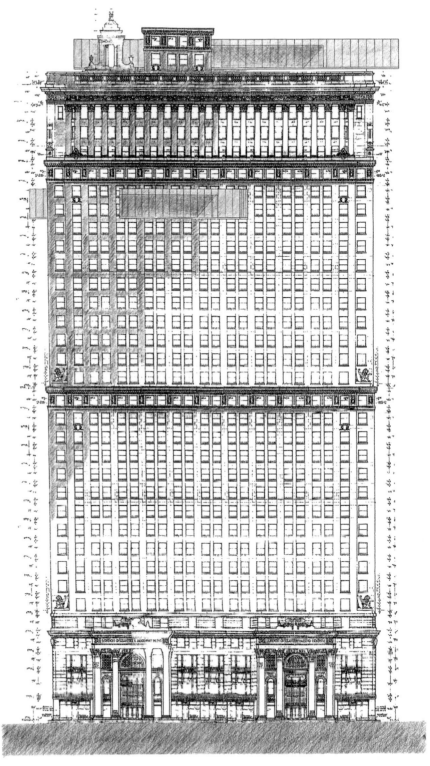

アメリカン・ボザール流の様式主義のファサードに突き刺さるガラスのシリンダー状ボックスと、屋上のペントハウス。マンハッタンの日常を切り裂くシャープな造形。

A rooftop penthouse, and a cylinder-shaped glass box that pierces an American Beaux-Arts-style facade. These sharp forms slice into the everyday life of Manhattan.

都市の隙間に住みつく——マンハッタンの上
空に忍び込むようにつくられたこの住宅は、
ある意味で、70年代の都市ゲリラ住居の正
統的な嫡子である。

Settling in an urban gap—made as
if sneaking into the Manhattan skies,
in a sense this house is the legitimate
offspring of the urban guerrilla
dwellings of the 1970s.

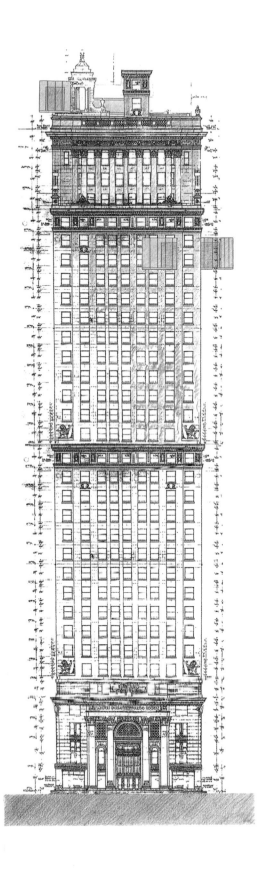

水庭越しに望む摩天楼の光。この場所ならではの借景。

A view of the lights of skyscrapers across the water garden. A "borrowed scenery" unique to this place.

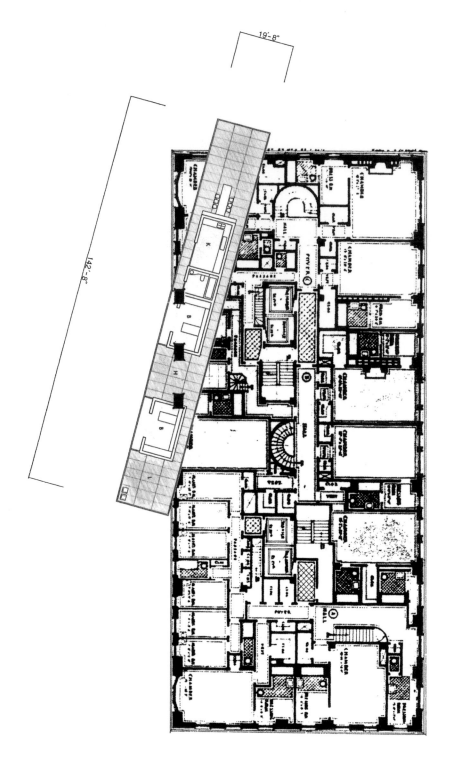

Lower floor plan

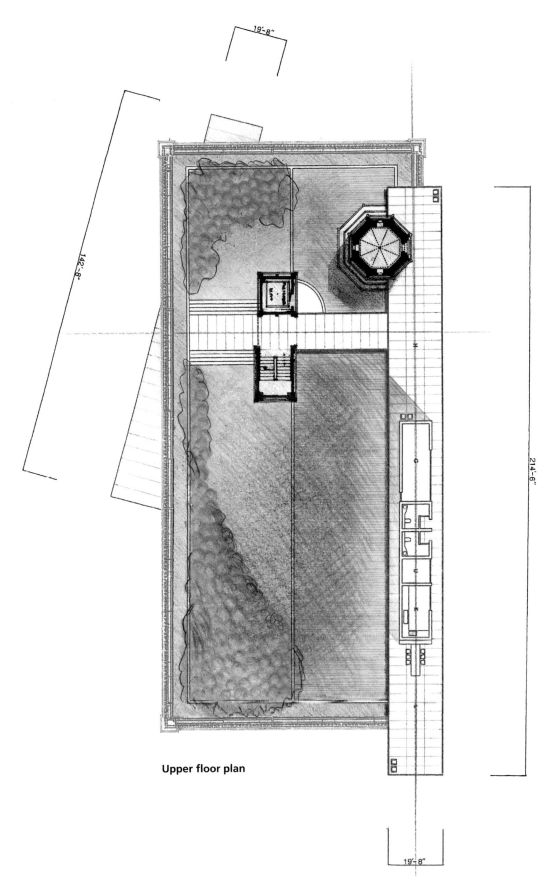

Upper floor plan

19'-8"

142'-8"

214'-6"

19'-8"

谷間の家

Crevice House
in Manhattan

| 2006-
アメリカ合衆国 ニューヨーク——
New York, U.S.A.

敷地はメトロポリタン美術館にほど近いマンハッタンのアッパーイーストに位置する。両側を高層ビルに挟まれた間口4m、奥行き30mほどのスペースにギャラリー兼住宅をつくる計画である。

　都市の谷間ともいうべき立地上、敷地には既存の隣接建物の採光確保のために、高さは2階以下にすべしとの制限があった。この立地の悪条件に対し、われわれは逆にそれを個性として活かすような建築イメージの提案を目標にした。

　全体は敷地の奥行きいっぱいに1階分沈めた直方体のヴォリュームと、その上部、敷地後方に設けられたペントハウスにより構成される。直方体内部は、奥行き方向に向かってセットバックしながら浮かぶ2枚のスラブによって区切られ、その段状の構成が最上階のペントハウスまで吹き抜け階段で連続する。ペントハウスに面する直方体の屋根部分は、全面プールとなっている。この水面を介して入り込む光、風、マンハッタンの空が、奥深く閉ざされた内部空間に住まいとして必要な自然の息吹と、都市の空気を伝えてくれる。

　「マンハッタンのペントハウス」と立地条件はまったく異なるが、ともに隙間から都市を生け捕りにしようと試みた実験住宅である。

The site is located on the upper east side of Manhattan, close to the Metropolitan Museum of Art. The plan is to construct a gallery and house in an approximately 4m wide by 30m deep space, interposed between high-rise buildings on either side.

In addition to being in a location that might be called an urban ravine, there is a height restriction of maximum two floors, in order to preserve light penetration to the existing buildings adjacent to the site. In response to this unfavorable site location, we aimed to propose an architectural image that made positive use of its characteristics.

Using the entire depth of the site, overall it comprises a sunken rectangular volume as the first floor, above which is a penthouse located to the rear of the site. The interior of the rectangular volume is divided by two slabs that float while stepping toward the rear of the site, and this tiered composition is linked to the penthouse on the topmost floor by an open stair. The entire surface of the rooftop area of the rectangular volume facing the penthouse is a pool. Light, wind, and the Manhattan sky penetrate through the medium of this water surface, conveying the urban atmosphere and bringing a necessary breath of nature to the deep, isolated dwelling.

Although having completely different site conditions from the Penthouse in Manhattan, these are both experimental houses that attempt to catch urban vitality through urban gaps.

都市のデッドスペースだからこそ生まれた、ビルの谷間の家。巧みに計算された光の効果により、奥行き方向に向かう空間の軸性が劇的に演出されている。

A house in a crevice between buildings that emerges precisely because of dead space in the city. The spatial axis perpendicular to the street is dramatically produced from a skillful calculation of the effects of light.

マリブの住宅

House in Malibu

2003-

アメリカ合衆国 マリブ—— Malibu, U.S.A.

<光と、音とともに暮らす家>

敷地はロサンジェルス郊外、マリブの太平洋を見下ろす岸壁上にある。

ここでは、光と音を主題に、その抑揚の操作による、建築空間の構築を試みた。

まず、岸壁にヴォイドを穿ち、プライバシーの確保と、海景への最大限の眺望と、2つの要件を満たす住空間を確保する。

そのヴォリュームは、直方体、三角柱、立方体の純粋な幾何学立体の組み合わせとして再構成され、内部においては、光のダイナミックな空間のシークエンスが体感される。幾何学立体の片鱗を覗かせる外部においては、人工と自然の強いコントラストが、場所性をより強化する風景の刺激となっている。

最も大きな空間容積をもつ立方体のヴォリュームでは、光とともに音が、空間を規定する重要な要素になっている。床から壁へ、段状に連続する放物双曲面によって空間は立体的に形づくられ、最良の音響効果を得る。かつてイアニス・クセナキスがコルビュジエと協同でつくり上げた『電子詩曲（1958年ブリュッセル博フィリップス館）』では、内部を包むHP面、円錐面がそのまま外形に現れていたが、この住宅では、そのすべてが立体内部に封じ込められ、部位によって異なる意味を与えられている。

音楽ばかりでなく、海の潮の音、風の音、雨の音といった、マリブの自然の音すべてが、丁寧に拾い上げられ、美しい音の洪水をつくり出す。

目に見えない光と、音から生まれた建築である。

Living with light and sound

The site is located in the suburbs of Los Angeles, on a Malibu cliff overlooking the Pacific.

This is an attempt to construct architectural space through manipulations of light and sound that consist the main theme of the project.

First, a void is cut in the cliff to ensure living spaces that would fulfill two requirements: protection of privacy and maximal view of the ocean.

This volume is then reorganized as a combination of purely geometrical bodies—rectangular solid, triangular prism and cube—which offers inside a sensation of dynamic spatial sequence of light. The outside gives a glimpse of the geometrical bodies. High contrast between the man-made and nature intensifies the locational and accents the landscape.

The cube is the largest in terms of spatial volume. There, light and sound are important elements that define the space. From the floor up to the wall, the tiered continuum of hyperbolic paraboloids molds the three-dimensional space where optimal acoustics is provided. In the past, 'Poeme Electronique (Philips Pavilion at the Brussels World Fair, 1958)' created by Iannis Xenakis in collaboration with Corbusier had featured direct external manifestation of hyperbolic paraboloid and conoid surfaces covering the inside. But with this residence. everything is contained inside the solids and given different significances according to regions.

Not only music but every natural sound of Malibu—sounds of the waves, the wind or the rain—is carefully picked up to create a beautiful sound flood.

An architecture born out of sightless light and sound.

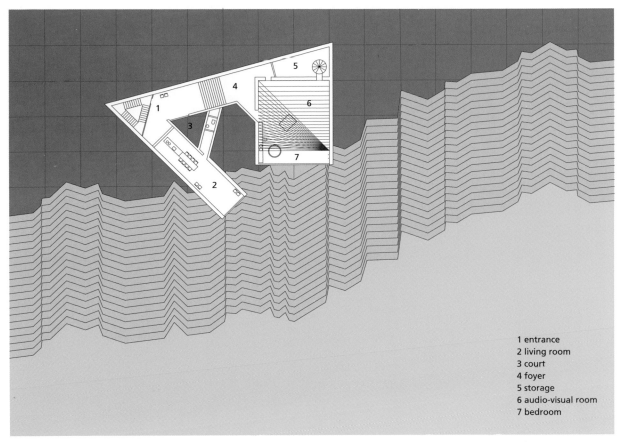

1 entrance
2 living room
3 court
4 foyer
5 storage
6 audio-visual room
7 bedroom

plan

岸壁に穿たれた幾何学形態のヴォイドの
連続がつくる住空間。
Living spaces are made by piercing the cliff with
a series of geometrically shaped voids.

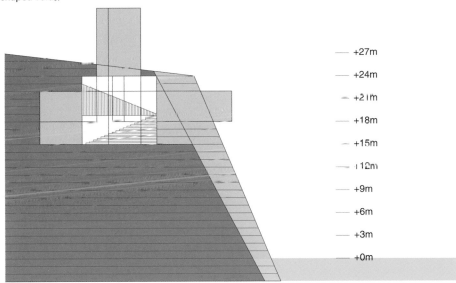

+27m
+24m
+21m
+18m
+15m
+12m
+9m
+6m
+3m
+0m

Section 1:500

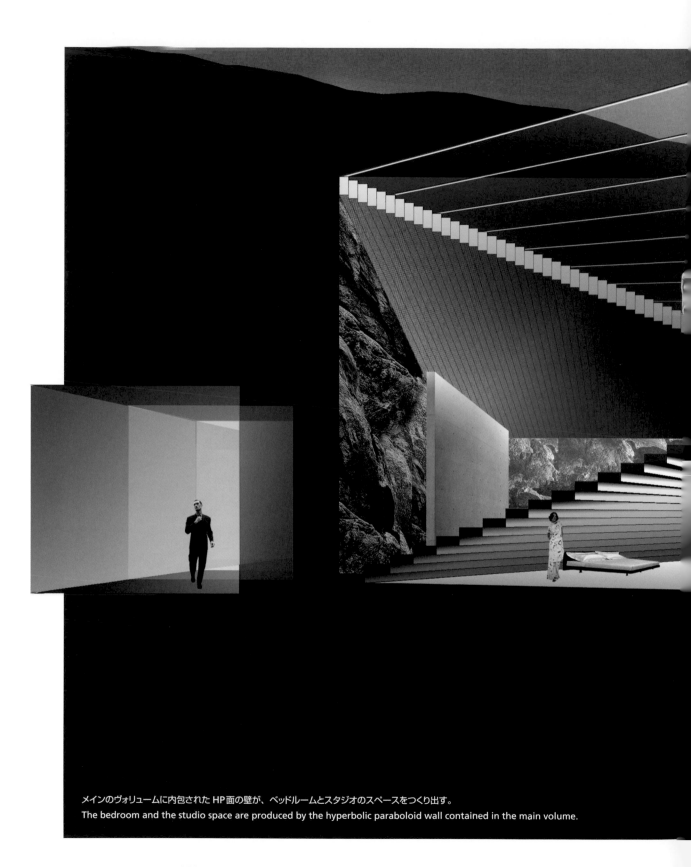

メインのヴォリュームに内包された HP面の壁が、ベッドルームとスタジオのスペースをつくり出す。
The bedroom and the studio space are produced by the hyperbolic paraboloid wall contained in the main volume.

岸壁に見え隠れする幾何学ヴォリュームの片鱗が、住居の存在を伝えるのとともに、人工と自然の対比による力強い風景をつくり出す。

As well as conveying the existence of the dwelling, the discontinuous glimpses of geometrical volumes in the cliff produce a powerful scene due to the contrast between the artificial and the natural.

敷地はサンフランシスコの太平洋を望む海岸にあり、自然がつくり出した変化の激しい地形が広がっている。この力強い風景をそのままに、生活空間に引き込むような建築を考えた。

　構成の幾何学は正方形グリッドを基本とし、異なるレベルにある3枚の水平面（1階、2階、屋根スラブ）を自然の地形の上に重ね合わせたかたちである。まず機能的に要求されるヴォリュームをグリッドに沿って、各水平面上に配置する。次に配置された機能の隙間にグリッド交点を結ぶ対角線の切り込みを穿つ。切り取られた水平面は部位によって床・ブリッジ・天井・庇といった、多様な建築要素へと意味を変え、穿たれたヴォイドは立体的にズレ、重なりながら建築の奥底まで入り込み、風や光の自然、そして周囲の景観を内部空間に引き込む。各水平面を断面的に連続させ、全体を統合するのは階段・プール・テラスといった内外を緩やかにつなぐ中間領域である。

　海面と呼応する水平面の重ね合わせを原イメージに生まれたアイディアだった。水平面による、抑制された幾何学的構成によって、光と影、景観が空間内部に鮮やかに明滅する。この場所の力を最大限引き出す装置としての建築である。

ゴールデン・ゲート・ブリッジの住宅

Golden Gate Bridge House

2004-

アメリカ合衆国 サンフランシスコ ── San Francisco, U.S.A.

The site is situated along the Pacific coast of San Francisco, within a rugged topography that nature has prepared. I have pictured an architecture that would draw this dynamic landscape into the space of living.

　The structural geometry is based on square grids, with three planes on different levels (1F, 2F, roof slab) superimposed over the natural topography. First, the volumes required in terms of function are placed along the grids on each horizontal plane. Next, incisions are cut diagonally, connecting the grids' nodes, between these functions. Cut surfaces are then interpreted as various architectural elements such as the floor, bridge, ceiling and eaves. Voids are layered, out of alignment, and penetrate deep into the bottom of the architecture, dragging along the surrounding landscape, nature, wind and light into the interior. What provides the cross-sectional continuity to each horizontal plane and unifies the entirety is the intermediate region that loosely connects the interior and exterior, such as the stairs, pool and terrace.

　This idea is a result of an original image of layering horizontal planes that call and respond to the surface of sea. The horizontal plane's subdued geometrical structure accounts for the lively flicker of light, shadow and landscape inside the space. This architecture is an apparatus to draw the maximum potential out of this place.

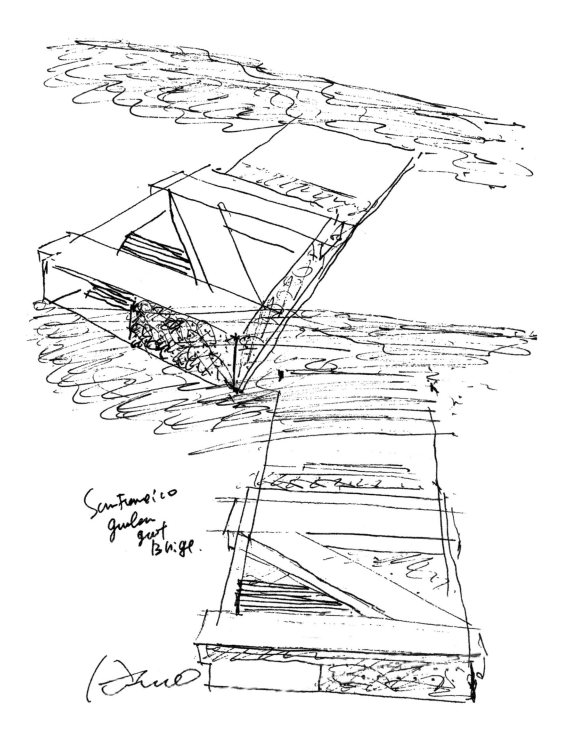

イメージスケッチ。太平洋との空間的な連続性と、斜線により切り取られるヴォリュームとヴォイドとの入れ子状の空間イメージが端的に描かれている。

Image sketch. A spatial continuity with the Pacific Ocean is clearly depicted, as well as an image of nested spaces of volumes and voids sliced by a diagonal line.

激しい岸壁の風景に突如現れた幾何学的なコンク
リートの箱。それ自体自立した存在としてありながら、
そこここに穿たれたヴォイドを通じて、周囲の自然と
大いに交歓する。

A geometrical concrete box that suddenly
appears in the scenery of rugged cliffs. While
having an autonomous presence, it acts in
concert with the natural surroundings through
the penetrating void.

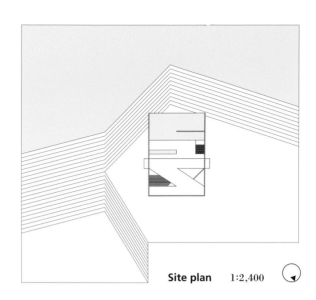

Site plan   1:2,400

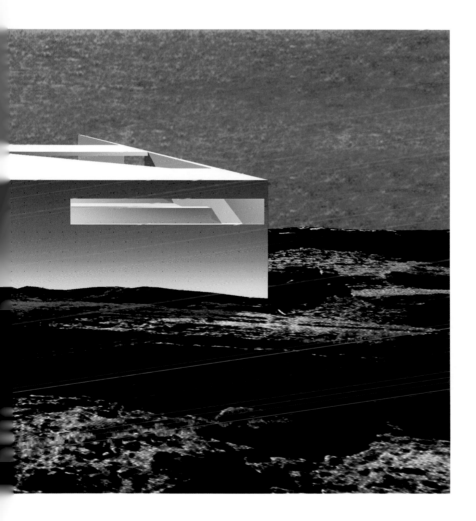

グリッドに従う静的なプランの住居に、角度を振っている屋根スラブが架け渡されることで、空間に劇的な変化が生まれる。

Dramatic changes are generated in the spaces by diagonally spanning a roof slab across the static, grid-aligned plan of the dwelling.

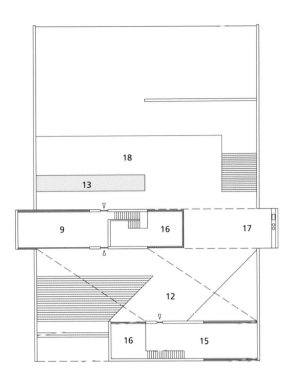

Upper level plan

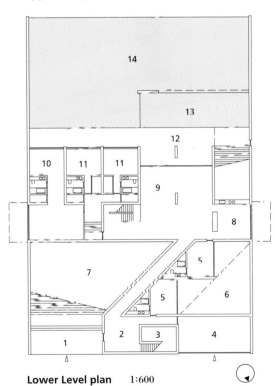

Lower Level plan   1:600

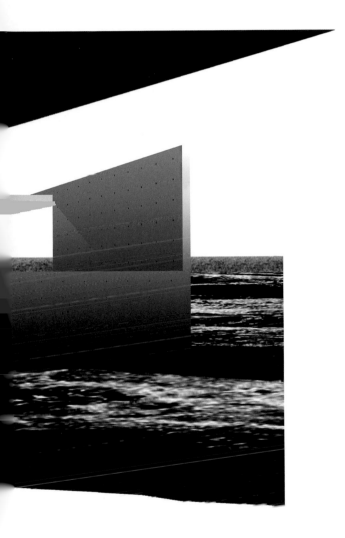

1 entrance gate
2 entrance
3 maid room
4 garage
5 guest room
6 court
7 mechanical / storage
8 dining / kitchen
9 living room

10 master bedroom
11 bedroom
12 outdoor living
13 pool
14 water
15 audio-visual room
16 void
17 outdoor kitchen
18 roof terrace

切り取られた３枚のスラブ（１階床、２階床、屋根）の重なりの内に展開する、岸壁の住まい。

This cliff dwelling expands within the layering of the three sliced slabs (first floor, second floor, roof).

ANDO by ANDO

　自身の建築を客観的に評価するのは得意でない。私にとって建築とは、あくまで
それぞれの状況下における個別の解答を探すことであり、とりわけ特定の個人を相
手に手探りでつくってきた住宅においては、そのプロセスを私的な感情抜きに語り
得ないからだ。

　そこで、手法の分析や分類といった視点は他に譲るとして、代わりに建築活動を
スタートしてから今まで辿ってきた道程を、節目となった住宅の仕事を軸に振り返っ
てみることにする。

　時系列を追って書くつもりで、結局記憶の断片をつないだ切れ切れの文章になっ
てしまったが、住宅という等身大の建築を通じて、自分が何を考え抱えながら走っ
てきたかは正直に書き表せたと思う。

独学という出発地点―――孤独ゆえの不安

　「本当に独学なのか」「独りでどのように学んだのか」国内のみならず海外でも
一番よく聞かれるのはこの質問だ。

　その通り、私は専門教育を受けることなく建築家としてのスタートを切った。学
歴が重視される現代社会においては、建築も大学の建築学科進学から始めるのが常
識である。人々が、その常識から外れた独学というキャリアに興味をもつのは当然
といえば当然だろう。

　ただ、私は意図して独学の道を選択したわけではない。10代の後半で次第に建築
への興味が増していったとき、私も大学の建築学科進学を考えていた。しかし家庭
の経済的事情、また自身の学力不足により、進学は諦めざるを得なかった。そこか
ら始まった＜独学＞である。知識も人脈もなく、学ぶのはもちろん実社会に出て働
きながら――先のまったく見えない、不安でいっぱいの出発だった。

　まず「何を学んだらよいのか」という根本的な問題から始めねばならなかった。
学ぶべき対象を把握するために、建築系の大学で用いられる教科書を買い集め、こ
れを1年で読破する計画を立てた。何かに追われるように頁をめくり、ともかく期
限通り目標は達成した。正直、理解できたのは半分がいいところだったが、それで
も建築学の体系はおぼろげながら掴めたので、無駄ではない1年だった。

　一方で、大学進学を諦めた時点から、インテリア設計やプロダクトデザインなど、
建築にこだわらず少しでも興味惹かれる仕事には、手当たり次第アルバイトで挑戦
し、それぞれの職能の通信教育も受けた。それらの実践を通じ、デザイン、設計とい

う行為自体は徐々に身体が覚えていった。しかし、いくら本を読んでも、やはり「建築とは何なのか」という問いの答えは見つからなかった。

　結局、私は「本質を掴むには、自身の目指す建築を実際に訪れ、その空間を体験し、それを身体に記憶していく、経験的学習を重ねていくしかない」という結論に達した。まずは日本国内を歩き回り、古民家から伝統建築、丹下健三先生らの近代建築を時間をかけて巡った。そして1965年、日本で一般の海外渡航が解禁になった翌年に、ついに私はヨーロッパに渡った。この旅が、本当の意味での私の独学の始まりだった。

自己流のグランドツアー

　初めてのグランドツアーは、横浜港から船で出発してナホトカを経由し、シベリア鉄道に乗ってモスクワに入り、そこから北欧、スイス、イタリア、ギリシア、フランス、スペインを回り、マルセイユからアフリカを経由してインド、タイ、フィリピン、そして横浜に戻るという、7カ月ほどの行程だった。

　グランドツアーといっても、例えばル・コルビュジエやルイス・カーンがそれぞれの旅で西欧建築の源泉に触れ開眼したというほどに、劇的なエピソードがあったわけではない。見知らぬ土地を歩く不安で絶えず緊張していたし、何より建築の世界は、私が簡単に掴めるほど底の浅いものではなかった。歩けば歩くほど、探していた答えが見つかるどころか、逆に建築への問いが深まっていく、そんな旅だった。

　パリに入り、真っ先にサヴォア邸に向かった。このモダニズムの名作を訪ねることは、旅の最重要目標のひとつだった。建築がわからずに独り苦しんでいたとき、現代建築の面白さ、その可能性を私に教えてくれたのが、古本屋で見つけたル・コルビュジエの作品集だったからだ。

　しかし、初めて見たサヴォア邸から、期待していたほどの発見は得られなかった。当時は、文化財として保護される前の廃墟のような状態であり、空間より前に建物に刻まれた時間ばかりが目についてしまったのだ。加えて私は、ドミノ構造の歴史的意味や、近代建築5原則の問題についての充分な教養をもち合わせていなかった。といって、わからないまま帰るわけにはいかない。「わかるまでは」と自分を奮い立たせ、訪問を繰り返した。

　廃墟が、建築に見えるようになったのは3回目くらいだったと思う。剥げ落ちた外観の向こうに、自然に逆らって建築を立ち上げる、建築家の意思を強く感じた。

廃墟であることが、逆に建築の力を浮き彫りにしているようにすら思えた。新たな発見に感動するのと同時に、「自分は一体何をつくりたいのか」と深く自らに問いかけながら、パリに戻った。

目前の建築を受け止めきれず、なかなか次の場所に行けなかったのは、ギリシア、ローマからイタリア・ルネッサンス、バロックに至る西欧古典の歴史に触れたときも同じだった。例えばギリシアのパルテノン神殿。

私が建築を始めた当時の建築とは即ち西欧建築のことであったから、その原点ともいうべきギリシアの建築は、出発前につくった「旅で見るべき建築リスト」の筆頭に挙げられた存在だった。

しかしアテネに入り、市街からアクロポリスの丘を目指して胸を躍らせ足を進めていたものの、いざ目の前に立つと、やはり「わからない」。陰影深い列柱の空間が何を伝えようとしているのか、その本質を掴もうと、サヴォア邸のときと同じくしばらくのアテネ滞在を覚悟した。

数日目の早朝、独り丘を登り、数人の観光客の佇む神殿をぼんやりと眺めていたとき、ようやく自分なりの答えが見つかった。「この場所を支配しているのは数学だ」。

数学とは即ち、建築に潜む人間の理性の力である。それが古代から近代のコルビュジエにまで連綿と続く西欧建築の本質であり、それこそが自身の生まれ育った日本の建築と西欧のそれとの決定的な差異なのだと。無論このように言葉にして整理できるようになったのは、旅から帰ってさらに数カ月後の話であるが……。

あの頃もう少しでも予備知識をもっていれば、もっとスムーズな旅ができたろう。遠回りすることばかりで、実際「見るべき建築リスト」に入れていたのに、準備不足で探しても見つからずじまいだったものもいくつかあった。

それでも、自分の感性だけを頼りに体当たりでぶつかっていったことは、やはり間違いではなかったと思っている。時間はかかったし、不安に押しつぶされそうになることも少なくなかったが、その分、旅での出会いと発見を深く噛み締め、自分のものにすることができた。若き日の旅の時間に身体に刻まれた建築の記憶が、今に至る私の建築活動の原動力になっているのは確かである。

モダニズムとの距離

独学という言葉から、制度にとらわれない自由な生き方を想像する人は多いだろ

う。しかし、自由を選んだがゆえの孤独の本当の苦しさを知る人は少ない。独学で私が一番つらかったのは、ともに学び、互いの成果を確かめ合える同級生がいないことだった。自分が一体どのような場所を歩いているのか、どこまで進んで来たのかがわからない、その孤独ゆえの不安がいつも胸にあった。それなりに経験を積んだ今も、完全にそれを拭い切れない。一方では、その不安感があるからこそ、いつまでも緊張感を絶やさずに現役のままでいられる部分もあるのだが……。

　大学に行ったとして、4年間で学べることなど知れていよう。だが、そこで同じ目的の同士を得られれば、この独りの不安から逃れることはできる。それこそが大学教育の意味だろうと私は思う。

　独りよがりに陥るのを避けようと、若い頃から情報収集には熱心だった。読めもしない海外の雑誌でも、気になればアルバイトで貯めた金をはたいて、是が非でも手に入れた。

　そんな私が、短いアンテナを精一杯巡らして調べた挙句、時代を見る目を養う教科書として選んだのがジークフリート・ギーディオンの『空間・時間・建築』だった。当時は既にポストモダンの萌芽が始まろうとしていたときで、かつてのモダニズムのバイブルも、その独善的な歴史観に対し異議を唱えられていたが、私には良い入門書だった。初めての渡欧の際にも大切に携えていき、移動中に繰り返し読んだ。ギーディオンのいう、全体から部分へと一貫した論理で語り得るモダニズムの理想、その意味を考えながら拙い建築行脚の旅を続けた。

　だが、現実に近代建築の名作の数々を訪ね歩いてみると、近代建築主義としての共通点よりも、個々の建築の差異点の方が強く印象に残った。同じモダニズムだといいながら、フィンランドのアルヴァ・アアルトの建築と、コルビュジエの建築とでは、その空間の性格に大きな開きがある。また、同じコルビュジエの建築でも、白の時代の住宅と晩年のロンシャン礼拝堂とでは、まったく異質の空間性を備えている。「これほど多様な広がりをもつモダニズムとは一体何なのか、その答えを現代建築は果たして示し得たといえるのか」。旅を経て、建築への問いかけは一層深まってしまった。

　その後、アメリカ、ヨーロッパを中心に数回の建築行脚の旅を実行した後、探していた答えを見つけられないまま、1969年に自分の事務所を開設し、設計活動をスタートした。

　当時、日本の同世代の建築家の多くは、いかにしてモダニズムを超克するかというテーマで、それぞれに独自の展開を試みようとしていた。いまだモダニズムの間

題を整理しきれていなかった私は、彼らの活躍を横目に、モダニズムをもう一度原点から問い直し、その可能性を見つめ直すことを自身の建築の目標に据えた。このスタート地点におけるモダニズムとの距離の測り方の違いが、それぞれのその後の建築活動のありようを決定づけることになったのだと思う。

仕事はつくるもの──草の根からのスタート

　建築家の「仕事がない」という愚痴は、今も昔も変わらず聞かれるものだ。とりわけ都市成長が一段落し、社会的な需要そのものが減ってきている現代の日本では、問題は深刻である。始める前に諦めてしまうという人も少なくない。

　私も29才で事務所を開設した直後しばらくは、何もできない状態が続いた。だが最初から外れた道を歩んできた私は、期待をしていなかった。悩む間もなく、道を切り拓く努力を始めた。

　まず、暇にまかせて周辺の空き地に架空のプロジェクトを描いた。それを見ず知らずの土地所有者にプレゼンテーションして、事業計画として提案した。無論、計画が受け入れられることはついぞなかった。が、そうするうちに次第に小住宅設計の依頼がポツポツと舞い込むようになった。文字通り、草の根からのスタートだった。

　今思えば、何とも乱暴な営業活動である。しかし建築家という職業を考える上では、実に有効なトレーニングだった。

　「建築は座して待っていてはつくれない」

　「仕事は自分でつくり出すものだ」

　私の持論である。その気持ちで走り続けてきたことが、IV期にわたる神戸の六甲でのプロジェクトにつながり、ゴルフ場の計画から一転、環境再生をテーマにした淡路夢舞台の計画につながった。

　建築家はもっと積極的に社会に発信していくべきだ。自身の理想を社会に問い、何をつくるべきかという構想から参画していくことで、建築はもっともっと大きな役割を社会に果たすことができる。次代の建築への道を切り拓くのは、建築家自身の意識改革なのだと、私にはそう思えてならない。

都市ゲリラ住居

　事務所開設後の初めての仕事は、学生時代の友人からの依頼だった。敷地は長屋街区の角地、延床面積30坪、総工費300万円と厳しい条件ながら、私なりの建築をつくろうと全力で取り組んだ。

　計画から1年足らずで、四周をコンクリートの壁で囲った垂直型の洞窟のような構成の家が完成した。主たる開口部は吹き抜け上部のトップライトのみ。開放性よりも閉鎖性を、光よりも闇を指向した家は、当時流行のいわゆるモダンリビングのイメージと正反対の方向を向いていた。

　完成の翌年、ふとしたことから雑誌『都市住宅』の植田実さんにこの住宅を見てもらうことができ、幸運にも発表の機会を得た。初めて書いた原稿のタイトルは「都市ゲリラ住居」。トロッキーやチェ・ゲバラの影響でつけたタイトルで、自分は強大な都市に立ち向かうゲリラであり、同じく都市に住みつこうと踏ん張る共闘者たちの「抵抗の砦」をつくっていくのだという趣旨の内容だった。

　70年代当時は、歴史的に見ればモダニズムの教条主義への反発から、それを乗り越えるべくポストモダンムーブメントが世界を席巻し始めたときである。周囲は私の書いた論文と掲載された写真の攻撃的なイメージとを重ねて、既成の社会、既成の建築概念に対する建築家の強固な意思表明として受け取り、私はモダニズムへ異議を唱える1人に数えられるようになった。

　正直、私自身はいわゆるポストモダンムーブメントにはまったく興味はなかった。むしろ言葉ばかりが先行する風潮にある種の嫌悪感を抱いていた。しかし、ゲリラを名乗ったのは、モダニズムという建築主義に抗うためではなかった。私が挑みたかったのは、モダニズムの透明な論理で御しきれない矛盾に満ちた現実の都市であり、つくりたかったのは剥き出しの生命力に満ちた不条理の空間だった。今思えば、建築というよりも彫刻をつくっているような感覚だった気がする。その都市ゲリラ住居の延長線上でつくったのが、1976年の住吉の長屋だった。

住吉の長屋―――私の原点

　住吉の長屋については、国内外のさまざまな評論家がそれぞれに深読みして複雑なクリティックを書いてくれている。しかし、当事者としてはともかくつくりたいものに精一杯取り組んだというのが正直なところで、それほど戦略的な意識はな

かった。設計をスタートしたのは1974年の初めだった。両隣と壁1枚で隔てられた3軒長屋の真ん中1軒の建て替えという工事の難しさといい、間口2間、奥行き7間という特異な敷地形状といい、最初につくった友人の家をしのぐほどの条件の悪さだった。が、一寸の油断も1ミリの無駄も許されない、その極限の緊張状態が、逆に問題を徹底的に考え抜き、自身を琢磨する絶好の機会となった。若さゆえの向こう見ずの勇気が可能にした建築だった。

「住宅」というテーマに対し、当時考えていたのは人間が主体的に意思をもって住まう場所づくりだった。寒ければ着る。暑かったら脱ぐ。重要なのは、環境制御のための装置としてではない、人間の生を受け止める空間の確かさだと。

住まい手の側からすれば、時代錯誤な、ある意味建築家の傲慢だったが、クライアントとの多少の摩擦などものともせず、私は自分の考えを貫いた。この辺が、独学の建築家の短所であり、長所でもあるのだろう。そして、既存長屋を取り壊した後、現れた敷地を3分割し、その真ん中を中庭として開放した構成の住吉の長屋をつくった。

無論、クライアントの理解を得た上での計画だったが、住空間を中央で分断してしまう、非近代的な構成は、あくまで私の意志だった。通風、採光、日照という最低限の条件が確保された後、機能性の問題は住まい手に任せたらいい。重要なのはそこで人間が精神的、身体的にいかに己を育んでいけるかだと考えていた。

私は人間社会が制度的、技術的にいかに進歩しようと、中で自然を感じられる住居が、人間生活のあるべき姿だと考えている。住吉の長屋の中庭は、機能性という面では、ときに厳しい生活を人間に強いる。だが、同時に開け放たれた中庭は、自然の移ろいというかけがえのない刺激を生活内部に引き込む、呼吸する住まいの心臓ともなり得る。

「狭いからこそ、非合理を承知で中庭を中心に据える」

それぞれの長屋暮らしを通じ、中庭のもたらす空間の豊かさを身体で知っていたクライアントと私には、その決断が誤りでないという確信があった。

しかし、雑誌メディアに発表すると、常軌を逸した構成に対し、数多くの批判が寄せられた。予想外の反響の大きさに驚くとともに、私はいかに小さくささやかな建築であっても、そこに確固たるメッセージがあれば、社会に問題提起し得ることを知った。住吉の長屋が、建築家としての私の実質上のデビュー作となった。

この頃から、故毛綱毅曠さん、渡辺豊和さんや石井和紘さん、石山修武さんといった、同世代の建築家たちと知り合うようになった。個性的な彼らとの対話は、独り

でいた私には得がたい刺激だった。

　伊東豊雄さんには1977年に出会った。とある建築雑誌の特集企画で私が取り上げられた際の、インタビュアーが伊東さんだった。住吉の長屋や完成直後の神戸のローズガーデンなどを案内していると、引き渡し後の建物に自分の家のように入り込んでいく私の様子に心底驚いていた。大阪のクライアントと建築家の親密さが、カルチャーショックだったらしい。

　そもそも最初からクライアントに対する遠慮はなかった。打ち合わせでも、間取りや仕様などさまざまな要望を挙げる彼らを押さえ付け、自身のアイディアを優先させるのが常だった。

　そのクライアントの大切さに気づいたきっかけも、住吉の長屋だった。といっても、完成するまでは、それまで通り。さすがに中庭の存在は説明をして、納得はしてもらっていたが、その他の部分では基本的な間取りの合意を得た後、一切こちらの意図通りに進めていた。

　それが完成後、吉田五十八賞の最終審査に、建物を見に来られた村野藤吾さんから予想外の批評の言葉を頂いた。建物の良し悪しには触れず、一言「これはつくらせた施主が偉い」と。そのとき初めて、自分につくる機会を与えてくれるクライアントという存在に気づいた。住吉の長屋の建築批評として、最高の一言だったと今も思う。

建築の両義性──小篠邸での試み

　住吉の長屋の後、自身の目指すべき方向性は明らかになり、事務所もある程度安定していた。が、一方で新しいことへの挑戦という意味では、ある種のマンネリに陥っていた。その状況を打破する契機となったのが、1981年の小篠邸だった。

　それまでの仕事の大半が、猥雑な都市環境の中にある極小の敷地でいかに＜豊かな＞住空間を切り取れるかというテーマだった。対して小篠邸は芦屋、奥池の広大な敷地で、規模設定もプログラムも縛りのない──すなわち住吉の長屋とはまったく正反対の視点で、自身の目指す建築の原型を追及できる好機だったのだ。

　抗うべき都市はない、豊かな自然に包まれた風景を前に、私は初めて建築と外部空間の関係、いわゆる庭の問題に行き当たった。

　「このなだらかな丘の風景の魅力を最大限活かせるのはいかなる建築か」

　自然と建築とを融和させた建築空間は、日本の伝統的建築の最大の美徳である。

その日本建築の流動的空間を、現代建築で再現しようと思うのは自然な発想だった。それを都市ゲリラ住居から追及してきた西欧的な、一貫した構成の原理による力強い壁の表現で実現したいと考えた。その結果が、地形に沿ってレベルを変えて並列する、2本のコンクリートボックスによる構成だった。

目指したのは日本建築の柔らかさと西欧建築の強さを重ね合わせた建築——即ち自然と大らかな対話を交わしながら、その環境に埋没することなく確固たる存在の意思を明示する、そんな両義的な建築のあり方だった。

建築としての自立性を高めるために、それまでの小住宅同様、無装飾なコンクリートによる構成の幾何学を徹底して純化させていく一方で、その人工的世界と向き合う自然の現象がいかなる影響をもたらすか、図面上で考えられる限りのスタディを行った。

「夏の光の変化は空間にどのような表情をもたらすか」

「冬の光はどのような角度で差し込むか」

形態的な装飾を捨て去った後では、光が空間を性格づける重要な役割を担うことになる。そのような問題を踏まえつつ、再度抽象的な幾何学の操作に戻り、微細な修正を加えていった。どちらも諦めきれない、抽象的世界での思考と現実の具象的世界での思考とのギリギリの葛藤の中で建築がつくられていった。

抽象と具象という主題

この抽象と具象の葛藤は、私にとって建築における永遠の主題である。10年ほど前、新建築の住宅特集でこの問題について論じた「抽象と具象の重ね合わせ」という論文を掲載してもらった。ここで私は、建築は抽象的なものと具象的なものの葛藤の中にあるとした上で、抽象を表徴するものとしてアルバースの「正方形礼賛」を、具象を表徴するものとしてピラネージの「幻想の牢獄」を挙げ、最後に「アルバース的な骨格の内にピラネージ的幻想の迷路を潜ませたような」抽象と具象を同時に表現する建築が自分にとっての永遠の建築の課題だという言葉で締めくくった。

建築に＜強さ＞をもたらす抽象的な世界への志向と、＜深み＞を与える具象的世界への眼差し。自身の内にある、この相反する志向のギリギリのバランスをそれぞれの建築で探っていく——言い換えれば、幾何学的構成を遵守し、使用する材料も限定した上でいかに自然と交信する豊かな空間を生み出せるか、その場所に刻まれた歴史や人々の記憶をいかにして建築で受け継いでいけるかという主題である。

住吉の長屋は、この抽象と具象の問題を自分なりに追及し、そのプロトタイプともいうべき究極解を示し得た仕事だったと思う。対して小篠邸はその方法論の拡張化、一般化に挑戦した仕事だった。その建築は後にケネス・フランプトンによって彼の言うクリティカル・リージョナリズム（批判的地域主義）の代表例として評価を受けることとなる。

六甲ハウジング──初めての集合住宅

小篠邸の完成と同時期に、私にとって初めての集合住宅計画である六甲の集合住宅の建設がスタートした。

この斜面地集合住宅の計画は、当初山裾の造成された平地での建設を依頼してきた施主を説き伏せ、背後の60度の急斜面を敷地に選び直したことから始まった。

計画にあたり私が目標としていたのは、斜面地という立地特性を活かした構成とした上で、各住戸の面積、間取りがすべて異なるようなヴァリエーション豊かなプランをつくること、そして集合住宅内部に路地を引き込んだような人間的で親密なパブリックスペースをつくることだった。

それをかたちにしていく手段として、私は平面形状も断面形状も不規則な自然の地形に、あえて等質なフレームの構成をはめ込むことを考えた。不規則なものに、規則的なかたちをもち込むことで、当然そこに立体的なズレが生じてくる。そのズレによってできる隙間を結んで、パブリックスペースとし、これに多様な形式の住戸が独立住居のように接続していくというアイディアだ。

言葉にすると簡単だが、立体フレームという単純なユニットの操作で、しかもそれを地形に沿わせながら、豊富な住戸プランをつくり、その隙間を使って変化に富んだパブリックスペースをつくるのは容易な仕事ではなかった。最終構成に煮詰まるまで何案ものプランをスタディし、いくつもの模型をつくった。住吉の長屋から小篠邸まで一貫して取り組んできた「抽象と具象の重ね合わせ」という主題の集大成とすべく、密度の高い建築を目指した。

完成した建物は斜面にあわせ各住宅がセットバックしながら段状に折り重なる構成で、建物全体は、中ほどに設けた広場によって上階部分と下階部分の2つの棟に分けられる。

最下階からすれば約10階建ての高さとなる、この集合住宅のメインアプローチを、私は中央の隙間を貫く階段に託した。あらゆる住戸へのアプローチは、この中

央階段を核として建物の隙間を巡る階段によっている。

　急傾斜の崖を背に立つ建物で、10階建てとくれば、垂直動線はエレベーターによるのが常識だ。しかし、私は集合住宅にとって最も大切な「集まって住むがゆえの豊かさ」を体感させる装置として、この屋外に開放された階段広場を、あえて中心に据えた。

　クライアントたっての要望で、目立たぬようエレベーターも設けたが、完成後の建物では、上下階のほぼすべての住民が日常の移動に階段を利用し、そこでの隣人との触れ合いを楽しんでくれている。

　建築における場所性、地域性の問題や、個と公、部分と全体の問題など、このプロジェクトで、実に多くの問題に気づき、実に多くを学んだ。

共同体の再生───生活空間の象徴化

　先日亡くなられた篠原一男さんが、1962年に『新建築』で発表された「住宅は芸術である」という重要な発言がある。建築の言語論的分析が盛んな時代に、空間の象徴性を謳ったこのテーゼは、建築界に少なからぬ衝撃を与えた。

　視点はやや異なるが、私が六甲の集合住宅の階段で試みたのもまた生活空間の象徴化である。ここでいう象徴とは、建築表現の手段ではない、家族なり地域といった共同体の目に見えないかたちの、文字通りの象徴だ。

　70年代あたりから黒沢隆さんの個室群住居に象徴されるようなプライバシーを重んじる気運が高まり、社会全体でいわゆるコミュニティーが崩壊していく傾向が目立った。そのコミュニティーを取り戻すひとつの手がかりとして、建築空間、それも日常の住空間の内に象徴的空間をもち込むことを、個人住宅の設計を通じて提案してきた。そのコミュニティーの対象を家族から集住体へと発展させた最初の試みが、六甲の集合住宅だった。

　実は、六甲の集合住宅が完成に近づく頃から、この斜面地一体を連続する集合住宅共同体として再編できないか、という思いで、隣接する敷地での集合住宅計画を勝手に始めていた。いつもながらの無謀な試みだったが、その積極性がここでは功を奏し、六甲の集合住宅は II 期、III 期と20年近くの間に、段階的な成長を遂げることとなった。

　ひとつの場所の成長に継続的に関われるというまたとない好機を得て、私は斜面地を活かした構成という一貫した主題のもと、規模の拡張とともにパブリックスペー

スの充実に努めてきた。その成果が今、各期にかたちを変えて設けた階段広場の織りなす日常の風景に、確実に現れてきている。

建築の原点が住宅にある

独学で建築を志す決心で活動をスタートしてから、今日までに40年の歳月が過ぎた。その間、住吉の長屋のクライアントは変わらぬ姿であの極小住宅を住みこなしてくれており、小篠邸は昨年3度目の増築工事を終えたところだ。六甲の集合住宅はIV期目となるプロジェクトの建設が現在進行中である。

ここまで原稿を書き進めてきて、改めて私という人間の核をつくったのが、独学という状況であり、その不安と闘いながら必死で建築を追い続けた20代の日々にあったことを痛感した。同時に、スタートした時点から今まで、自身の建築活動の軸は、いつもその時々での住宅の仕事での挑戦にあったことを再認識した。

小住宅の設計から都市に闘いを挑んだ私が、今は国内外の公共建築を中心とした施設の建築を手がける一方で、東京の都市再生構想にも建築家として参加している。小さな事務所に比してかなりの仕事量で、何とか日々悪戦苦闘している状況だが、それでも、住宅は年に数件のペースでつくり続けている。若い所員のトレーニングの機会でもあるし、私自身のバランス感覚を保つのに必要な仕事であるから、事務所の運営という面でのデメリットを承知で、積極的に依頼を受けるようにしている。

今抱えている仕事の目処がつき、落ち着いてきたら徐々に仕事の規模を落として、自身のスタート地点に立ち戻ってみたいと今は考えている。ともあれ、私の最後の仕事は住宅だと、これだけは強く心に決めている。

Ando by Ando

I cannot pretend to be an objective judge of my own work. Architecture to me is the pursuit of individual solutions under specific circumstances. I design houses in particular with certain individuals in mind, and in any discussion of my design process I must include the role played by my own emotions.

Leaving it to others to analyze or classify my method, I have chosen instead to use works that have been turning points in my career to retrace the route I have taken since I began my architectural activities.

Although I began with the intention of dealing with matters chronologically, the result has turned out to be a fragmentary text joined together primarily in my memory. However, I believe I have succeeded in honestly expressing what I have held fast to in the course of my life.

Self-Education as a Point of Departure: The Anxiety of Solitude

"Are you really self-taught?" "How did you teach yourself?" Those are the questions I am asked most often, whether in Japan or overseas.

I did in fact begin to practice without a formal education in architecture. In contemporary society, schooling is regarded as important; it is conventional wisdom to begin architecture by entering the architecture department of some university. Inevitably, people are intrigued by my unconventional, self-taught background.

However, I did not deliberately set out to be an autodidact. In my late teens, as my interest in architecture gradually grew, I too thought about studying the subject at a university. I had to abandon the idea because of financial circumstances in my family and my own academic shortcomings. That is how my self-education began. Lacking any knowledge or connections, I learned while working in the real world. At the start, I did not know what to expect and was tormented by anxiety.

I was faced with a fundamental question: What exactly should I study? To get an idea of what I ought to learn, I purchased all the textbooks used at a university with an architecture department and devised a program to read them all in one year. Like a man driven, I went through the books and finished them all on schedule. In truth, I understood at best only half of what I had read, but the year was not wasted, as I had a vague grasp of the system of architectural studies.

Around the time I abandoned the idea of entering a university, I began to accept any interesting part-time work that came my way in not just architecture but interior design and product design: I also took correspondence courses in those fields. Through such practical experience, I gradually became versed in the act of design. Nevertheless, no matter how many books I read, I still had no answer to the question, "What is architecture?"

In the end, I came to the conclusion that the only way to grasp the essence of architecture was through repeated empirical study, that is, by actually visiting buildings I admired, experiencing their spaces and inscribing those experiences in my memory. First, I traveled around Japan to everything from old folkhouses and traditional buildings to works of modern architecture by Kenzo Tange and others. In 1965, a year after the general public in

Japan was first permitted to travel overseas, I went to Europe. That journey was the beginning of my self-education in a true sense.

Undertaking a Grand Tour in My Own Way

On my first grand tour, I went by ship from Yokohama to Nahodka, took the Siberian Railway to Moscow, and from there traveled around Scandinavia, Switzerland, Italy, Greece, France and Spain. From Marseilles, I made my way back to Yokohama via Africa, India, Thailand, and the Philippines. The entire trip took approximately seven months.

I call it a grand tour, but compared with, for example, the journeys that opened the eyes of Le Corbusier and Louis Kahn to the source of Western architecture, it was absent of any dramatic episodes. Traveling in unfamiliar lands, I experienced continual stress. Not only that, the world of architecture proved recondite and did not readily yield its secrets. Far from discovering the answer I sought, I found myself more puzzled by architecture the more I traveled.

I did not immediately find the answer, even at the Villa Savoye to which I headed immediately after arriving in Paris. Visiting this masterpiece of modernism was one of the most important objectives of my journey. That was because, at a time when I was struggling alone to understand architecture, Corbusier's collected works, found in a used bookstore, had taught me the delights and the possibilities of contemporary architecture.

However, I did not discover as much as I had hoped on my first visit to the house. At the time, the building, not yet protected as a cultural asset, was in a state of near ruin; I saw, not the spaces, but the ravages of time. In addition, I was not yet sufficiently educated in the historical significance of the Dom-ino structure or the question of the Five Points of a New Architecture. Nevertheless, I could not leave, still ignorant. I repeatedly went back to the building, swearing I would do so until I understood it.

I believe it was around my third visit that I was able to see the ruin as architecture. I could finally see past the exfoliated exterior and sense the intention of the architect to defy nature and erect a building. The fact that it was in ruin seemed to me to reveal all the more the power of architecture. Moved by this discovery and asking myself what did I really want to create, I returned to Paris.

I experienced this same inability to immediately absorb the full significance of a building and move on to the next stop on my itinerary upon visiting classical works in Greece and Rome. For example, there was the Parthenon in Greece.

When I began my self-education, architecture to me meant Western architecture. Naturally, Greek architecture, its point of origin, was at the top of the list of must-see buildings I had compiled before my departure.

I arrived in Athens and excitedly ascended the Acropolis, but once I stood in front of the Parthenon, I could not understand it. Determined to grasp its essence and learn what the shadowy space of its colonnade was trying to communicate, I resigned myself to a stay as prolonged as that made necessary by the Villa Savoye.

Early in the morning several days later I climbed the hill alone and stood staring at the temple, where a number of tourists were wandering. At last, a sort of answer occurred to me: *It is mathematics that rules this place.* Mathematics is the power of human reason that is hidden in architecture. It has been the essence of Western architecture from ancient times to the modern works of Corbusier and is what distinguishes Western architecture from that of my native Japan. Of course, it was only after I had returned to Japan several months later that I was able to articulate those thoughts fully.

If I had had a bit more prior knowledge, the journey would have been much smoother. I took a roundabout route, and from lack of proper preparation was unable to find a number of buildings on my list.

Nevertheless, I do not believe it was a mistake to confront those buildings directly, armed only with my sensibility. It took time, and anxiety often threatened to overwhelm me. However, to that extent, I was able to appreciate and assimilate the encounters I had and the discoveries I made during the journey. The memories of architecture I have from that journey in my youth have definitely been the driving force in my subsequent architectural activities.

Distance from Modernism

For many, the word "self-education" suggests a free way of life, one not bound by the social system. However, choosing freedom means choosing solitude, and few know how painful that solitude can be. The most difficult aspect of self-education for me was the absence of any classmates with whom I could study and ascertain what I had learned. I was always plagued by anxiety because of my solitude; I did not know what sort of path I had taken or how far I had come. I am not completely free of anxiety even now that I have considerable more experience. Of course, it is thanks to that anxiety that I am able to continue to work with undiminished intensity.

There is a limit to what I could have learned in four years at a university, but the company of others with similar objectives would have freed me from the anxiety of solitude. I believe that having such company is the true value of a university education.

In an effort to avoid complacency, I have been an avid collector of information since my youth. Using all the money I earned from part-time work, I would acquire foreign magazines that intrigued me, even though I could not read them.

After a search that tested my limited powers to gather information, I chose Sigfried Giedion's *Time, Space and Architecture* as a textbook so that I might learn to see the true nature of the times. Postmodernism was already starting to emerge at that time, and there were those who objected to the self-righteous view of history expressed in the erstwhile bible of modernism. For me, however, it proved a good introduction. I carried it with me on my first visit to the West and read it repeatedly as I traveled. During my architectural pilgrimage, I thought about the ideals and the significance of modernism, which was, according to Giedion, characterized in both its details and its entirety by a consistent logic.

On visiting a number of masterpieces of modern architecture, I was struck more by their differences than by what they had in common. Though Alvar Aalto of Finland and Corbusier are both modernists, their spaces are very different in character. Even among works by Corbusier, the houses of his white period and Ronchamp Chapel from his last years are entirely different in the character of their spaces. What exactly is this modernism which encompasses such diversity? Has that question been answered by contemporary architecture? The journey only raised more questions about architecture.

After undertaking several more architectural pilgrimages, mainly to the United States and Europe, I opened my own office in 1969 and began to practice architecture without having found the answers to my questions.

At the time, many architects of my generation in Japan were attempting in their separate ways to go beyond modernism. Not having fully resolved the question of modernism in my mind, I looked askance at their activities. I made it my own architectural objective to go back to square one and reexamine the potential of modernism. The difference in the distance we put between ourselves and modernism determined, I believe, the different nature of our subsequent architectural activities.

Work Is Something to Be Created: Starting at the Grass Roots

The architects' complaint that work is scarce is a familiar one. The problem is particularly severe in contemporary Japan, where urban growth has leveled off and social demand for new construction has itself decreased. Not a few aspirants quit architecture even before they have started.

I too had no work for quite some time after I opened my office at the age of 29. However, having strayed off the beaten path, I had no expectations. I immediately began attempts to make my own way.

First, I took advantage of my spare time to develop an imaginary project for a nearby empty lot. This I presented to the owner of the lot, a complete stranger, as a project proposal. Not surprisingly, the proposal was rejected. However, in pursuing such activities I gradually began to receive commissions to design small houses. I literally started at the grass roots.

Looking back, I see how reckless my activities were, but given the nature of the architectural profession, they provided a quite effective training.

It is my belief that you cannot sit back and wait, if you want to design architecture; work is something you have to create yourself. It is because I have lived by that belief that I ended up doing a four-phased project in the Rokko district of Kobe and the Awaji Yumebutai project, which was originally supposed to be a golf course but eventually became a project with environmental regeneration as its theme.

Architects ought to be more aggressive in making their opinions known to society. Architecture can play a much bigger role in society if architects took the initiative and suggested, each in accordance with his or her ideals, what should be created. I believe a change in awareness among architects themselves is necessary if the next generation is to make any headway.

Urban Guerrilla House

A friend from my student days gave me my first job after I opened my office. The conditions were restrictive: a corner site in a district of rowhouses; a total floor area of 100 square meters; and a total construction cost of three million yen. However, I dedicated myself to the project and attempted to create my sort of building.

Less than a year later, a house built like a vertical cave, surrounded on four sides by concrete walls, was completed. The main opening was just a skylight at the top of the void space. Closed rather than open, dark instead of light, this house had nothing of the image of "modern living" then in fashion.

A year after the house was completed, I had an opportunity to show it to Makoto Ueda of the magazine *Toshi Jutaku* and was fortunate enough to have it published. The title of my first published text was "Urban Guerrilla House". I was under the influence then of Trotsky and Che Guevara; the text was about how I was a guerrilla confronting the powerful city and creating "strongholds of resistance" for people struggling to live in the city.

The 1970s was a time when, in reaction to modernist doctrinairism, the postmodern movement which sought to go beyond modernism began to sweep across the world. The essay I had written and the aggressive image projected by the published photographs were interpreted by people as an expression of an architect's rejection of the existing social order and established architectural concepts, and I found myself included among those in disagreement with modernism.

In truth, I had not the slightest interest in the so-called postmodern movement. In fact I loathed the tendency, so common in the movement, to verbalize things. I called myself a guerrilla, not out of a desire to oppose the architectural ideology called modernism. What I wanted to challenge was the city of reality, a city full of contradictions that could not be governed by the transparent logic of modernism. What I wanted to create was absurd spaces full of raw vitality. Looking back, I think I approached my work then more as sculpture than as architecture. The Rowhouse in Sumiyoshi of 1976 was an extension of that urban guerrilla house.

The Rowhouse in Sumiyoshi: My Point of Origin

Critics, both Japanese and foreign, have read a great deal into the Rowhouse in Sumiyoshi and have written complex critiques. In truth, however, I simply did my best to create what I wanted to create; I do not recall being all that calculating in what I was doing.

I began to design at the start of 1974. The conditions were perhaps even more restrictive than those for the first house I had designed for my friend. The construction work was difficult, involving as it did the rebuilding of the middle unit of three rowhouses; only a single wall separated the house from the one next door on either side. The site configuration too was peculiar; it was two *ken* wide and seven *ken* deep (approximately 3.6 meters by 12.6 meters). However, these extreme, stressful conditions—the fact that I had to be alert at all times and could not let even a millimeter go to waste—provided me with an opportunity to think through problems and improve my skills. The building was made possible by the reckless courage of youth.

At the time, I thought of residential design as the creation of a place where people can dwell as they themselves intend. If they feel cold, they can put on an additional layer of clothing. If they feel warm, they can discard extraneous clothing. What is important is that space be, not a device for environmental control, but something definite and responsive to human life. From the point of view of the inhabitant, it may have been an anachronism— in some respects an act of arrogance on the part of the architect. However, I stuck to my beliefs despite some friction with the client. That is perhaps the shortcoming as well as the strength of a self-educated architect. After the existing rowhouse was demolished, the site was divided into three parts. The Rowhouse in Sumiyoshi was then built, with the middle third of the site made into an open courtyard.

The project was naturally carried out with the client's approval, but I was determined to give the house this anti-modern organization, with the dwelling space cut in the middle. After satisfying the minimum conditions of ventilation, daylighting and exposure to sunlight, I thought the question of functionality could be left to the inhabitant. I believed that the important thing was to permit people to nurture themselves there spiritually and physically.

No matter how advanced society becomes, institutionally or technologically, a house in which nature can be sensed represents for me the ideal environment in which to live. From a functional viewpoint, the courtyard of the Rowhouse in Sumiyoshi forces the inhabitant to endure occasional hardships. At the same time, however, the open courtyard is capable of becoming the house's vital organ, introducing into everyday life and assimilating precious stimuli such as changes in nature.

I placed the courtyard at the center in full knowledge of the irrationality of such a decision, precisely because the house was small.

The client and I both knew from experience living in rowhouses how a courtyard can enrich space; we were confident that the decision to organize the house around a courtyard was not a mistake.

Once the house was published in magazines, however, many people criticized its unconventional organization. The huge reaction surprised me and taught me that even a small building can have an impact on society if it has a definite message. The Rowhouse in Sumiyoshi was in effect my debut work as an architect.

From around that time, I became acquainted with other architects of my generation such as the late Kiko Mozuna, Toyokazu Watanabe, Kazuhiro Ishii and Osamu Ishiyama. Conversations with these individualistic architects provided much needed stimuli for a loner like myself.

I met Toyo Ito in 1977. He interviewed me when I was taken up by a special issue of an architectural magazine. I showed him my work such as the Rowhouse in Sumiyoshi and Rose Garden in Kobe, which had just been completed. He was amazed by the way I dropped into houses that were already occupied as if they were my own. The closeness of the relationship between a client and an architect in Osaka apparently came as a culture shock to him.

Early in my career I did not stand on ceremony with clients. In discussions, I would usually keep in check clients who made various demands about layouts or finishes and give priority to my own ideas.

The Rowhouse in Sumiyoshi made me aware of the value of clients, though I behaved as I always had until it was completed. The courtyard did prompt me to make an effort to explain its presence to the client and gain his approval, but otherwise, I did pretty much as I wanted after he agreed to the basic layout.

After its completion, the house was nominated for the Isoya Yoshida Prize. On visiting the house prior to making his final decision, the architect Togo Murano who was judging the nominated works offered an unexpected critique. He said nothing about the building's merits or demerits but only remarked that "the client for this is to be commended." That was when I was first made aware of how clients give me opportunities to create. I still think Murano's remark was the best architectural criticism that has been provided of the Rowhouse in Sumiyoshi.

An Architecture Open to a Double Interpretation: The Koshino Residence

After the Rowhouse in Sumiyoshi, I knew the direction I should take. My practice stabilized to some extent. However, I found that I was not taking on new challenges; I had fallen into something of a rut. The Koshino Residence of 1981 provided me with a chance to break out of that established pattern.

In the majority of my works up to then, the theme had been how to carve out a "rich" dwelling space on an extremely small site in the middle of the vulgar urban environment. By contrast, the Koshino Residence was for an extensive site in the Okuike district in Ashiya City; there were no constraints on the size or the program. Thus the commission gave me, in the pursuit of my ideal architectural prototype, an opportunity to adopt a viewpoint that was the direct opposite of the one taken in the Rowhouse of Sumiyoshi.

In this verdant natural landscape, with no city to oppose, I confronted for the first time the question of the relationship between architecture and exterior space, that is, the question of gardens.

What sort of architecture can make the most of the attractive features of this gently sloping hillside?

Architectural spaces in which nature and architecture are in harmony are what is most admirable about traditional Japanese architecture. It was perhaps natural that I should conceive the idea of re-creating in contemporary architecture the flowing spaces of Japanese architecture. I wanted to achieve that through the use of forceful walls arranged in accordance with those consistent, Western principles of organization I had adhered to since the urban guerrilla house. The result was two concrete boxes arranged in parallel on different levels of the hillside.

My objective was an architecture that possessed both the softness of Japanese architecture and the strength of Western architecture; that is, an architecture open to a double interpretation, on the one hand engaged in a calm dialogue with nature, and on the other, clearly asserting its own presence in the environment.

As in earlier, smaller houses, I made the geometrical composition of the exposed concrete as pure as possible in order to make the building independent in character. At the same time, I made drawings to study every conceivable effect nature would have on that man-made world. How would changes in light in summer affect the appearance of the space? At what angle would light enter in winter?

Once a building has been stripped of formal ornament, light comes to play an important role in giving space its character. Taking into account such problems, I manipulated the abstract geometry once more and made fine adjustments. The building was created by balancing the conflicting demands of ideas in an abstract world and ideas in the representational world of reality.

Abstraction and Representation

For me, this conflict between abstraction and representation is an eternal theme of architecture. I wrote an essay on this subject entitled "Superimposition of Abstraction and Representation" about ten years ago in a special residential issue of *Shinkenchiku*. Asserting that architecture is based on the conflict between abstraction and representation, I cited Albers' "Homage to the Square" as an expression of abstraction and Piranesi's *Carceri* plates as an expression of representation. I concluded with a statement that an architecture that expressed simultaneously both abstraction and representation, "concealing a Piranesian visionary maze within an Albersesque framework", was for me the eternal theme of architecture.

My theme is to balance the conflicting demands made by two opposite tendencies: a predilection for an abstract world that gives architecture "strength" and a yearning for a representational world that provides "depth"; in other words, to see how a rich space that enters into a dialogue with nature can be created and how the history and memories of a place can be passed on to architecture, while adhering to a geometrical organization and using limited materials.

The Rowhouse in Sumiyoshi was a work in which I pursued this problem of abstraction and representation in my own way and, I believe, was able to suggest the ultimate, prototypical solution. By contrast, the Koshino Residence was an attempt to expand and generalize that methodology. The work was subsequently cited by Kenneth Frampton as a representative example of what he called "critical regionalism".

Rokko Housing: My First Multi-Unit Housing Project

The completion of the Koshino Residence coincided with the start of construction on Rokko Housing, my first multi-unit housing project.

This project began with my persuading the client, who had asked me to design an apartment building on level land, already prepared for development, at the foot of a mountain, to make the 60-degree slope behind that property the site instead.

My objective in the project was first to devise an organization that made the most of the sloping character of the site; I would then create a highly variegated plan in which no two units had the same floor area or layout and introduce into the project public spaces that had the human scale and intimacy of back streets.

As a way of giving shape to the project, I conceived the idea of inserting a uniform frame into the sloping site which was irregular in both plan and section. The introduction of a regular form into something irregular naturally generates three-dimensional displacements. I linked the interstices created by those displacements and made them into public spaces; the units with diverse forms are connected like detached houses to those spaces.

It sounds simple, but creating ample unit plans as well as diverse public spaces in the interstices between units by manipulating a three-dimensional frame adapted to the topography was not an easy task. We studied many different proposals and created many models before deciding on the final organization. My aim was to create a work that was designed down to the smallest details that would represent a compilation of all I had learned on the theme of superimposing abstraction and representation from the Rowhouse of Sumiyoshi to the Koshino Residence.

The completed building steps back and the individual units themselves are set back to follow the slope of the site. A plaza in the middle divides the building into an upper half and a lower half.

The main approach to this multi-unit housing project, which is approximately ten stories in height from the lowest floor, is a stairway threaded through an interstice in the middle. All units are accessed by stairs in interstices in the building organized around the central stairway.

Ordinarily, vertical circulation in a ten-story building constructed with its back to a steep slope is by elevator, but I deliberately located the open stairway/plaza in the middle so that residents would experience the richness that comes from living in close proximity to other persons, which is the greatest benefit of being in a multi-unit housing project.

The client insisted on having elevators, but I made them inconspicuous. Since the completion of the building, most residents, no matter which level they live on, use the stairs for moving up and down and enjoy encountering neighbors there.

Through this project I became aware of, and learned a great deal about, many issues in architecture such as the question of the character of a place or region, and the question of private versus public, or part versus the whole.

Reviving Community: Transforming the Space of Everyday Life into a Symbol

The architect Kazuo Shinohara, who died recently, published in *Shinkenchiku* in 1962 an important statement that "Houses are art". At a time when the semantic analyses of architecture were popular, his thesis celebrating the symbolic character of space had considerable impact on the architectural world.

Although my viewpoint was somewhat different from his, I too attempted to transform the space of everyday life into a symbol in the stairway of Rokko Housing. Here, the "symbol" is not a means of architectural expression but a thing that gives form to the invisible community, whether it be that of a family or a neighborhood.

From the early 1970s there was a tendency to place greater value on privacy, evidenced for example by Takashi Kurosawa's houses, which were clusters of individual bedrooms. Society as a whole seemed to be losing its sense of community. In the design of single-family houses, I proposed the introduction of a symbolic space in everyday dwelling spaces as a step toward the restoration of that sense of community. Rokko Housing was my first attempt to take that idea one step further, from the single-family house to a multi-unit housing project.

In fact, as Rokko Housing neared completion, I began to devise a plan on my own to develop adjacent land into a multi-unit housing project with the idea of reorganizing the entire hillside into one continuous multi-unit community. It was as usual a reckless endeavor, but this aggressiveness paid off. It took almost 20 years, but Rokko Housing was followed by two successive phases, Rokko Housing II and III. Given a unique opportunity to be continuously involved in the growth of one place, I worked not only to expand the scale of the project but to create ample public spaces; my theme has consistently been to devise an organization that makes the most of the sloping site. The results are evident in the everyday scenes to be encountered in the stepped plazas, which have taken a different form with each phase.

The House is the Point of Origin of Architecture

Forty years have passed since I began my activities, determined to pursue a profession in which I had educated myself. The client of the Rowhouse of Sumiyoshi continues to live a full life in that extremely small dwelling. A third addition to the Koshino Residence has just been completed last year. Construction on a project that will become the fourth phase of Rokko Housing is currently in progress.

In writing this text, I have been reminded once more of how at the core I am the product of my self-education and those years in my 20s when I fought anxiety born of that self-education and desperately pursued architecture. At the same time, I have confirmed for myself once more the fact that from the start of my career to the present day, the design of houses has always been the axis around which my architectural activities have revolved.

I, who challenged the city through the design of small houses, am now designing mainly public buildings in Japan and abroad on the one hand and participating as an architect in Tokyo's urban regeneration concept on the other. The work load is substantial for a small office like mine, and every day is a struggle. Nevertheless, I continue to design several houses each year. Houses are opportunities to train young staff members and help me preserve my own sense of balance. I therefore welcome such commissions despite their negative repercussions on the administration of my office.

Once the jobs I am committed to now are on track, I want to gradually reduce my work load and return once more to where I began. In any case, of one thing I am certain—my last work will be a house.

敷地は低層木造家屋がひしめきあう大阪の下町、その一角にある3軒長屋の中央の1軒を通し梁もろとも切り取って建て替えたものである。

　狭小な敷地に建つ極小の建築の内に、いかにしてミクロコスモスとしての住空間を実現するかという主題に対し、われわれが提案したのは、既存長屋を2層分のコンクリートの箱に置き換え、その箱を3分割した中央をヴォイドとする構成だった。

　中庭を挟んで、1階は居間と食堂・台所・浴室が、2階では子供室と主寝室が対峙し、それぞれの空間はブリッジと階段によって結ばれる。

　単純な構成とその内に展開する複雑多様な空間体験、コンクリート壁の閉ざされた表情とその内に息づく光、風による抽象化された自然の生命力。その後の私の建築の原点となるイメージを、この小さな都市住宅建設のプロセスの中で掴んだ。

　中庭を核とした構成上、あえて街路側のファサードは壁で閉じたが、唯一穿たれたエントランス開口から漏れる光が暗示するように、この住宅はあくまで、長屋という都市住宅形式の文脈の中で誕生したものである。

住吉の長屋
Row House in Sumiyoshi
1975-76
大阪府大阪市 —— Osaka, Osaka

Amid densely packed low-class wooden houses in an old working class district of Osaka, the site is the middle portion of three adjacent row houses on a corner, which was cut away together with its through-beams, and then rebuilt.

To implement the living spaces as a microcosm within a minimal building on a narrow site, our proposal was to replace the existing two-story row house with a concrete box, and to organize that box in three divisions with a central void.

The courtyard is interposed between the living room and the kitchen / dining room / bathroom on the first floor, and the child room and master bedroom on the second floor. The spaces are all linked by a bridge and flight of stairs.

This simple composition and the diverse and complex spatial experiences that unfold within, the closed expression of the concrete walls and the wind and light that breathe within, provide the vitality of an abstracted nature.

In addition to a composition with the central courtyard as the core, the street facade is boldly closed off with a wall, but as suggested by the hint of light escaping from the sole opening of the entrance, this house has still emerged from within the context of the urban housing model known as the row house.

3軒長屋の中央部分を切り取り、挿入されたコンクリートのボックス。隣家との間隔は人も入れないほどで、コンクリートの型枠は撤去されていない。施工的にも限界に挑戦した住宅。

The central part of three row houses was excised, and a concrete box was inserted. The gaps between the box and the neighboring houses are not even wide enough for a person to enter, so the formwork for the concrete could not be removed. This is a house that challenged limits even during its construction.

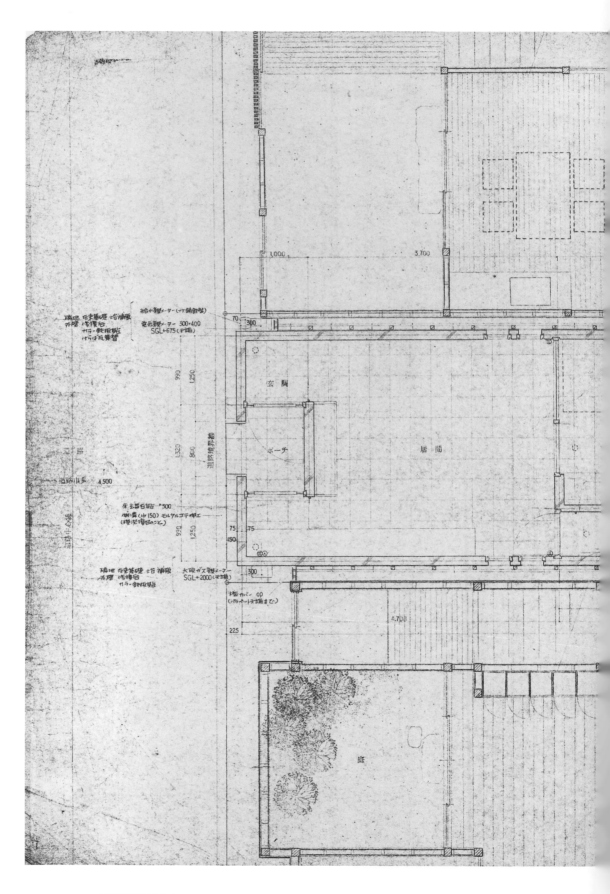

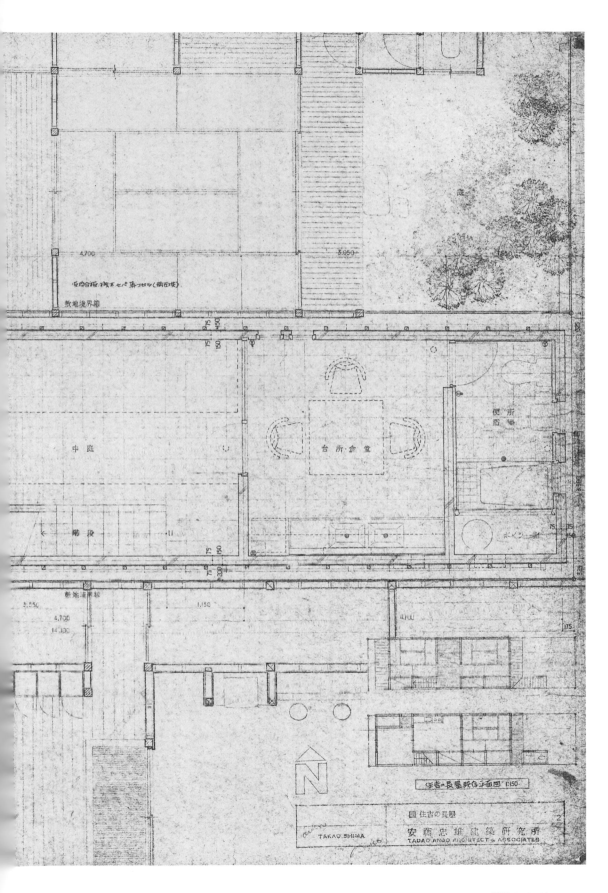

4,700

3,050

1,550

佐官台板 挽木セパ葉コロン(調色塗).

敷地境界線

75 450

75 150

中庭

便所
簡易

台所・食堂

階段

75 150

75 200

75 75 150

敷地境界線

3,550

4,700

14,100

1,150

4,700

175

住吉の長屋既往平面図 1:150

N

□ 住吉の長屋

2

TAKAO SHIMA

安藤忠雄建築研究所
TADAO ANDO ARCHITECT & ASSOCIATES

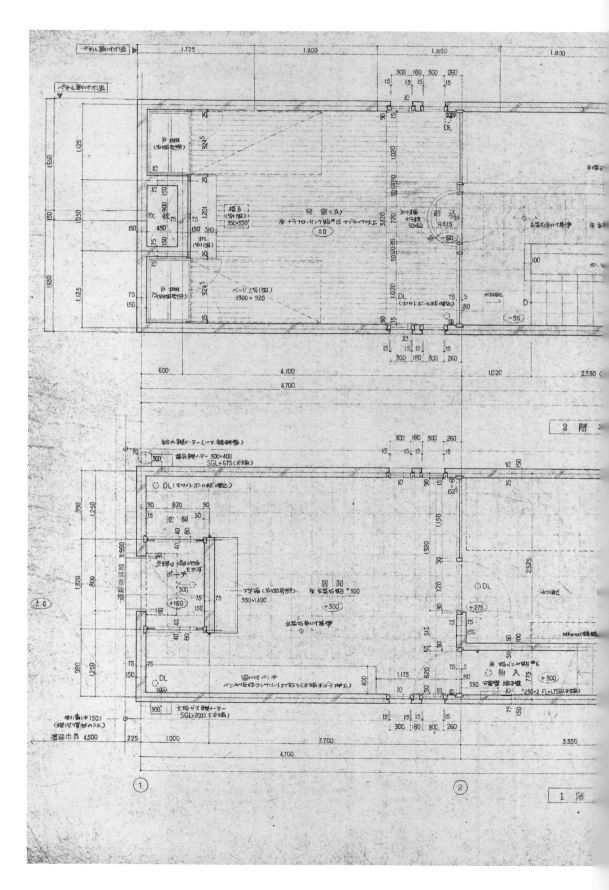

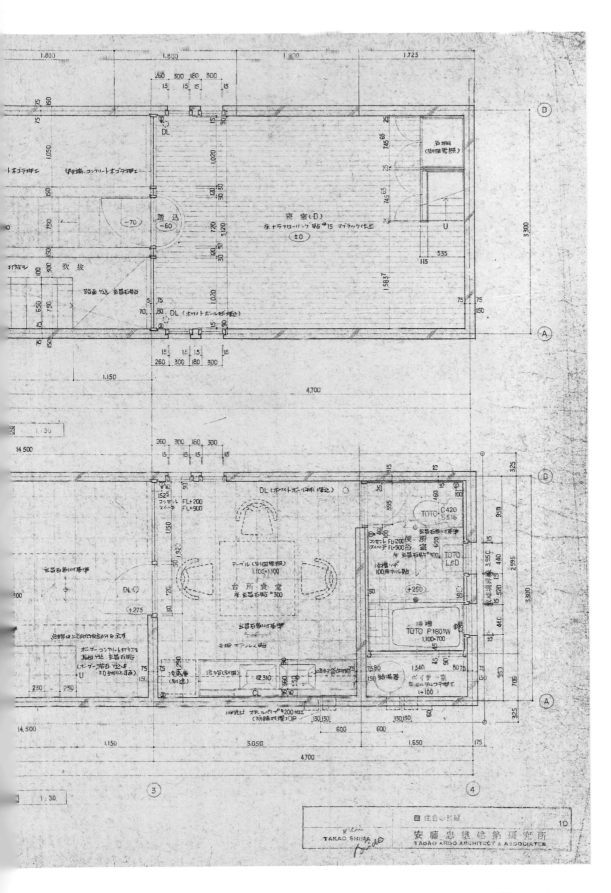

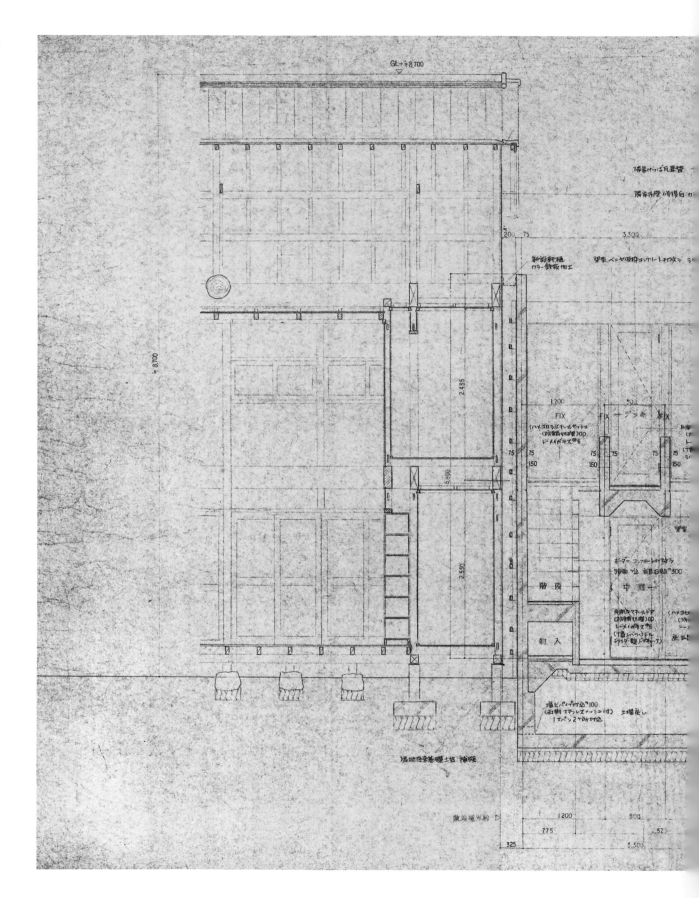

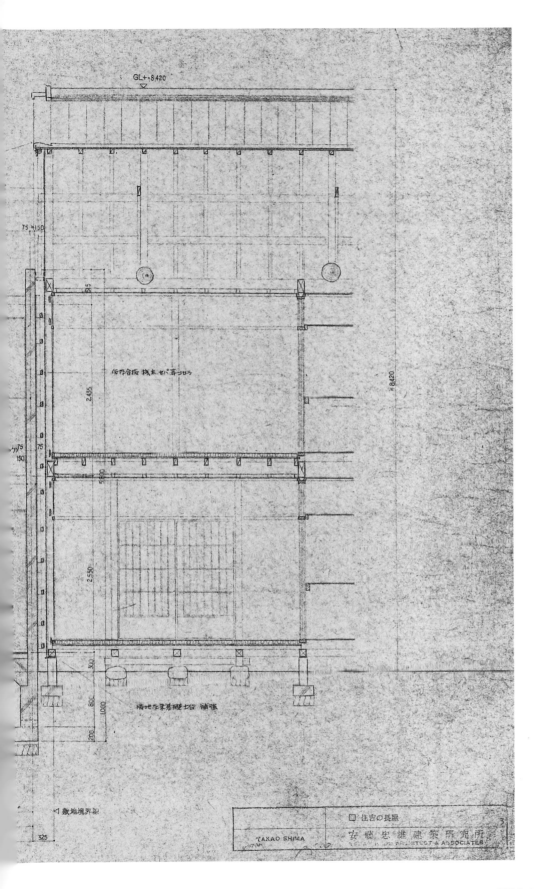

GL+.8420

75 =150

515

仮作合板 桟木.セパ葺コロシ

2.455

75

150

5300

2.550

=8420

300

800

1000

200

隣地住家基礎土台 補強

敷地境界線

325

TAKAO SHIMA

住吉の長屋

3

安藤忠雄建築研究所
TADAO ANDO ARCHITECT & ASSOCIATES

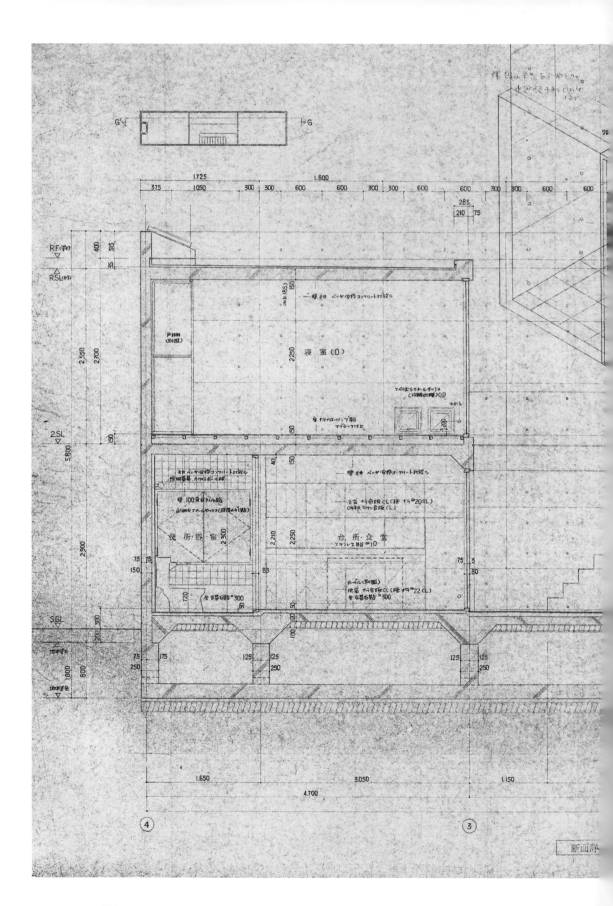

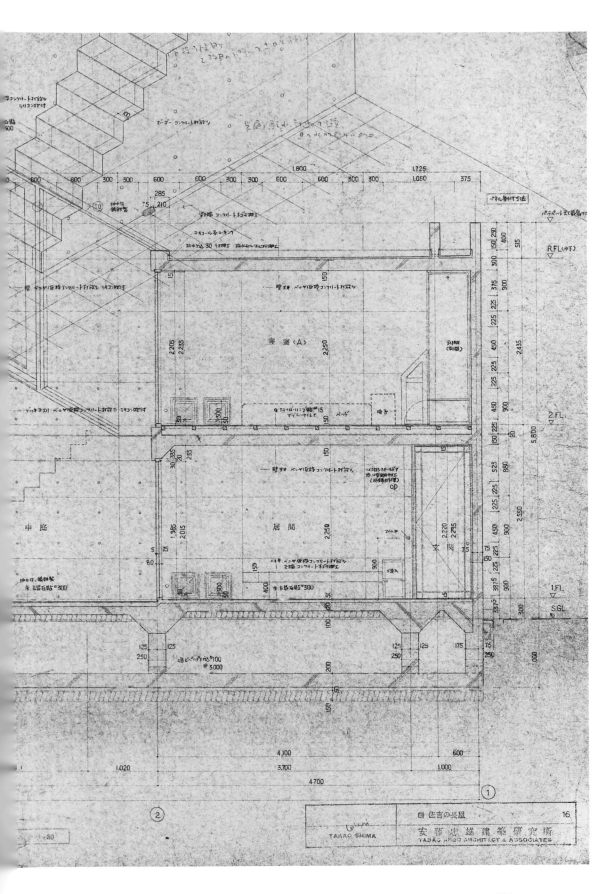

中庭に浮かぶブリッジと、階段の造形。極めて単純な
構成の中、最小限の要素が織り成す多様な空間のシー
クエンス。

The sculpting of the stair and the bridge that floats
above the courtyard. Varied spatial sequences and
minimal elements are interwoven in this extremely
simple composition.

中庭から食堂を見る。玄昌石貼りの床が、中庭から室内まで連続する。建築の内と外の概念を一変させた、小宇宙の空間。

Looking at the dining room from the courtyard. The slate floor surface continues from the courtyard to the interior. This is a microcosmic space that completely inverts the concepts of architecture's inside and outside.

2階床のフローリングを含め、インテリアの人間の手に触れる部分にはすべてナラ材が用いられている。コンクリートの壁、玄昌石の床、ナラの家具——人間とともに、時間の経過を刻んでいく、自然の材料。

All the interior parts touched by human hands are made from oak, including the wood floorboards on the second level. Concrete walls, slate floors, oak furniture—together with human beings, these natural materials are weathered by the passage of time.

中庭のヴォイドを介して相対する4つの部屋に、光、風が
入り込む。住居の中心部を占める中庭は、各スペースの
緩衝領域であるのと同時に、自然を引き込む装置である。

Light and wind enter the four rooms that confront
each other across the courtyard void. The courtyard
contained in the middle of the dwelling is a buffer
area for each space, and simultaneously a device
that draws in nature.

富島邸は実質上の私の処女作である。敷地は住吉の長屋と同様の長屋街区で、その端の1軒分を切り取って、コンクリートの箱型住宅に置き換えるという計画だった。ここでは、主たる開口部を屋上のスカイライトとして、その下に吹き抜け階段を設けて各部屋をスキップフロアでつなげる構成を試みている。この住宅で初めてコンクリートという素材を扱い、建築の壁のもつ力を実感した。

後に友人であるクライアントからこの住宅を譲り受け、自身のアトリエとすることになった。使いこなしていく過程で、逐次増改築を行い、第1期では屋上に屋根を架け、第2期では隣接地に新築棟を建てて連結、第3期には2棟間にヴォールト屋根のペントハウスを架け渡し、全体の印象を一変させた。即興的な改造の積み重ねは、来訪者の意表をつく不連続な空間をつくり出し、最終的にはいわゆる機能合理主義とはほど遠い迷宮的なアトリエ空間が生まれていた。この建築は、私にとって活動の拠点であるのと同時に、個人的な建築実験の場であった。その後、大淀のアトリエは全面取り壊し、新たに大淀のアトリエIIをつくることとなる。

冨島邸／大淀のアトリエ

Tomishima House / Atelier in Oyodo

1971-73, 80-81
大阪府大阪市——Osaka, Osaka

The Tomishima House is essentially my first work. The site is similar to the row house district of the Row House in Sumiyoshi, and the plan involved cutting one part from the end and replacing it with a concrete box house. With a rooftop skylight as the main aperture, and an open stair below it, I attempted a composition in which the various rooms are connected as skipped floors. In this house, I first dealt with the material of concrete, and I sensed the power possessed by the walls of architecture.

I later took over the house from the client, who was a friend, and converted it into my personal atelier. In the process of learning to use it, I made a series of extensions. In the first phase, I added a roof to the rooftop deck; in the second phase, I built a connected new wing on the adjacent site; in the third phase, I constructed a vaulted-roof penthouse spanning between the two wings, completely changing the entire impression. This accumulation of improvised extensions produced discontinuous spaces that surprised visitors, and finally resulted in a labyrinthine atelier space that is a long way from functional rationality. This architecture was my base of activity, and was simultaneously a place for personal architectural experimentation.

I later demolished the entire Atelier in Oyodo and constructed Atelier in Oyodo II.

冨島邸のアクソノメトリック・ドローイング。屋上のスカイライトの下に設けられた吹き抜け階段の踊場が、そのまま部屋となったような構成。

Axonometric drawing of the Tomishima House. A composition in which the landings of the stairwell established below the rooftop skylight are used as the rooms.

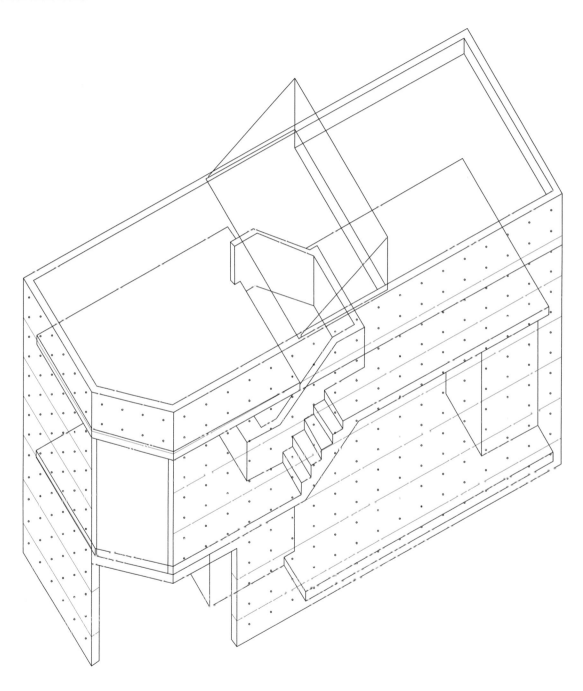

長屋街に挿入されたコンクリートの箱。1階にガレージ
と住居部への入口、2階のコーナーに唯一の窓がある。

A concrete box implanted in a row house
neighborhood. The entrance to the garage and
the residential part is on the first floor, and the
only window is on the corner of the second
floor.

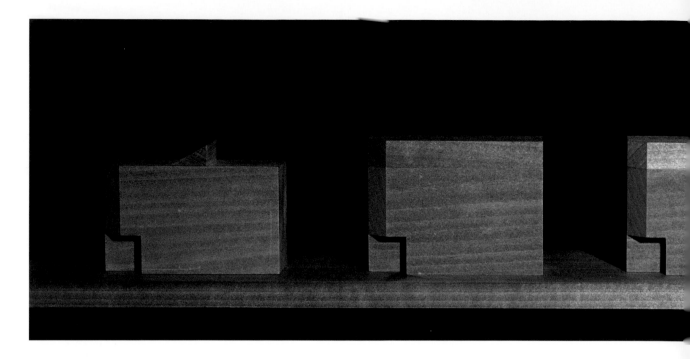

富島邸
Tomishima House

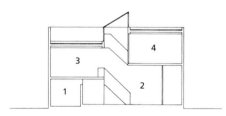

Section

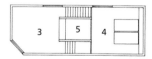

Second floor plan

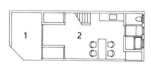

First floor plan   1:300

1 garage	5 void
2 dining room	6 atelier
3 living room	7 court
4 bedroom	

増築第I期
Addition phase I

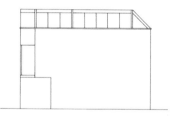

North elevation

冨島邸は後に安藤自身のアトリエとして再出発する。3度の増改築を重ねる中で、安藤は積極的に即興のデザインを楽しんでいた節がある。

The Tomishima House was later renovated as Ando's own atelier. Across a series of three extensions, Tadao Ando enjoyed a period of active design improvisation.

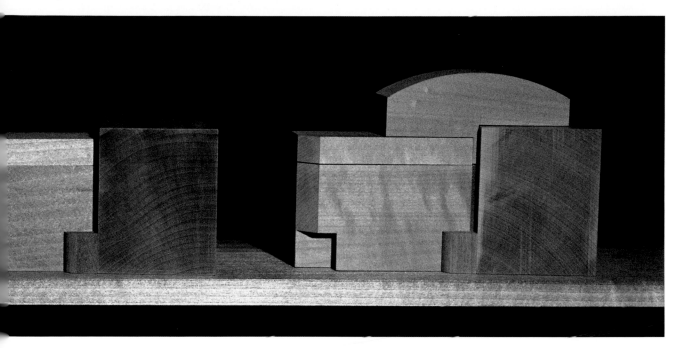

増築 II 期
Addition phase II

増築 III 期
Additon phase III

Second floor plan (phase II)

Fourth floor plan (phase III)

First floor plan (phase II)

Third floor plan (phase II)

大淀のアトリエの変遷。長屋街区に登場したコンクリートのボックスが生物のように増殖していく、
ダイナミックな建築のプロセス。

Transformations of the Atelier in Oyodo. In a dynamic architectural process,
the concrete box that appeared in this row house district proliferated like a living thing.

大淀のアトリエを解体し、全面的に新築したものである。建物の平面的な輪郭はそのまま、内部も基本的には前のアトリエのかたちを踏襲している。

　地上5階、地下1階の建物の構成の核となるのは、建物東側を占める1階から最上階までを貫く吹き抜け階段の空間である。各フロアはこの吹き抜けに面して、段状にセットバックしながら重ねられ、ブリッジを介して階段と結ばれる。全体が一体となったワンルームの構成で、各スペースの用途もあえて特定しておらず、常に全体が流動的な場となっている。吹き抜け階段の上部は全面トップライトが架けられており、そこから建物内部深くまで入り込む自然の光が、コンクリートの壁に繊細な自然の移ろいを映し出す。この光の井戸の底が私の仕事場である。

大淀のアトリエ Ⅱ

Atelier in Oyodo Ⅱ

1989-91
大阪府大阪市——Osaka, Osaka

The Atelier in Oyodo was demolished, and this is a completely new building. The plan profile of the building remains unchanged, and the interior also basically follows the shape of the previous atelier.

With five floors above ground and one floor below ground, the compositional core of the building is the stair space that occupies the east side of the building from the first floor up until the top. Every floor faces this void, layering up as they step back in a tiered shape, linking to the stairs through bridges. The whole is unified into a single-room composition. Without specifying the usage of any space, it is always a fluid place. The surface above the stair void consists entirely of a skylight, and natural light penetrates deep into the interior of the building, projecting the subtle shifts of nature onto the concrete walls. My workspace is at the bottom of this well of light.

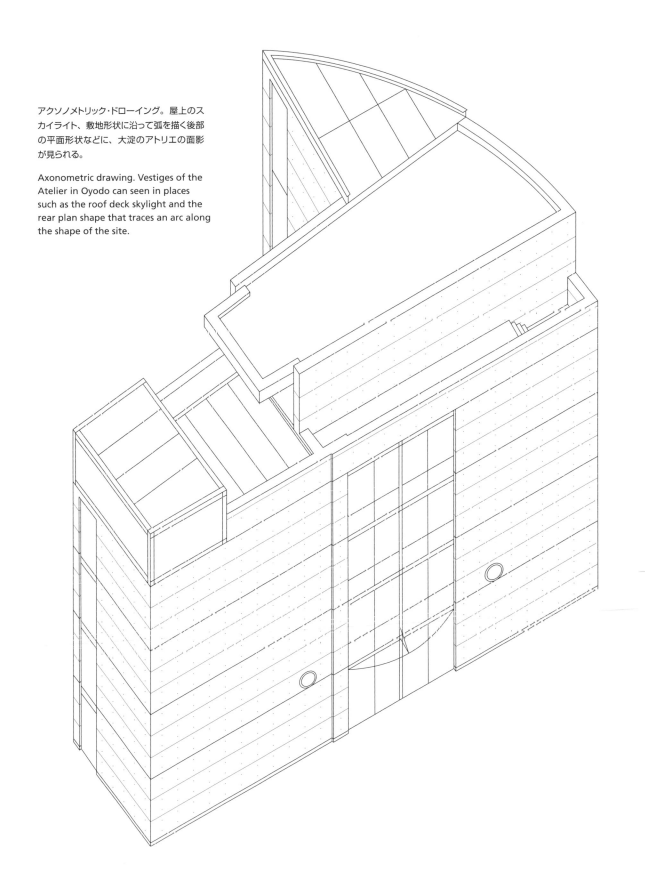

アクソノメトリック・ドローイング。屋上のス
カイライト、敷地形状に沿って弧を描く後部
の平面形状などに、大淀のアトリエの面影
が見られる。

Axonometric drawing. Vestiges of the
Atelier in Oyodo can seen in places
such as the roof deck skylight and the
rear plan shape that traces an arc along
the shape of the site.

5層吹き抜けの空間に、トップライトからの光が差し込む。　Light from the skylight streams into the five-level void space.

吹き抜けの底に見えるのが安藤のスペース。各階に座るスタッフとは吹き抜けを介して空間的につながっている。垂直方向に広がるワンルームのオフィス空間。

Tadao Ando's space can be seen at the bottom of the void. The staff members sitting on each floor are spatially linked by the void. This is a single continuous office space that expands in the vertical direction.

吹き抜け階段、ブリッジから各フロアを巡る壁は全面書架となっている。

There are bookshelves across all the wall surfaces surrounding
each floor, accessed by bridges and the stairwell.

4 階の打ち合わせスペース。　The fourth-floor meeting space.

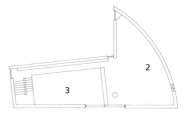

Fouth floor plan

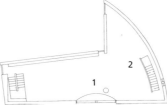

First floor plan

Third floor plan

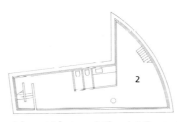

First basement floor plan

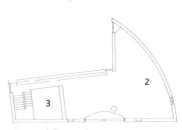

Second floor plan

1 entrance
2 atelier
3 void

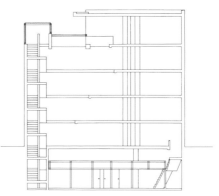

Second basement floor plan

Section 1:400

吹き抜け階段から見る4階レベルのオフィス。　The fourth level of the office, seen from the stairwell.

大淀のアトリエⅡの、道路を隔てた向かいの敷地に計画されたアトリエ・アネックスである。ゲスト
ハウスとしての機能もあわせもつ。

　全体は、不整形の敷地中央に、中庭を囲むように配されたＬ字型のコンクリートボックスと、そ
の北東側にとりつく敷地形状に沿った鋭角の壁により構成される。階段室や水廻り、倉庫などの
サービス空間は、各階の鋭角の壁によるスペースに納められる。Ｌ字型のコンクリートボックスは、
地階から２階までの３層にわたる居住空間と最上階のゲストルームとに分けられ、それぞれのスペー
スは吹き抜け、テラスにより、中庭のクスノキを中心に連続的に展開していく。

　半屋外の空間を手がかりとした空間の積層により、立体的な広がりをもつ居住空間をつくること
が主題だった。

大淀のアトリエ・アネックス

Atelier in Oyodo Annex

1994-95

大阪府大阪市——— Osaka, Osaka

Planned on a site just across the street from Oyodo Atelier II, this is the atelier annex. It also includes guesthouse facilities.

In the center of an irregularly shaped site, overall it is composed of an L-shaped concrete box arranged around a courtyard with acutely angled walls following the shape of the site attached to the northeast. The service spaces on each floor, such as the staircase, water utilities and storage, are accommodated in the spaces defined by the acutely angled walls. The L-shaped concrete box is divided into a guestroom on the top floor and a three-level living space from the basement up to the second level. Due to the voids and terraces, every space continuously extends toward the central courtyard, which has a camphor tree in the center.

The theme was to construct an expansive three-dimensional residential space by means of a spatial layering that leads to semi-outdoor spaces.

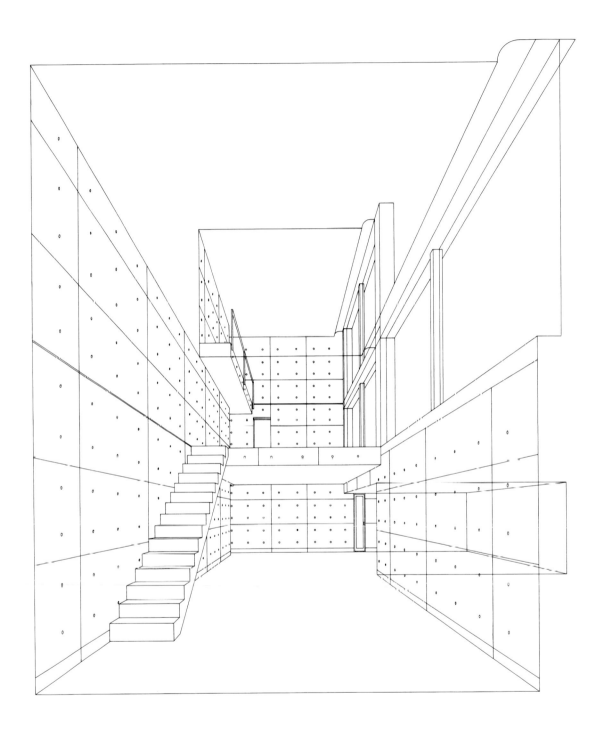

パースペクティブ・ドローイング。吹き抜け、中庭、テラスを介して3層にわたり連続するダイナミックな空間構成。

Perspective drawing. A dynamic spatial composition that is connected across three levels through the void, courtyard, and terrace.

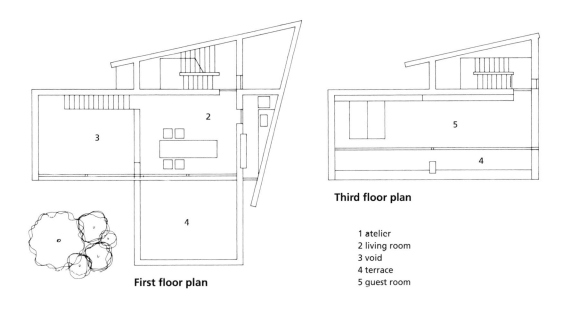

First floor plan

Third floor plan

1 atelier
2 living room
3 void
4 terrace
5 guest room

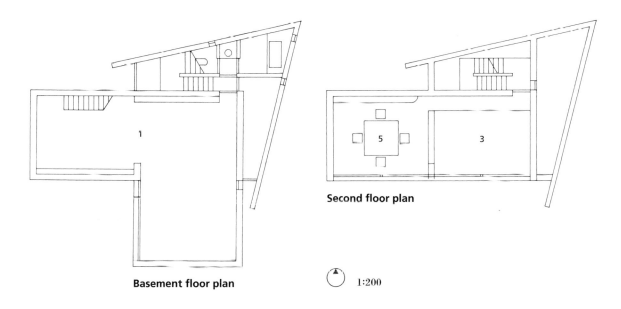

Basement floor plan

Second floor plan

1:200

西側ファサード。無機的なコンクリートの壁を背景に、
中庭のクスノキの緑が活き活きと繁っている。

West facade. The lush green of the camphor
tree in the courtyard spreads across the
backdrop of the inorganic concrete wall.

リビングから同面積のテラスを見る。テラス
に向かって右側は半階下がった中庭空間。

Looking from the living
room toward a terrace with the same
surface area. Facing the terrace to
the right is a courtyard space that
has been lowered by half a floor.

リビング越しに望むテラスと中庭。
Looking across the living room to the terrace and courtyard.

テラスから中庭のクスノキを見る。
Looking at the camphor tree in the terrace from the courtyard.

アトリエからリビングへ昇る階段から南側の庭を見る。入れ子状に連続する吹き抜けの空間。

Looking at the south garden while ascending the stairs from the atelier to the living room. A series of nested void spaces.

左：吹き抜けを介して2階ゲストルームを見る。
右：中庭に面したゲストルーム。

Left: Looking through the void at the second-floor guestroom.
Right: The guestroom facing the courtyard.

地階アトリエ。
奥の吹き抜け部分は天井高さ 5.1m。

Basement atelier.
The deeper void section has a
ceiling height of 5.1m.

敷地は、兵庫県芦屋の緑深い山の斜面に位置する。日本の著名なファッションデザイナーのための住宅である。自然豊かな立地環境、自由度の高いプログラムを受けて、われわれが目指したのは、建築が自律した存在としてありながら、周囲の自然環境と呼応するような建築と場所の関係性の創出だった。

構成は単純である。点在する樹木を避けながら、高さの異なるコンクリートのボックスが半ば埋もれたかたちで2本並置されている。ボックスの長手方向は敷地の傾斜面にも平行し、両者は地中の通路によって結ばれている。片方の棟は、下層にリビングと食堂、上層に主寝室を納め、もう一方の棟は、壁を隔てて連続する6室の個室を納めている。2棟に挟まれた階段状の中庭は、リビング棟の2階と個室棟の屋上をつなぎ、生活空間に広がりを与える装置として働く。

ボックス内部は、強い光を引き込むスリット窓、庭の風景を切り取る開口部など、限定された外部の自然との関わりによって、各々のスペースの性格づけがなされている。建築要素を徹底して純化することで、そこに入り込む自然の力を際立たせるような住まいを意図していた。

建物が竣工してから4年後にアトリエ棟を増築することになった。既存部分の直線的な構成に対して、増築部分は1/4の円弧を描く壁が地盤を受け止め、空間を囲い取る。円弧に沿って、天井にはスリット状のトップライトが穿たれ、コンクリートの壁に力強い光の幾何学が描かれる。この対比的な性格をもつ増築部分の介入により、この住宅の建築としての完結性はより高められることとなった。

小篠邸

Koshino House

1979-81, 83-84 (atelier),
2004-06 (guest house)
兵庫県芦屋市 —— Ashiya, Hyogo

The site is located on a verdant slope in Ashiya, Hyogo prefecture. It is a house for a well-known Japanese fashion designer. Taking on the abundant nature of the local environment, and a program with a high degree of freedom, we aimed to generate a relationship between architecture and place that allowed the architecture to have autonomy while acting in concert with the surrounding natural environment.

The composition is simple. While avoiding the scattered trees, two concrete boxes of different height have been juxtaposed in a half-buried shape. The long sides of the boxes run parallel with the slope of the site, and they are connected by means of an underground passage.

One wing contains the living room and dining room on the lower level, and the master bedroom on the upper level. The other wing contains a series of six private rooms isolated by walls. The tiered courtyard garden interposed between the two wings connects the second floor of the living wing with the rooftop of the private room wing, and acts as a device to give an expansive living space.

Inside the boxes, each space is given character by means of a relationship with the limited exterior nature, through slit windows letting in strong light and apertures that frame the garden scenery. The goal was a house in which the power of nature that penetrates it is made conspicuous by a thorough purification of the architectural elements.

Four years after the building was completed, an atelier wing was added. In contrast to the linear composition of the existing parts, the addition is enclosed by a wall that delineates a quarter circle, blocking the earth and embracing the space. The ceiling is pierced by a slit-shaped skylight that follows the arc, geometrically drawing powerful light on the concrete wall. The architectural completeness of this house was enhanced by the strongly contrasting character of the addition.

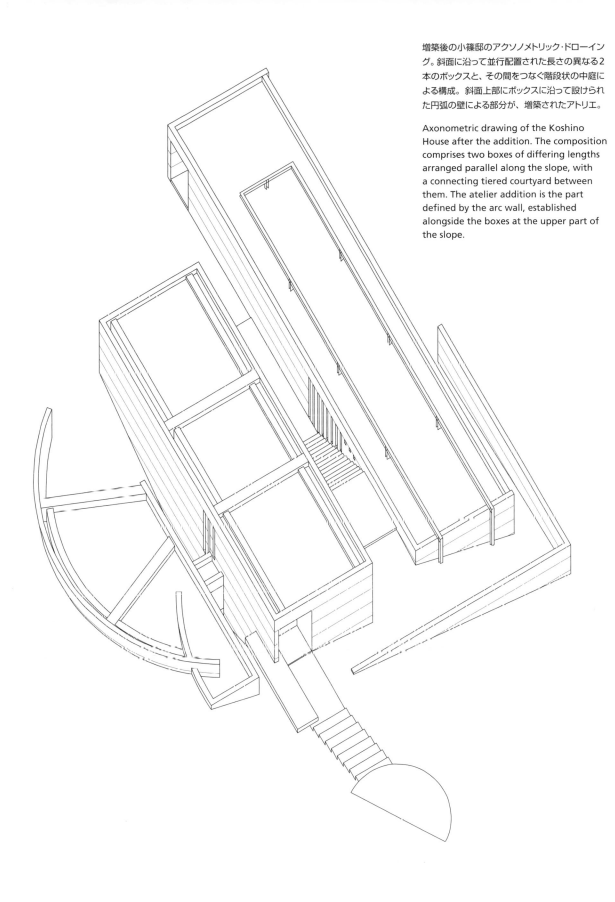

増築後の小篠邸のアクソノメトリック・ドローイング。斜面に沿って並行配置された長さの異なる2本のボックスと、その間をつなぐ階段状の中庭による構成。斜面上部にボックスに沿って設けられた円弧の壁による部分が、増築されたアトリエ。

Axonometric drawing of the Koshino House after the addition. The composition comprises two boxes of differing lengths arranged parallel along the slope, with a connecting tiered courtyard between them. The atelier addition is the part defined by the arc wall, established alongside the boxes at the upper part of the slope.

増築後の小篠邸の鳥瞰。地形に沿って埋め込まれたように配置されたコンクリートのボックス。
Bird's-eye view of the Koshino House after the addition. An array of buried concrete boxes, following the topography.

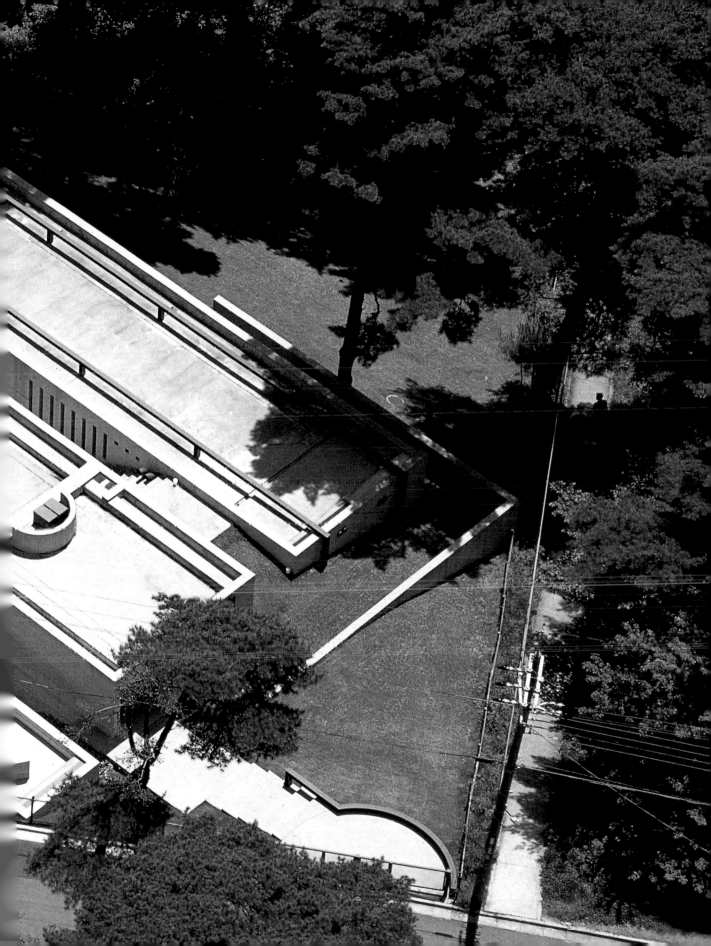

個室棟南側外観。列柱のワンスパンが個室1室分に相当する。
建物際の樹木はもとからあったもの。既存樹木を極力残すことを
前提に建物配置が計画された。

The south facade of the private room wing. One span of
the colonnade corresponds to one private room.
The trees at the edge of the building were pre-existing.
The building layout was premised on retaining as much
as possible of the existing trees and shrubs.

リビングに設けられた２つの開口部は、それぞれが切り取る
庭の風景を踏まえ、慎重にプロポーションが決定されている。

Each of the two openings created in the living
room have been determined based on framing
scenes of the garden with careful proportions.

壁際に設けられたスリット状のトップライトからの光が、
壁に自然の推移を映し出し、無機的なコンクリートの
箱に生命を吹き込む。

The light from the slit-shaped skylight on the
edge of the wall projects the transitions of nature
onto the wall, breathing life into an inorganic
concrete box.

廊下よりリビング方向を見る。
Looking in the direction of the living room from the corridor.

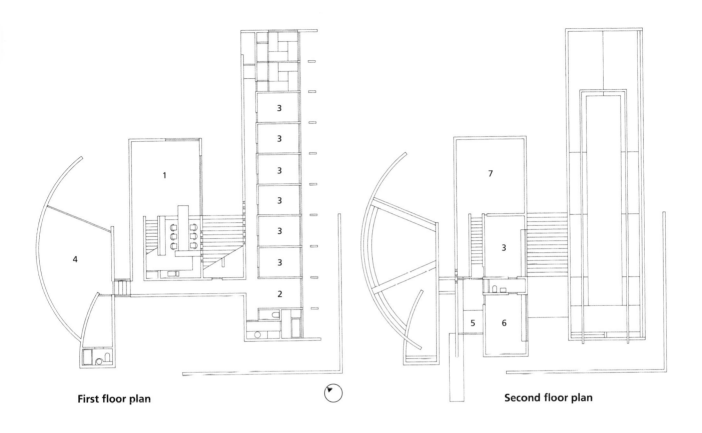

First floor plan

Second floor plan

1 living room
2 lobby
3 bedroom
4 atelier
5 entrance
6 study
7 void

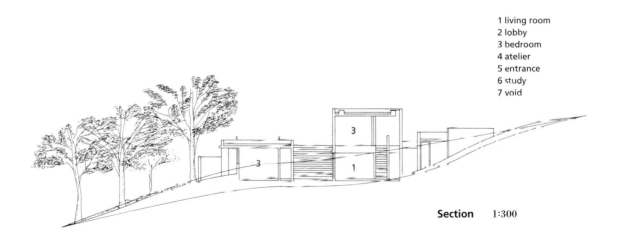

Section   1:300

厳格な幾何学による構成。増築部を形どる円弧も、既存棟の幾何学と一定の図学的関係を保っている。

A composition based on strict geometry. The addition part is modeled by an arc, and also maintains
a fixed relationship with the geometry of the existing wing.

増築されたアトリエ内部。曲面の壁にトップライトから光が差し込む。
Interior of the atelier addition. Light streams onto the curved wall from the skylight.

トップライトから差し込む光の表情は刻々と変化する。

The light penetrating from the skylight changes
in expression from moment to moment.

増築されたアトリエ部分。
庭と建物との関係は、増築においても踏襲されている。

Atelier addition.
The relationships between the garden and the
building are maintained in the addition.

兵庫県芦屋市の奥池に建つ小篠邸の2度目の改築である。

　アトリエ棟の増築から20年目、再びクライアントから建物の増築を依頼された。新たな要素の付加がテーマであった第Ⅱ期と異なり、今回は建物の一部を取り壊し、完全につくり変えるのが要望のプログラムだった。具体的には、家族の成長によりほとんど使われなくなった個室を納めた南側の棟を取り壊して、ファッションデザイナーであるクライアントの多彩な創造活動を受け止めるホールとする計画である。自身の意識の上でも、実際の空間構成の上でもいったん完結した建築であったが、既存の建物をも含めて敷地としてとらえて、スタディを始めた。

　まず、南側の棟を取り壊した後につくるヴォリュームを、かつての輪郭をなぞった上で、今回手を加えない北側の棟と同じ高さの2層の構成とするよう考えた。これにより、地形に沿う建物ヴォリュームによるサイトは失われるが、代わりに対のヴォリュームがつくり出す階段状中庭空間の自立性は高まる。内部においては、拡張した容積の中で、既存部分の構成原理を踏襲しつつ、幾何学による反復と対比のリズムの強化を試みた。目指したのは、人間の想像力を喚起するような繊細かつダイナミックな新たな空間の創造だった。

小篠邸ゲストハウス
Guest House for Koshino House
2004-06

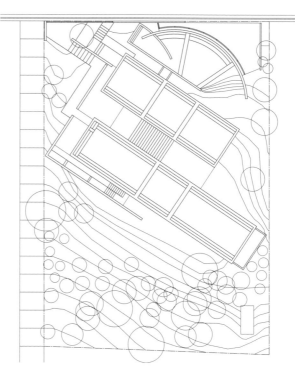

This is the second extension to the Koshino House, built in Okuike, Ashiya City in Hyogo prefecture.

　Twenty years after the addition of the atelier wing, the client again commissioned me to make an addition to the building. As opposed to phase Ⅱ, in which the theme was the addition of a new element, the program this time required part of the building to be demolished and completely reconstructed. Since the children grew up, the private rooms contained in the south wing were rarely being used, so essentially the plan was to demolish it and make a hall that would contain the diverse creative activities of the fashion-designer client. In my personal consciousness, and in its practical spatial composition, this had been a finished building, but I begun to make studies by perceiving it as a site that included existing buildings.

　For the volume that would be constructed after the south wing was demolished, I first retraced the former profile, and then devised a two-level structure with the same height as the untouched north wing. While the building volume following the site topography would be lost as a result, the autonomy of the tiered inner-court space created by the replacement volume would be enhanced. Within the expanded volume of the interior, while following the compositional principles of the existing parts, I attempted a strengthened rhythm of contrast and repetition due to geometry. The aim was to create a subtle and dynamic new space that arouses the power of the human imagination.

新築されたゲストハウスの玄関アプローチ。奥に見えるのは既存の小篠邸。

Approach to the entrance of the newly built guesthouse.
The existing Koshino House can be seen further in.

ゲストハウス新築後の中庭。2棟の高さが揃えられたことで、
空間の求心力が高められた。

The courtyard after the guesthouse was built.
The centripetal force of the space has been
enhanced by aligning the heights of the two wings.

かつての個室棟の輪郭をなぞりながら、高さ方向にヴォリュームを拡張して生まれたゲストハウス。
While tracing the outline of the former private room wing, the guest house is produced by enlarging the volume in the vertical direction.

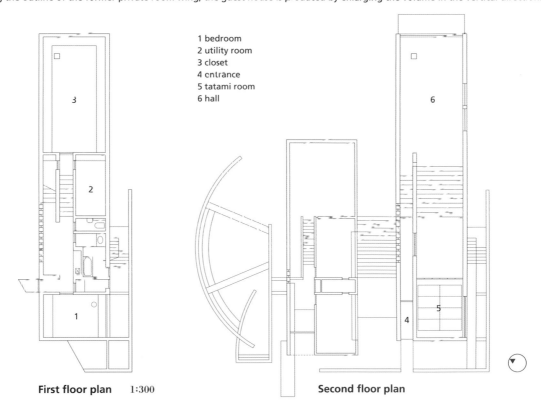

1 bedroom
2 utility room
3 closet
4 entrance
5 tatami room
6 hall

First floor plan　1:300

Second floor plan

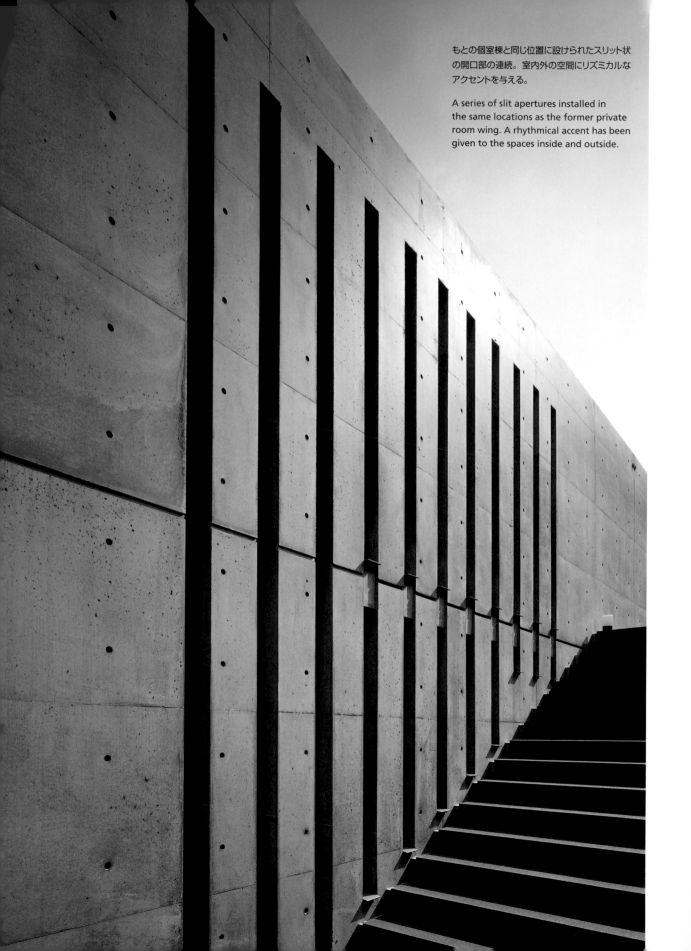

もとの個室棟と同じ位置に設けられたスリット状の開口部の連続。室内外の空間にリズミカルなアクセントを与える。

A series of slit apertures installed in the same locations as the former private room wing. A rhythmical accent has been given to the spaces inside and outside.

ホールを西側から見る。既存部の居間と同じ建築言語を用いながら、まったく異なる印象の空間をつくり上げている。

Looking at the hall from the west. While using the same architectural language as the living room in the existing section, they have been reproduced a completely different spatial impression has been created.

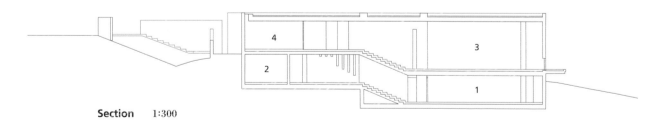

Section 1:300

1 closet
2 bedroom
3 hall
4 tatami room

南側の庭に向かって大きく穿たれた開口部と、対面のスリ
ット状トップライトからの光を受ける壁の表情との対比が、
空間に緊張感を与えている。

The contrast between the large opening toward the south
garden and the expression of light from the slit-shaped
skylight on the opposite wall gives a tension to the space.

東面の壁いっぱいに穿たれた地窓。テラスとして突き出したスラブが、鮮やかに風景を切り取る。

A window pierces through the full width of the east wall.
The projecting slab forms a terrace that vividly slices the scenery.

東側テラスから南側庭を見る。
Looking at the south garden from the east terrace.

南側外観。南東に見える松の木は、1981年の建設から時を越えて立ち続けている。
South facade. The pine tree visible to the southeast has continued to stand since construction in 1981, transcending time.

建物は、京都と奈良の県境の新興住宅地に位置する。ここでは静謐な居住空間の確保を主題として、囲われた壁の内に自立するミクロコスモスの創出を試みた。

　周囲の散漫な風景を断ち切り、壁が囲いとるのは短辺7m、長辺19mで南北に伸びる2層分の高さの直方体である。これを縦に2分割し、一方を中庭にあて、他方を居住スペースとする。1階は居間と食堂とし、2階は中庭に面した居室部分をさらに2等分して寝室とテラスとする。

　全体のヴォリュームの内の3/5を占める、このコンクリートに囲まれたヴォイドスペースが、囲われた住まいに光、風といった純化された自然を引き込み、空間に無限の奥行きをもたらす。住吉の長屋以来、試みてきたボックスの内にスペースとヴォイドを等分に配する手法を最も端的に展開できた住宅だった。

中山邸

Nakayama House

1983-85

奈良県奈良市——Nara, Nara

This house is located in a new residential area on the border between Nara and Kyoto Prefectures. With the theme of ensuring a quiet residential space, this is an attempt to generate an independent microcosm within an enclosing wall.

Severed from the diffuse surrounding scenery, walls enclose a two-story rectangular volume measuring 7m by 19m and extending north-south. It is divided in two along its length, with one half as a courtyard garden and the other half as a living space. The living room and dining room are on the first floor, while on the second floor the living space facing the courtyard garden is once more divided into two equal parts, a terrace and a bedroom.

Comprising 3/5th of the entire interior volume, the void space enclosed by concrete draws purified natural light and wind into the enclosed dwelling, bringing an infinite depth to the spaces. Since the Row House in Sumiyoshi, this house is the most direct development of the technique of dividing the interior of a box into equal parts of space and void.

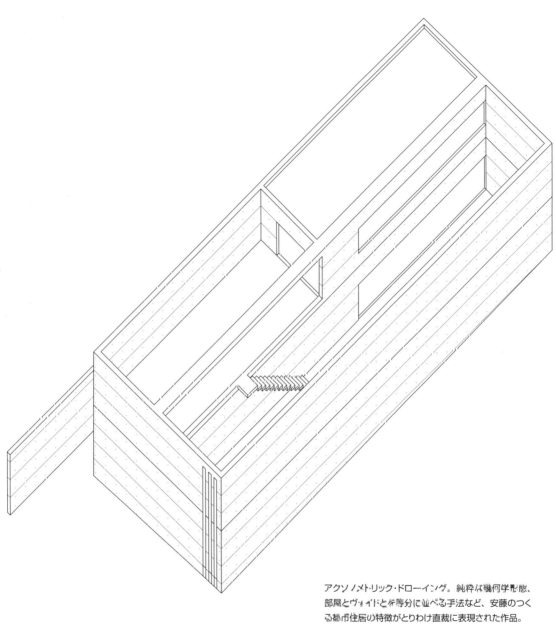

アクソノメトリック・ドローイング。純粋な幾何学形態、部屋とヴォイドとを等分に並べる手法など、安藤のつくる都市住居の特徴がとりわけ直截に表現された作品。

Axonometric drawing. In its method of aligning an equal division of room and void, as well as its pure geometrical form, this work is an exemplary expression of the character of Ando-designed urban dwellings.

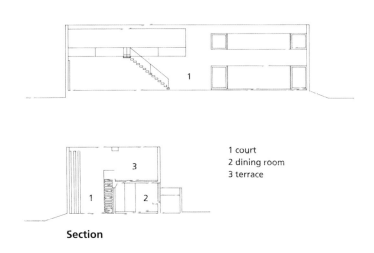

1 court
2 dining room
3 terrace

Section

左：北側から遠望する。右上：南側のアプローチ
を見る。散漫な風景の広がる周辺環境から、空
間を囲いとる高さ約 6m のコンクリートの壁。

Left: Distant view from the north.
Upper right. Looking at the southern
approach route. A concrete wall about
6m in height separates the space
from the surrounding environment of
desultory scenery.

左：直方体のボックス全体の1/2のヴォリュームを占める中庭。
右：中庭に向かって全面開放された居間。

Left: The courtyard occupies half the volume of the entire rectangular box.
Right: The wall of the living room facing the courtyard is entirely open.

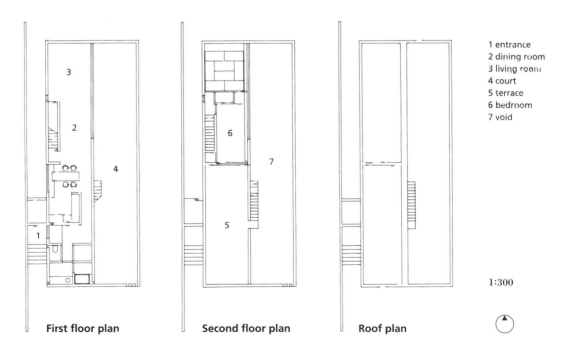

1 entrance
2 dining room
3 living room
4 court
5 terrace
6 bedroom
7 void

1:300

First floor plan　　**Second floor plan**　　**Roof plan**

寝室より2階テラスを見る。ヴォイドを形どってコンクリートの梁が飛ばされている。

Looking at the second-floor terrace from the bedroom. A flying concrete beam defines the void.

敷地は世田谷区の閑静な住宅地の中に位置する。クライアント夫婦とその両親たち3世帯のための住宅である。それぞれの家族が、プライバシーを確保して独立しながらも、ひとつに結びあった生活を営めるような、3世帯のための集合住宅として計画を進めた。

建物は、12m角の立方体と、敷地の形状に従って周囲を囲む高いコンクリートの壁面で構成される。立方体は、敷地のほぼ中央部に置かれ、北側と南側には余白が生まれる。その北側を住戸へのアプローチ空間、南側を中庭とする。この2つのヴォイドを軸に、各戸の生活空間が展開する。

アプローチに面する壁は、前面の坂道を登ってくる人を導き入れるように、内側に円弧を描いて入り込む。アプローチ動線は、道路面より下降する幅の広い階段と、上昇する狭い階段によって2分される。下降する動線は、両親たちの住戸のある1階の前庭へと続く。アプローチの狭い方の上昇する階段を昇ると、夫婦の住戸のエントランスがある。各戸はそれぞれに高いプライバシーを確保しているが、同時にそれらを立体的に結ぶ中庭空間の存在によって、確かな共棲感覚をも満たしている。

北側の前庭と南側の中庭には、以前繁っていたものと同じ樹木を、再び植えた。周囲の眺望をあえて断ち切る高いコンクリートの壁が、その1枚の葉に現れる陽の変化、四季の移り変わりを敏感にすくい取る。

城戸崎邸

Kidosaki House

1982-86
東京都世田谷区 —— Setagaya, Tokyo

The site is located in a quiet residential district in Setagaya ward. It is a three-household residence for the client couple and their respective parents. While ensuring privacy and independence for each family, we developed a housing plan that allowed the three households to carry on an interwoven lifestyle.

The building is composed of a 12m-cube and a tall concrete wall following the site shape to enclose the surroundings. The cube is located near the center of the site, leaving margins to the north and south. To the north is the approach space for the dwelling, and to the south is a courtyard garden. The living spaces of each dwelling expand along the axis of these two voids.

The wall facing the approach route curves inward as if to draw people ascending the sloping road in front, delineating the inner part with an arc. The approach route is split in two, with wide steps descending from street level, and narrow steps leading upward. The descending steps lead to the first-floor front garden of the parent dwellings. Ascending the narrow stair from the approach leads to the entrance of the client couple's dwelling. A high level of privacy is ensured for each household, but at the same time, a sense of communal living is satisfied by the existence of the connecting three-dimensional inner courtyard space.

The same kinds of trees and shrubs that used to grow in this area have been planted in the courtyard garden to the south and in the front garden to the north. The changing expression of single high concrete wall that completely blocks the surrounding view skims a sense of the changing seasons.

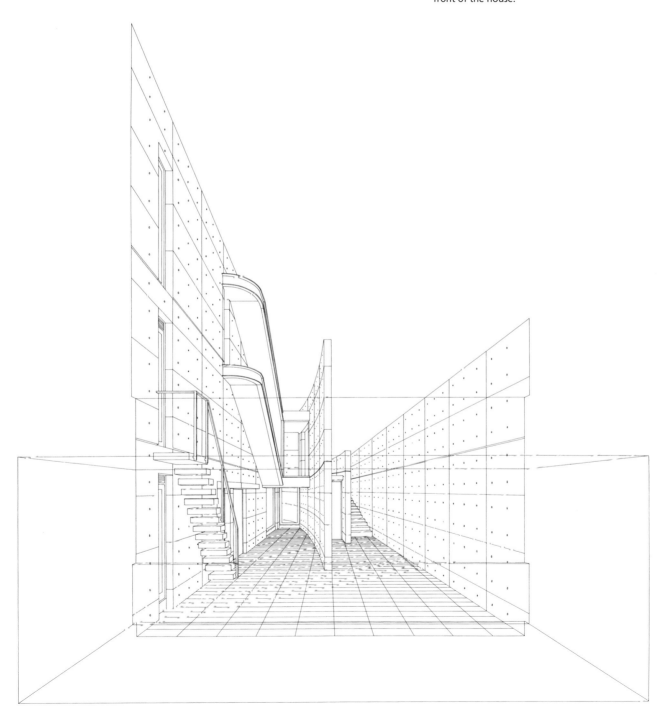

パースペクティブ・ドローイング。住戸A（父の住居）と
住戸B（義母の住居）の玄関に面した前庭。右手奥にあ
る階段が前面道路からのアクセス。

Perspective drawing. The front garden faces the
entries to unit A (father's dwelling) and unit B
(mother-in-law's dwelling). The stairs beyond
on the right provide access from the road in
front of the house.

西側に設けられた玄関アプローチ。左手の階段を降りていくと住戸A・Bの住居へ、2枚の曲面壁の間を入ると住戸C（夫妻の住居）へアプローチできる。

The approach route to the entrance established on the west. Going down the stairs on the left side leads to units A and B. Unit C (the couple's dwelling) may be accessed by entering between the two curved walls.

中庭より住戸Bを見る。左が居間、右が食堂。老婦人の生活感覚に対する
配慮から、内部はコンクリートに仕上げがなされている。

Looking at unit B from the courtyard. To the left is the living
room and to the right is the dining room. Out for consideration
for the lifestyle sense of an elderly woman, the interior is
finished in concrete.

住戸Aの居間より南東側の庭を見る。　Looking at the southeast garden from the living room of unit A.

中庭より住戸Bの居間を見る。　Looking at the living room of unit B from the courtyard.

住戸Cの2階テラスより中庭を見る。各戸のプライバシーを確保しながら、吹き抜け、中庭を介して充分な空間の広がりを得ている。

Looking at the courtyard from the second-floor terrace of unit C. While ensuring the privacy of each unit, a satisfactory spatial expansiveness is obtained through the voids and courtyards.

住戸Bの寝室より玄関前のスペースを見る。地窓の高さは床から900mm。

Looking at the space in front of the entrance from the bedroom of unit B.
The height of the window opening is 900mm from the floor.

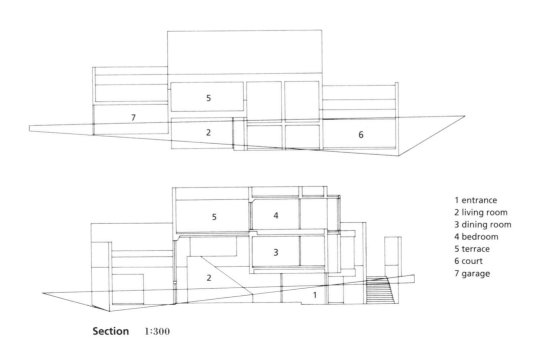

1 entrance
2 living room
3 dining room
4 bedroom
5 terrace
6 court
7 garage

Section 1:300

South elevation

左：住戸Bの食堂より見た中庭。右：住戸Aの居間より見た中庭。
ケヤキは、もとの敷地に立っていたときと同じ場所に植えられている。

Left: The courtyard seen from dining room of unit B.
Right: The courtyard seen from the living room of unit A.
The oak tree is growing in its original location on the site.

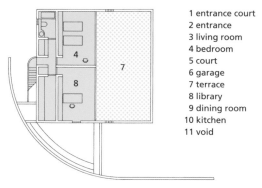

1 entrance court
2 entrance
3 living room
4 bedroom
5 court
6 garage
7 terrace
8 library
9 dining room
10 kitchen
11 void

Third floor plan

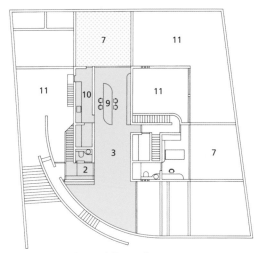

Second floor plan

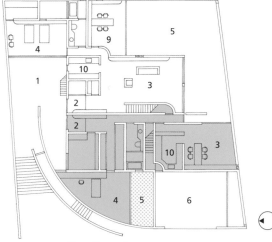

First floor plan   1:400

住戸 A
住戸 B
住戸 C

住戸Cの居間より食堂を見る。奥行きの深さに対し、抑えられた天井高さが空間に落ち着きをもたらしている。

Looking at the dining room from the living room of unit C. In response to its depth, a lower ceiling height brings calm to the space.

住戸Cの居間。天井スリットから落ちる陽光を受ける曲面の
RC壁が食堂からリビング部分へとつながる空間に劇的な変化
を与えている。

The living room of unit C. Sunshine falls from the
slot in the ceiling onto the curved reinforced
concrete wall, giving dramatic changes to the space
that connects the dining room to the living area.

左：食堂からリビングを見る。
右：エントランスを構成する曲面の RC 壁が
リビング内部にまで入り込む。

Left: Looking at the living room from the dining room.
Right: The curved reinforced concrete wall along the
entrance approach also penetrates the living room.

3階の住戸Cの寝室。2つの部屋ともコートに全面ガラス
で開かれている。コート南側の外壁にはあえて開口部を
設けず、静寂な空間性を獲得している。

The bedrooms of unit C on the third floor. Both of the rooms are opened to the court with entirely glass walls. A silent spatial character is attained by boldly omitting openings in the exterior wall of the roof court.

鳥瞰。3世帯の生活空間が複雑に入り組む多様な空間のシークエンスとは裏腹に、1辺12mの正方形平面のヴォリュームとその周囲を囲うコンクリートの壁による単純明快な構成が見てとれる。

Bird's-eye view. The living spaces for the three households are a complex intertwining of varied spatial sequences, yet conversely, it is clearly a simple and lucid composition, due to the square plan volume of 12m per side and the concrete wall that encloses its setting.

Axonometric

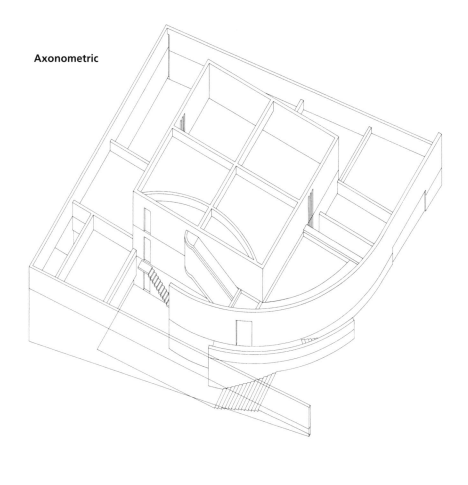

敷地は閑静な住宅街の、緑に囲まれた高台に位置する。韓国出身のクライアントのための住宅である。プログラムに対してゆとりのある敷地条件を活かし、ここでは各室をつなぐ動線部分を確かな空間性をもったギャラリーと見立て、このパブリックゾーンを中心として諸室が展開する伸びやかな構成を試みた。

　全体は、緑の庭の中に長く伸びる建物と、その表裏にとりつく壁がつくり出す、中庭空間を中心とする構成をもつ。ハナミズキの樹を抱く三角形平面のドライコートに面する建物の最下階は居間とし、玄関から居間までは、建物の奥行きに沿ったスロープでつなぐ。豊かな緑を設えた北側の庭には傾斜をつけ、それを受け止める奥のスペースを食堂にあてる。建物2階レベルの中央は屋根のない屋外テラスとし、下階同様のスロープによって、ヴォイドを介して向き合う上階の居室とテラスとを結ぶ。テラスと南側の庭とは縦長窓の連続による巨大なガラススクリーンを介して視覚的に連続している。

　インテリアには、クライアントの文化的・民族的背景を踏まえ、李朝の家具と韓国の調度品を配した。幾何学的モチーフを用いた李朝の家具は、確固たる民族性と同時に、現代につながる普遍性を有している。要所に配されたこの家具の存在が、回遊性の高いギャラリーのような空間に住まいとしての落ち着きをもたらしている。

李邸

Lee House

1991-93
千葉県船橋市——Funabashi, Chiba

The site is located on high ground surrounded by greenery, in a quiet residential area. This is a house for a client born in Korea. Making use of the freedom of the site conditions, with regard to the program, a gallery with a definite spatiality was selected as a circulation element to connect the various rooms, attempting a comfortably extended composition of various rooms focused on this public space.

The overall composition is centered on a courtyard garden space, with a long building extending through a green garden and walls attached to either side. A dogwood tree is contained in the center, and the building's lowest level is the living room, which faces the triangular dry court to the south. The entrance hall and the living room are connected by a ramp along the depth of the building. A slope has been established in the abundant greenery of the north part of the garden, and it captures a deep space that has become the dining room. The middle of the building's second level is a roofless outdoor terrace, which is connected by means of a ramp, similar to the one on the floor below, to the terrace and the upper level rooms, which face each other across a void. The terrace and the south garden are visually connected through an enormous glass screen composed of a series of long rectangular windows.

Influenced by the client's cultural and ethnic background, the interior was furnished with Korean fittings and Yi-dynasty furniture. The geometrical motifs of the Yi-dynasty furniture display a strong ethnicity, and simultaneously have a universality linked to the present day. The presence of furniture in key places creates a dwelling with a sense of serenity, in a space similar to a gallery with good circulation.

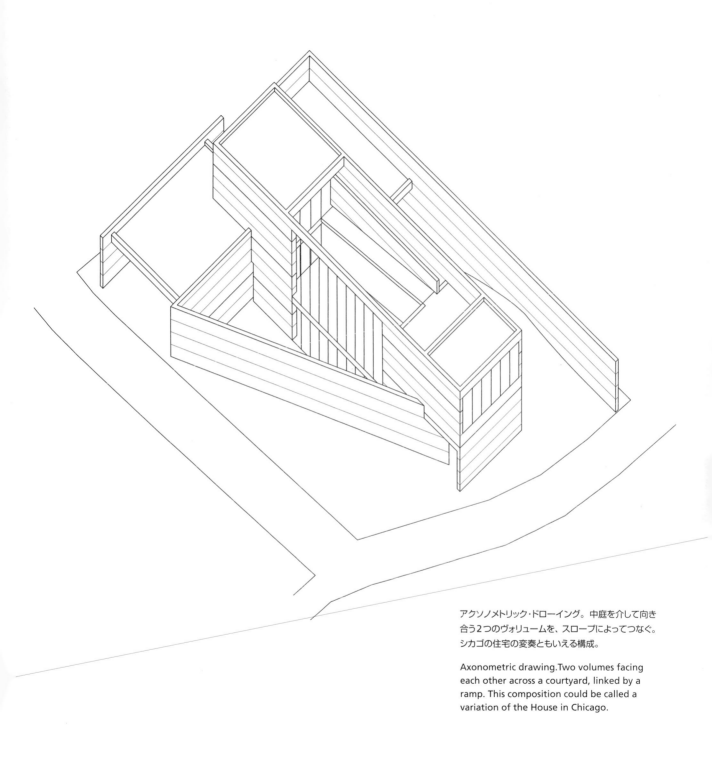

アクソノメトリック・ドローイング。中庭を介して向き合う2つのヴォリュームを、スロープによってつなぐ。シカゴの住宅の変奏ともいえる構成。

Axonometric drawing.Two volumes facing each other across a courtyard, linked by a ramp. This composition could be called a variation of the House in Chicago.

南から見る。閑静な住宅地にあって、緑に囲まれた住まい。

Looking from the south. A dwelling enclosed by greenery, in a quiet residential district.

楔形平面の壁に囲われた中庭に面するリビング。上階へ誘うスロープが、住まいにギャラリーのような回遊性をもたらしている。

The living room faces a courtyard enclosed by walls defining a wedge shape in plan. The ramp inviting us to the upper level brings a gallery-like circulation loop into the dwelling.

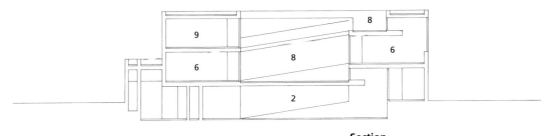

Section

1 entrance
2 living room
3 dining room
4 court
5 garage
6 bedroom
7 void
8 terrace
9 tatami room
10 atelier

Third floor plan

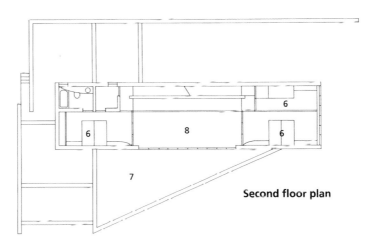

Second floor plan

黒の御影石が敷き詰められた中
庭。鋭角に入り込む壁が、空間に
緊張感をもたらしている。

The courtyard lined with black
granite. The walls meet at an
acute angle, bringing a tension
to the space.

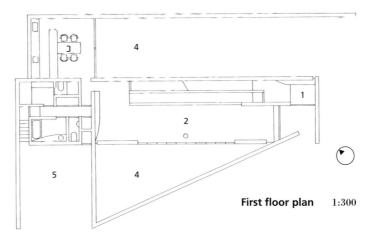

First floor plan   1:300

クライアントの民族的背景から、ここでは李朝の家具が採用されている。幾何学をモチーフとした家具がアクセントとなり、空間の回遊性がさらに高められている。

Due to the ethnic background of the client, Yi-dynasty furniture has been selected. With geometrical motifs, these items of furniture become accent points that further enhance the circulation loop of the space.

コートと2層分のサッシュを介して接する2階テラス。
住まいの中に大胆に引き入れたヴォイド空間である。

The second-floor terrace comes into contact with the
court through the double-height window.
The void space is audaciously brought into the residence.

1階食堂から見た中庭。斜面に植えられた緑が空間に入り込んでくる。

The courtyard seen from the first-floor dining room.
The greenery planted on the slope enters the space.

平野区の町家

Town House in Hirano

1995-96

大阪府大阪市——Osaka, Osaka

敷地は大阪市郊外、戦前からの旧い木造の長屋や町工場が建ち並ぶ下町の一画にある。若い夫婦とその母親のための2世帯住宅である。ここでは、限られたスペースの中で、各スペースに空間的広がりをもたせつつ、いかにして2世帯のプライバシーを確保するかが主題となった。それに対し、われわれが提案したのは四周を壁で囲って得られるヴォリュームの半分を屋外空間として、そのヴォイドを介した立体的な動線処理により2世帯の居住スペースのプライバシーを図るというアイディアである。

　2層分の高さをもつコンクリートの壁に唯一設けられた開口部をくぐると、まずエントランスコートに出る。ここから階段を昇ると2階のテラスに面した居間・食堂に導かれる。夫婦の寝室ゾーンへは、そこを抜けて反対側の階段を降りた先の、中庭空間からアプローチする。一方、母親の寝室ゾーンへは、エントランスコートから直接、半透明のスクリーンで隔てられた隣のコートに入りアプローチする。

　階段の昇り降りや、中庭という外部を通ることを半ば強いる構成は、機能的とはいい難いが、それによって住み手は変化に富んだ空間体験と、閉塞しないプライバシーを手に入れることができる。

The site is a section in an old working class district on the outskirts of Osaka, amid an array of wooden row houses and backstreet workshops that date from before World War II. It is a two-generation house, for a young couple and their mother. Here, in this limited space, the theme was ensuring the privacy of the two generations while maintaining the expansiveness of each space. In response, we proposed making half of the volume obtained by the enclosing peripheral walls into an outdoor space, with the idea of devising privacy for the two-generation residential spaces with a three-dimensional circulation arrangement through the void.

Passing through the only aperture established in the two-story-high concrete wall, one first emerges in the entrance court. Ascending the stairs from here, one is led to the living and dining room facing the second floor terrace. The bedroom zone of the couple is approached through the courtyard space that lies at the bottom of the stairs located at the opposite end. On the other hand, the bedroom zone of the mother is approached directly from the entrance court by entering an adjacent court separated by a translucent screen.

It is difficult to describe as functional a composition that half-compels one to ascend and descend stairs and pass through exterior courtyard gardens, but in this way the occupants gain a rich variety of spatial experiences and a non-isolated privacy.

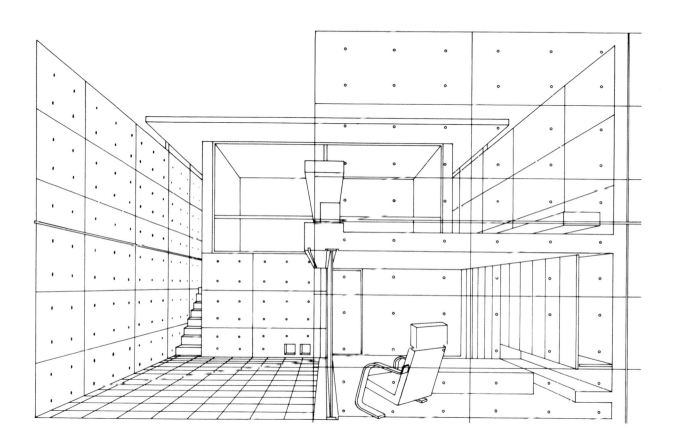

パースペクティブ・ドローイング。中庭を介して立体的
につなげられた夫婦の生活ゾーンと、2階のパブリック
ゾーンとの相互関係が見てとれる。

Perspective drawing. Three-dimensionally linked
by the courtyard, the interrelationship of the
couple's living zone and the second-floor public
zone can be clearly seen.

東側より遠望する。周囲には日本瓦の屋根を載せた木造の長屋や町工場が建ち並ぶ。

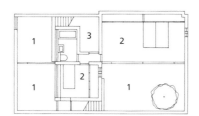

First floor plan   1:300

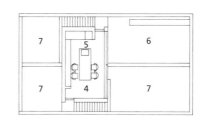

Second floor plan

1 court
2 bedroom
3 storage
4 living room
5 kitchen
6 terrace
7 void

Distant view from the east. Backstreet factories and wooden row houses roofed with Japanese tiles stand in the surroundings.

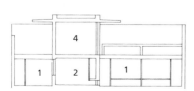

Section

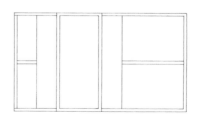

Roof plan

左頁：東側コート。壁に挟まれた隙間の階段を昇ると、2階の居間に至る。右頁：西側角の入口から見る。母親の寝室に面したコートの先に2階居間へのアプローチとなる外階段、その奥はテラスとなっている。

Left page: East court. The stair inserted in the gap between the walls leads up to the second-floor living room. Right page: Looking from the west corner entrance. At the edge of the court facing the mother's bedroom is an exterior stair that leads to the second-floor living room, and beyond it is a terrace.

2階居間より東側テラスを見る。
The east terrace seen from the second-floor living room.

1階東側コート。左手は寝室に面する。コートは壁、床ともにコンクリート仕上げ。
East court of the first floor. To the left, it faces a bedroom.
The walls and floors of the court have a concrete finish.

2 階居間から東側を見る。　Looking east from the second-floor living room.

左：コート、テラスには安藤のデザインによるベンチが設けられている。右：母親の前庭の見上げ。西側の道路に面する壁は、街並みのスケールに合わせ、高さを抑えている。

Left: Benches designed by Ando have been installed in the court and the terrace. Right: Looking up at the mother's front garden. The wall facing the road to the west has been lowered in height to fit the scale of the townscape.

2 階居間の夜景。テラスから見る。
Night view of the second floor living room, looking from the terrace.

敷地は滋賀県大津市の郊外、琵琶湖を望む高台の新興住宅地の一画にある。クライアントの家族とその母親が住む2世帯住宅である。

　異なる世代の2世帯住宅というプログラムに対し空間構成でいかに応えるか、その上で、眺望にすぐれた立地を活かす開放的な住空間をいかにして実現するかという主題に対し、われわれが提案したのは丘の上に周囲を見渡すように浮かぶ住まいのイメージである。

　建物は、敷地形状に沿った台形のヴォリュームと、その上に四方をはね出して載る同形のヴォリュームの2層の構成をとる。下階のヴォリュームは、3分割した中央をヴォイドとして、片側に母親の個室と上階への垂直動線を、もう片方に和室・書斎を設ける。上階は、台形平面の隣地に接する3辺を閉じた上で、琵琶湖を向いた残りの1辺を全面開放とし、このスペースを住まいの核となる家族室にあてる。

　キャンティレヴァーで水平方向に延びるバルコニーから、光、風が存分に入り込む、明るく開放的な上階の空間に対し、深い庇の下の下階の空間は、柔らかい光と影に包まれた落ち着いた雰囲気をもつ。その外周を緩やかな曲線を描きながら囲うコンクリートブロック積みの塀が、住まいを周囲から切り取る、緩やかな閾となっている。

滋賀の住宅
House in Shiga
2004-06
滋賀県大津市——Otsu, Shiga

The site is located in the suburbs of Otsu, Shiga prefecture, in a new residential area developed on top of a hill looking out over Lake Biwa. This is a two-generation house for the client family and their mother.

In responding to a program for a residence with two households of different generations, and also with regard to the theme of implementing an open living space that makes use of a superior location in terms of view, we proposed the image of a house floating above the hill looking out over the surroundings.

The building consists of two levels: a trapezoidal volume that follows the shape of the site, and above it a similarly shaped volume that spreads in every direction. The lower volume is divided in three, with a central void. On one side is the mother's private room as well as the vertical circulation toward the upper floor, and on the other side is a Japanese-style room and a study. The top floor is closed to the adjoining land on three sides of the trapezoidal plan, while the remaining side is made entirely open facing Lake Biwa. This space is the family room that constitutes the core of the house.

Wind and light enter freely from the horizontally extending cantilevered balcony, and the lower floor space under the deep eaves has a calm atmosphere shrouded in soft light and shadow, contrasting with the bright and open upper floor. A wall of stacked concrete blocks encompasses the perimeter with a soft curve, severing the house from its surroundings and becoming a lenient threshold.

アクソノメトリック・ドローイング。鋸歯状の塀が囲いとる
スペースに、板状のヴォリュームが浮かぶ。

Axonometric drawing. A plate-shaped volume
floats above a space enclosed by a serrated fence.

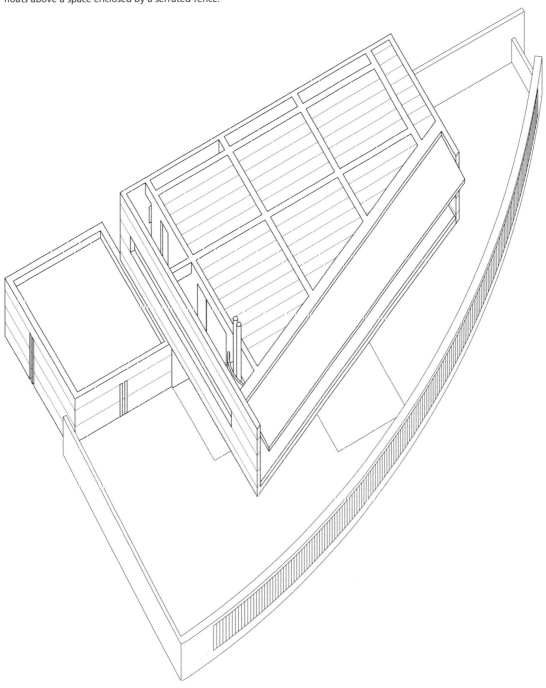

東側外観。庇とはねだしのバルコニーによる、水平
方向の広がりが強調されたデザイン。

East facade. Due to the eaves and projecting
balcony, the design emphasizes extension in
the horizontal direction.

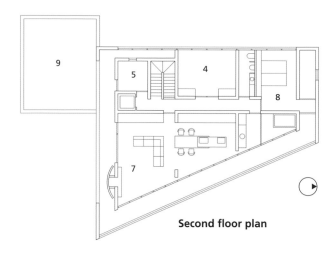

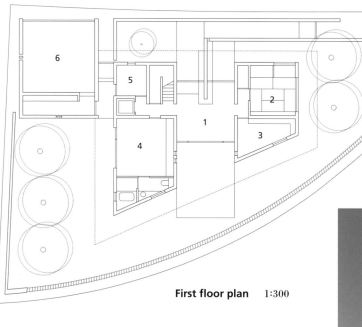

1 entrance hall
2 tatami room
3 study
4 bedroom
5 storage
6 garage
7 living room
8 master bedroom
9 planting

Second floor plan

First floor plan 1:300

1階には、東西に抜けた玄関ホールを挟んで
母親の寝室と客室が、2階にはリビング・キッ
チンと若夫婦の寝室が納められる。
右頁上：1階玄関ホール。

On the first floor, the entrance hall penetrating from east to west is interposed between the mother's bedroom and the guestroom, and the second floor is dedicated to the young couple's bedroom and a combined living room and kitchen. Right page : Entrance hall on the first floor.

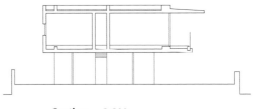

Section   1:300

左上：2層をつなぐ階段室。トップライトが空間の移動
を劇的に演出する。左下：寝室。
右：和室。水平窓からの光が、各室の空間を特徴づける。

Upper left: The staircase that connects the two levels.
The skylight produces dramatic movement in the
space. Lower left: Bedroom.
Right: Tatami room. The spaces of each room
are characterized by light from horizontal windows.

2階リビングの南面を見る。正面のコンクリート打ち放しの壁には炉台と暖炉が設けられている。

Looking at the south wall of the second-floor living room. A balcony and fireplace have been created in the exposed concrete wall of the facade.

North elevation　1:300

2階リビングの東面を見る。すりガラスの手摺越しに琵琶湖が見える。縦長の連続掃き出し窓は、全面開放が可能。

Looking at the east wall of the second-floor living room. Lake Biwa is visible through the frosted glass balustrade. It is possible to open the entire surface of this series of rectangular windows.

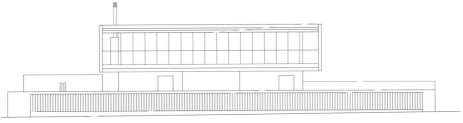

West elevation

神戸市垂水区の、瀬戸内海を見晴らす海岸沿いに建つ＜極小の＞個人住宅である。

　本来の敷地は、防波堤をまたいで数10mの奥行きがあったが、海に侵食され、大部分は水没していた。護岸の法規制から建設が許されたのは、残されたわずか5m角程のスペースだった。この矮小な敷地で、いかにして立地を活かした＜豊かな＞住空間を獲得するかが主題だった。

　建物は、敷地内で建設可能な最大限の正方形平面を、地上4階まで積み上げた、塔状の構成をとる。1階を玄関ユーティリティ、2階を寝室、3階を書斎として、住まいの核となるリビング・キッチンを最上階に設けた。

　極小ゆえに単純明快な構成となったが、海側を全面開口とした最上階だけは天井高さを平面の1辺と同じくし、さらに海に向かって1m迫り出させて、瀬戸内の海景を存分に取り込めるよう考えた。

　1mmの無駄も許さず、ささいな造作のディテールの決定にも非常な緊張を要したが、人間の生活空間の限界を改めて思い知る、良い経験となった。

4×4の住宅

4×4 House

2001-03
兵庫県神戸市——— Kobe, Hyogo

A 'minimum' private residence in Tarumi, Kobe City standing along the coast looking over Seto Inland Sea.

The site has once measured several dozen meter in depth past the breakwater, but a good part of it is now submerged under water, eroded by the sea. Recent bank protection regulations have permitted construction on a scanty space of 5m by 5m. Our primary concern was to achieve a 'rich' living space on this postage-stamp plot of land, taking advantage of itslocational conditions.

The building is a tower-shaped structure where a square plan with the largest possible size allowed to be constructed within this site, is piled up onto four levels overground. The ground level accommodates the entrance utilities; the second level the bedroom; the third level the study; and the top level the living room and kitchen that is the core of this house.

Scarcity of space has resulted in a simple and straightforward structure, but efforts were made for optimal ocean views, by giving the ceiling height of the top level the same length as the plan's side and projecting the front opening to the sea by a meter.

Trimmed to a millimeter, the project has required a great amount of concentration in the decisions over the smallest of details, but has turned out to be a good experience of acknowledging the limits of the human living space.

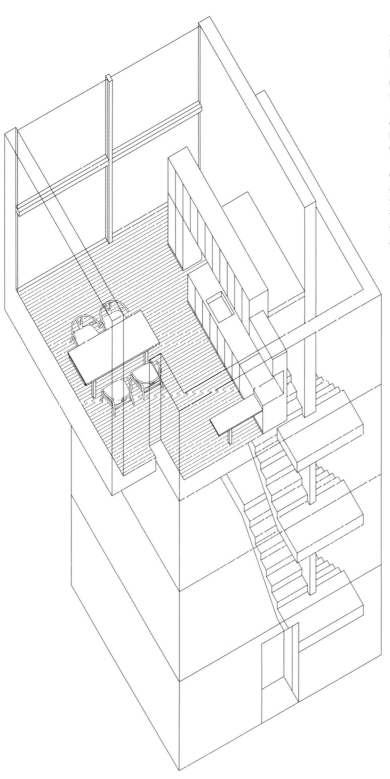

アクソノメトリック・ドローイング。4m角の平面が4層重ねられ、最上階のみ前後左右に1mずつずれている。1階が浴室・トイレなどの水廻り、2階が寝室、3階が書斎、4階がリビング・キッチン。

Axonometric drawing. A 4m-square plan is stacked up in four layers, with only the topmost floor displaced by 1m in each direction. The first floor contains water-related functions such as bathroom and toilet, the second floor contains a bedroom, the third floor contains a study, and the fourth floor contains a combined living room and kitchen.

南面いっぱいをガラス壁とした4階のリビング・キッチン。海を借景とした無限の広がりをもつ空間。

The south wall of the combined living room and kitchen on the fourth floor is entirely glazed. With the sea as "borrowed scenery," this is an infinitely expanding space.

リビング・キッチン東側を見る。北面には空だけをフレーミングする窓。
コンクリート打ち放し仕上げの天井高は4,150mm。

Looking at the east side of the combined living
room and kitchen. The north side has a window
that frames only the sky. The bare concrete ceiling
is 4,150mm high.

左：4階リビング・キッチン東側開口部の眺め。
右：リビング・キッチンから見る午後の海景。文字通り瀬戸内海とともにある生活空間。

Left: View from the opening on the east side of the fourth-floor combined living room and kitchen.
Right: The afternoon seascape seen from the combined living room and kitchen. This is literally a space for living with the Inland Sea.

4階リビング・キッチン西側を見る。窓外に広がる海は
刻々と表情を変え、どれだけ眺めていても飽きない。

Looking at the west side of the fourth-floor
combined living room and kitchen. The sea
extending outside the window changes expression
from moment to moment, and no matter how
long you gaze, it never becomes dull.

Sectional detail

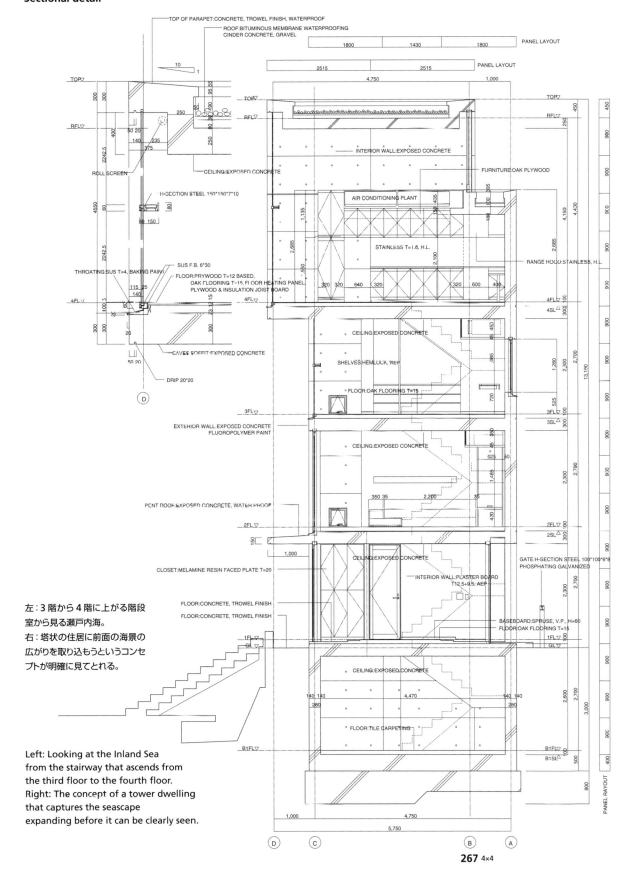

左：3階から4階に上がる階段
室から見る瀬戸内海。
右：塔状の住居に前面の海景の
広がりを取り込もうというコンセ
プトが明確に見てとれる。

Left: Looking at the Inland Sea
from the stairway that ascends from
the third floor to the fourth floor.
Right: The concept of a tower dwelling
that captures the seascape
expanding before it can be clearly seen.

天井高さを抑え、落ち着きのある3階の書斎。ここでも南面の全面開口部から淡路島までの眺望を取り入れている。

The third-floor study has a lower ceiling and a sense of calm. Even here, the completely open south wall provides a view to Awaji Island.

Fourth floor plan

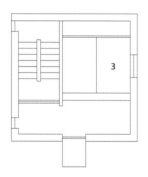

Third floor plan

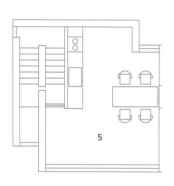

Second floor plan

First floor plan   1:150

1 bathroom
2 utility room
3 bedroom
4 study
5 living / kitchen

北側からの眺め。瀬戸内海、左に明石海峡大橋、そして対岸に
淡路島と、絶好のロケーションを眼前にこの家は佇んでいる。

View from the north side. The house stands
in an ideal location, with the Inland Sea in front,
the Akashi Kaikyo Bridge to the left, and the
shoreline of Awaji Island opposite.

左：鳥瞰。建物の完成から1年後、当初より予定されていた正方形
平面のデッキテラスが設けられ、海との連続性がより高められた。
右：南側外観の夜景。

Left: Bird's-eye view. The initially planned square-shaped
deck terrace was installed one year after completion
of the building, further improving its continuity with the
sea. Right: Night view of the south facade.

夕暮れ時の瀬戸内海を望む4×4の住宅。

The 4×4 House commanding a view of
the Inland Sea in the evening.

安藤忠雄の包容力

「4×4の住宅」の施主
中田義成氏の談話

私は祖父の代から続く神戸の工務店に生まれました。子どもの頃から父親の建設現場によく遊びに行っていたので、建築はとても身近な存在でした。建築の勉強をしようと大学に入学したのが1987年です。その頃はちょうどバブル経済がポストモダン建築の流行と重なり、隈研吾さんの「M2」とか、アイゼンマンの「布谷ビル」など、カラフルで複雑な、解釈の難しい建築が主流でした。もちろん安藤さんは既に有名でしたが、どちらかというとモノクロームで落ち着いた印象でした。

建築学科に入って間もなく、近現代の有名な20軒ほどの日本の住宅の中から1軒を選んでトレースする課題がありました。もちろん安藤さんの「住吉の長屋」も

The Open-Minded Tadao Ando:

A Conversation with Yoshinari Nakata, Client of the 4x4 House

Ando's Buildings Make Great Demands on Craftsmen

I was born to a family in Kobe that runs a construction firm started by my grandfather. As a child, I often visited my father's construction sites; as a result, buildings have always been a part of my life. In 1987 I entered a university with the idea of studying architecture. It was the era of the bubble economy and postmodern architecture. Colorful, complex and esoteric buildings such as M2 by Kengo Kuma and the Nunotani Building by Peter Eisenman were the mainstream. Ando of course was already well-known, but his buildings seemed monochromatic and quiet by comparison.

Not long after I entered the architecture department, students were given a list of 20 famous Japanese houses of the modern or contemporary era and told to trace drawings of one of them. Ando's Rowhouse in Sumiyoshi was of course on the list, but few students

入っていたのですが、選んでいる学生は少なかった。安藤さんの人気がなかったというより、建築学科に入りたての素人には、コンクリート打ち放しの四角い建物は、住宅として理解しにくかったのではないかと思うのです。安藤さんの図面はとてもシンプルですからね。

しかし後になって、安藤さんの建築には図面からは想像もできない空間があることがわかります。トレース課題の後、実際に建物を見てレポートする課題がありました。私は大阪の心斎橋にある安藤さんの「GALLERIA [akka]」を選びました。プランは四角い箱の中に緩い曲面壁があるだけの非常にシンプルなもの。しかし建物に入ってみると、縦や横への予想外の広がりがあったり、逆に天井が低く抑えられている部分があったりして、想像以上にダイナミックな空間だったのです。それから「住吉の長屋」もたまたま外側から見る機会があったのですが、実物を見ると物言わぬ迫力がありました。しかし、それで安藤建築のファンになったわけではなく、そのときは「こんな建築もあるんだ」くらいの認識でした。

その後もいろいろな建物を見ましたが、安藤さんの打ち放しコンクリートは、どの建物を見てもシャープで見事でした。それだけに施工は難しかったはずで、「すごく職人さんは頑張ってるな」と思いました。子どもの頃から打ち放しは見馴れていましたが、当時の打ち放しは、倉庫や駐車場の中など人目につかないところばかり。仕上げをしないやりっ放しを打ち放しと呼んでいたのだと思います。安藤さんの打ち放しはPコンの跡がきちんと計画されて配置されていますが、そのように施工するのは通常より手間がかかるのです。また安藤さんの

selected it. It was not that Ando was unpopular; I think to neophytes, the squarish exposed concrete building was difficult to think of as a house. The fact that Ando's drawings were extremely simple may have contributed to that difficulty.

Later, however, I discovered that Ando's buildings have spaces that are unimaginable from his drawings. After the tracing problem, we were given the task of actually going to a building and reporting on it. I chose GALLERIA [akka] by Ando in the Shinsaibashi district in Osaka. The scheme is quite simple: a box enclosing gently curving walls. However, once I entered the building, the space turned out to be much more dynamic than I had imagined; the space was unexpectedly wide and deep, while the ceiling by contrast was in places deliberately kept low. I also had a chance to look at the outside of the Rowhouse in Sumiyoshi; the building was full of silence but exuded power. However, I did not become an admirer of Ando then; at the time, the experience only made me realize building like those existed.

I subsequently looked at other buildings by Ando. The exposed concrete was superb in every work. The construction must have been difficult; I admired the workmanship. I have been familiar with exposed concrete since I was a child. When I was young, exposed concrete tended to be used in places no one looked at such as the insides of warehouses and parking garages. Exposed concrete tended to be just concrete that no one had bothered to put a finish on. In Ando's exposed concrete, the locations of the round indentations left by separators have all been carefully planned beforehand; such care means more work. Ando's exposed concrete also has crisp corners; constructing concrete so that there are no rounded corners is also quite difficult. Ando's exposed concrete was something entirely different from ordinary exposed concrete.

打ち放しはピシッと角が出ていますが、角を欠けないようにつくるのも非常に難しい。同じ打ち放しといっても、安藤さんのはまったく違うものだったのです。

この敷地には安藤さんしかない

1997年の暮れ、取引のあった不動産業者から「開発が頓挫した土地を買わないか」という相談を持ちかけられました。面積は363m²。目の前に瀬戸内海が広がり、明石大橋と淡路島を望む絶好のロケーションです。ところが詳しく話を聞いてみるとかなり特殊な土地で、海辺の砂浜まで敷地なのですが、法的に住宅を建てられるのは道路と堤防の間だけなのです。それでも建築可能な面積が65m²あり、値段も手頃でした。いずれ自分で設計した自宅を建てるつもりで、思い切って購入したのです。

「海辺だから、コンクリートに白いモルタルを厚く塗った地中海風の家がいいかな」などと思案しながら簡単な図面を描いているうちに数年が経っていました。そんな頃に雑誌『ブルータス』の「約束建築」という特集号（2001年11月1日号）を目にしたのです。安藤さんをはじめ、伊東豊雄さんや高松伸さんなど、有名建築家10人から1人を選んで応募し、選ばれたら実際に自宅を設計してもらえるという企画。それまで雲の上の存在だった建築家に設計してもらえるかもしれないチャンスでした。

誰に応募したらいいのか大いに悩みました。そのときに考えたのは、建築の強さです。私が学生のときに多く見たカラフルな建築は、時代の流れとともに取り壊され

This Site Calls for Ando

At the end of 1997, a real estate agent I have had dealings with asked me if I would be interested in buying a property on which development had stalled. It was 363 square meters in area and looked out over the Inland Sea; it had a fantastic view of the bridge Akashi Ohashi and Awaji Island. However, as the agent went on to describe the property in detail, it became apparent that the site was somewhat peculiar. The site extended all the way to the beach, but construction of a house was permitted by law only between the road and the embankment. Nevertheless, there was still 65 square meters of usable land, and the price was reasonable. I purchased the land with the intention of eventually designing a house for myself there.

Thinking that a house in the Mediterranean style, with a thick coat of white plaster on concrete, might

be appropriate because of the seaside location, I made simple sketches. Several years went by. Then I came across a special issue entitled "Promissory Architecture" (November 1, 2001) of the magazine *Brutus*. The magazine listed ten well-known architects (including not only Ando, but people such as Toyo Ito and Shin Takamatsu). You could apply for consideration by one of them; if you were picked from among the applicants, the architect would actually design a house for you. It was an opportunity to have a distinguished architect design my house.

I had great difficulty deciding to whom I ought to apply, but I thought the building needed to be durable. With the passing of time, many of the colorful works of architecture I had looked at as a student had been demolished or, if still standing, were in bad repair. The light and airy buildings that one saw a lot of these days would probably require a great deal of maintenance in a harsh,

たり、残っていてもボロボロになっているものばかりです。また、最近見られるような軽い建築は、海に面した厳しい環境ではメンテナンスが大変だろう。そのように考えてみると、一貫してしっかりとした建築をつくってこられた安藤さんにお願いしたいと思ったのです。

もともと自分で設計するつもりでしたから、安藤さんに断られたとしても他の建築家に依頼する気持ちはありませんでした。幸いなことに、安藤さんはこの敷地が阪神淡路大震災の震源地に近いこともあって、設計を引き受けてくれることになったのです。

これも安藤ブランド？

最初の打ち合わせは大阪の安藤事務所で行われました。持参した敷地の図面と写真を見せて「砂浜まで敷地ですが、実際に建てられるのはこの部分です」と説明をしたのですが、安藤さんは「そうか、この土地か」というなり、実際には建てられない海辺の方ばかりに描き込みをしていました（笑）。さすがに私の設計案は見せなかったのですが、安藤さんは「建築の勉強をしているんだったら、自分でもチャレンジしてみたらいい」といわれました。そのときは不遜にも、「敷地の小ささを考えると誰が設計してもプランはほぼ同じ。敷地への思い入れの強さがある分だけ、自分の方がいい設計になるのでは」くらいに思っていたのです。ですから、「安藤さん、なんとかお願いします」という気持ちが半分、ありきたりな案が出てきたらお断りしようという気持ちも半分でした。

最初の打ち合わせから約3カ月後、安藤さんから出

seaside environment. These thoughts led me to feel that Ando, who has consistently designed sound buildings, was the architect I wanted.

Since I had originally intended to design the house myself, I had no intention of asking another architect if Ando turned me down. Fortunately, Ando agreed to design the house, in part because the site was near the epicenter of the Hanshin-Awaji Earthquake, which was such a significant event in his life.

Is This too an Ando Brand?

The first meeting took place in Ando's office in Osaka. I showed him drawings and photographs of the site and explained that, though the property extended to the sea, construction was restricted to a part of the land. Ando said, "So, this is the site," but in fact began to draw sketches of the part by the sea on which nothing could be built [laughing]. I did not show him my own scheme, but he remarked, "You should try it, since you studied architecture." I was presumptuous enough to think that, because the site was small, the scheme would be the same no matter who designed it. My design might in fact be better because I was more attached to the property. Although I was still eager to have him design the house, I was also prepared to reject his scheme if it turned out to be nothing out of the ordinary.

The scheme he produced approximately three months after our first meeting was entirely unexpected. I had been anticipating a three-story house, taking up the full width of the site. His scheme was instead a vertically-oriented, four-story house, with each floor accommodating one room. He used only 22.5 square meters of the 65 square meters of usable land. Not only that, the house was completely glazed on the third and fourth floors on the side facing the sea. I had imagined only a limited

てきた案はまったく予想外のものでした。私は敷地の横手いっぱいを使った3階建てを想定していましたが、安藤さんの案はワンフロアひと部屋で、縦長の4階建て。65m²の建築可能な敷地のうち、わずか22.5m²しか使っていません。しかも3階と4階は海に面する壁がなくて、全面ガラスになっている……。私は壁に窓が開いていて、見たいときに海が見えるというのが海と建物との関係性くらいに思っていました。安藤さんの案では、海を見て楽しむというよりも、海と一体になって暮らすような感じです。「なんと大胆な！　家でここまでやっていいの？」と、びっくりしました。

一方、私が思い描いていた安藤建築の造形的な建築言語──軸線に対して壁を斜めにズラして隙間がつくられていたり、曲面壁が挿入されていたり、思いがけない高さの吹き抜けがあったり──が全然使われていなくて、少しさびしいなとも思いました。ヴィトンで買った鞄に、ヴィトンのマークがなかった感じですね（笑）。これまで私が勝手に思い描いていた安藤スタイルにはまったくこだわりがなく、海際の住宅のあり方をまっすぐとらえて余計なものはすべて削ぎ落とされていました。自分の考えとはるかにかけ離れた設計に感銘し、この案で進めていくことになりました。

建築家の肺活量

設計の大部分は、私が見せてもらう前に非常によく練られていましたので、私から大きな変更を迫る必要はありませんでした。細かい間取りや家具のことなど、私の要望は全部伝えました。でも安藤さんは、こちらの要望

relationship existing between the sea and the building; that is, windows punched in walls from which one could look at the sea when one wanted. In Ando's scheme, one did not so much enjoy a view of the sea as live at one with the sea. I was amazed by the boldness of the idea. It seemed so extreme for a house.

On the other hand, I was a trifle disappointed to find no trace of what I had imagined to be his architectural vocabulary; e.g. a wall placed at an angle with respect to the axis, creating a gap; the insertion of a curved wall; and an unexpectedly high, multi-level space. It was like purchasing a bag at Louis Vuitton and not finding the Vuitton pattern on it [laughing]. He was not fixated on what I had thought of as the Ando Style; he produced a straightforward response to the problem of a house by the sea and eliminated all superfluous elements. I was profoundly impressed by this design which far surpassed my own ideas; I decided to go ahead with the scheme.

The Lung Capacity of an Architect

I did not need to ask for any major changes, since the design had been so thoroughly worked out before I saw it. I communicated all my wishes with regard to details about layouts and furniture. Ando did not simply listen to my wishes but responded in ways I had not imagined. I was impressed: architects have a deeper understanding of these things; they have what I would call a greater lung capacity.

Suppose I and Ando both dived into the "sea of thought" in an effort to accommodate the living and dining areas in one room. I would combine the parts as I would pieces in a puzzle; the moment I came up with a "living-dining space", I would be satisfied and immediately surface. Ando, on the other hand, would let out air a bit at a time and sink to the bottom of the sea; he would not surface for some time. By the time he rose to

をそのまま聞き入れるのではなくて、想像以上のかたち
で応えてくれるのです。やっぱり建築家は考えが深いし、
＜肺活量＞が違うなと思いました。

　例えばリビングとダイニングをひと部屋に納めようとし
て、＜思考の海＞に私と安藤さんが一緒に潜ったとします。私はパズルのようにそれぞれのピースをパッと組み
合わせて、いわゆるリビング・ダイニングを思いついた
時点で満足して、すぐに浮かび上がってしまう。でも安
藤さんは、ボコボコと少しずつ息を吐き出しながらジッ
と海底に沈み、なかなか上がってきません。ようやく海
面に浮かび上がったときには、リビングでもダイニング
でもない、まったく新しいかたちになっている。かたち
自体はむしろ非常にシンプルになり、私の思いを解決し
て、安藤さんのスタイルも崩すこともなく「これ以外にど

んなかたちがあるんだ」と思うような姿になっているの
です。

　＜肺活量＞の大きさは、1階のプランに強く感じます。
最初は玄関が海側だけでした。でも日常のアプローチと
して、陸側（道路側）にも玄関をつけて欲しいと伝えま
した。お願いはしてみたものの、交通量の多い国道に面
しているので落ち着いた玄関にはなりにくいし、庇がな
いと雨の日はつらい……。私にはどうしても不格好な玄
関しか思いつきません。ところが安藤さんの示したかた
ちは、とてもスマートでした。陸側から海側に抜ける廊
下を中心に通し、陸側の玄関ドアを少し内側に引っ込
めて、余計な庇をつけることもなく静かに陸側から入れ
る。これしかない、というような見事な解答でした。

　細かいところも随分配慮してもらいました。例えば4

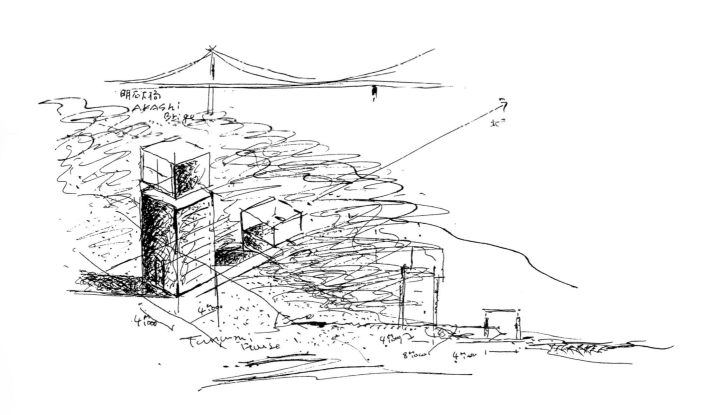

階から屋上へ上がるメンテナンス用の階段です。最初は外階段だったのですが、怖くて上がれないと思ったのです。安藤事務所の担当スタッフに「内階段にできないか」と相談したところ、「外階段の方が納まりが綺麗だから、それはあり得ないだろう」と。スタッフがそういうのだから安藤さんにいってもアカンだろうなと諦めていたら、安藤さんは、「それも一理ある。中でいいじゃないか」とあっさり変更してくれたのです。実際には、階段室上部のロフトへ上がれるハシゴが用意されていて、ロフト上のトップライトから屋上にハシゴで出られるようになっています。

　また、2階寝室のベッド脇にサイドテーブルを置けないかと、狭さも考えずに無理を承知でお願いをしてみたのです。そうしたらなんと、ベッド自体の幅が大きくなっ

て、枕もとに棚をつくってくれました（笑）。ベッドと棚をうまく組み合わせて、サイドテーブルの機能を満足する逆転の発想には、本当に感心しました。

　安藤さんの住宅は「施主泣かせで住まい手に厳しい」と想像している人も多いと思います。私も安藤さんに依頼する前は、自分のスタイルを通して、施工者はもちろん施主にも「自分に合わせろ」というやり方なのではないかと半信半疑の思いでした。実際はむしろ逆で、「そんなに施主のいうことを真剣に受け止めていいんですか？」と思うくらいでした。設計当時、私は独身だったのですが、安藤さんが「中田さん、結婚したら子どもができるなあ」といわれたので、「そうしたらどうしましょう？」と聞いたところ、「3階に机を並べてこうしたら……。あ、いける！」と（笑）。安藤さんは先々のことまで結構考え

the surface, his solution would be, neither a living room nor a dining room, but something entirely new. The form itself would be extremely simple and seem somehow inevitable; it would answer my need but still be consistent with Ando's style.

I think the first floor plan in particular shows his large "lung capacity". At first, there was only an entrance on the seaward side. I said I wanted an entrance on the landward (road) side as well for everyday access. However, I realized that creating a tranquil entrance space would be difficult, since the front of the house faces a heavily-trafficked national road. In addition, an entrance would probably require an overhang to keep off rain. Try as I might, I could only imagine an awkwardly designed entrance. However, Ando's solution was quite smart. He introduced a corridor running through the middle of the house from the landward side to the seaward side; the entrance door on the landward side was slightly recessed

to provide cover, obviating the addition of an overhang. It was a superb (the only) solution.

Ando was quite accommodating about small details; for example, there was the matter of the stairs from the fourth floor to the rooftop for maintenance purposes. It was an open stairway at first, but I thought it would be too scary to climb. I asked the staff member in charge of the project at Ando's office whether the stairs could be brought indoors but was told that an outdoor stairway was a better fit. I thought it would be no use asking Ando himself and had given up on the idea. However, apprised of my wish, he said the idea had merit; why not put it indoors? Just like that, he changed the design. There is now a ladder for climbing up to the loft above the stairway, and using the ladder, one can go up to the rooftop by way of a skylight above the loft. I also asked if a side table could be installed by the bed in the second-floor bedroom, despite the limited size of the space.

てくれているのです。

　でも決して、安藤さんが迎合しているわけではありません。最初に「自分のスタイルはこういうものです。本当にこのスタイルで進めていいですか?」と施主に意見を求め、徹底的に意見を闘わせた上で、お互いに納得したらスタートする。どちらかの意見を曲げて擦り合わせるのではなく、袂を分かつ覚悟で話し合うという感じでした。

　しかし、実際に設計を進める段階に入ると、「無理をいったけれど、こうしてくれたんだな」という配慮や優しさが、図面に滲み出ていますね。安藤さんは何事にも常に厳しい人ですが、根は優しい人なのだと感じました。もちろん、直に優しい言葉を投げかけてくれるわけではありませんけれど(笑)。

安藤コンクリートに挑む

　施工は私の工務店で行いました。実施設計図をもとに施工図を描き起こしてみると、寸法がかなり細かく押えられていることに驚きました。普通の実施設計図より格段に描き込まれていました。例えば4階の東側の壁。幅が約5mありますが、1,800mmの普通の型枠を使ったら端数が出て、3枚の割り付けになります。でも安藤さんから「2枚でつくれる型枠はないか?」といわれて、通常より長い型枠を調達しました。壁のセンターに目地が入って、それだけでも綺麗な割り付けになります。ところがその目地のラインが、キッチンやテーブルの端部とピッタリ合うのです。型枠の割り付けのラインと、その他のさまざまな寸法の納まりがお互いに関係し合ってい

Suddenly, the bed itself became wider, and shelves were provided by the bed [laughing]. I was impressed by the way he cleverly combined the bed and the shelves and made the latter serve the function of a side table.

Many probably imagine that Ando's houses cause clients no end of worries and occupants many hardships. Before I asked Ando to design my house, I too suspected that he would not be accommodating in any way and demand that the client as well as the builder do precisely as he wanted. In reality, however, it was just the opposite; I almost began to worry that he was too receptive to my requests. I was single at the time, but Ando said, "You will no doubt have a child when you get married." "What will I do then?" I asked. He said, "If we line up the desks on the third floor in this way...ah, that should do it" [laughing]. Ando will anticipate things for you.

Nevertheless, Ando did not compromise. He first tells a client, "This is what my style is like. Is this really acceptable to you?" Only when views have been thoroughly aired and both sides are convinced will he begin. Instead of trying to reach an agreement at all costs, we entered into discussions prepared to disagree and have the project fall through. However, Ando made an effort to accommodate my wishes, however unreasonable, and that showed up in the drawings. Ando is strict about everything, but deep down he is gentle. Of course, he is not one to speak gently to you at first [laughing].

Taking up the Challenge of Ando's Concrete

My firm did the construction work. Preparing shop drawings from his working drawings, I was surprised by the extent to which dimensions were specified. His working drawings were remarkably more detailed than ordinary ones. Take, for example, the east wall on the fourth floor. The wall is approximately five meters in

る。こうした寸法への厳しいこだわりが、安藤建築の美学を支えているのですね。

また構造図を見ると、タイル目地が描かれているのかと思うくらい、鉄筋がぎっしり入っています。しかも、スランプ15の固いコンクリートを打つように要求されたのです。「15はちょっと厳しいと思うんですよ……」と伝えたところ、「シャブコンを打ってどないするんだ！　そんなコンクリートはすぐボロボロになる」と怒られました（笑）。学生時代から安藤さんの建築を目にしているので、ある程度の覚悟はしていました。しかし実際に施工をしてみて、改めて安藤さんの打ち放しコンクリートは想像以上に気を配らないとつくれないことがよくわかりましたね。

緊張感のある現場でしたが、私の工務店のスタッフも、職人も、みんな楽しそうに働いていました。安藤さんもときどき現場に来られたのですが、「おう、ご苦労さん」と、みんなに気軽に声をかけていました。型枠を外して、綺麗なコンクリートが姿を現した瞬間は、みんなでニッコリ（笑）。設計者、施工者、職人、みんなの気持ちが一緒にならないと、こうしたコンクリートはつくれません。安藤さんの打ち放しコンクリートを施工してみて、先々まで残る気持ちの入った建築をつくるための心構えを随分勉強させてもらいました。

建築を続けるヴァイタリティー

安藤さんと一緒に仕事をして驚いたのは、判断のスピードです。例えば、施工図をもとに私の工務店で1/20の模型をつくり、安藤事務所で打ち合わせをしたときの

width. With ordinary form panels, each 1800 millimeters in width, you would need three panels. However, Ando asked if this could be done with just two panels; I therefore procured form panels of extra width. The wall would have looked nice with just the joint coming in the middle. However, the joint was perfectly aligned with the kitchen and one end of the table. The arrangement of the concrete forms had been coordinated with various other dimensions. This perfectionism with respect to dimensions is the basis for Ando's architectural aesthetic.

Then there were the structural drawings, which showed steel reinforcements packed together so tightly they looked like drawings of tile joints. In addition, he wanted a hard concrete with a slump of 15. When I told him 15 seemed a bit severe, he replied angrily, "Why would you want watery concrete? Concrete like that will crumble in no time" [laughing]. Having looked at Ando's buildings since I was a student, I was prepared to some extent. However, through actual experience, I now understand that enormous care must be paid to create Ando's exposed concrete.

The construction site was stressful, but everyone from my own staff to the craftsmen enjoyed working there. Ando visited the site occasionally and would cheerfully greet everyone. Everyone smiled when forms were removed, revealing a beautifully produced concrete [laughing]. Concrete like that is impossible to create unless everyone—the architect, the builder, and the workmen—is on the same page. Building Ando's exposed concrete taught me a great deal about the mental preparation that is needed to create a lasting building that is full of feeling.

Vitality Needed to Continue Practicing Architecture

The thing that surprised me, working together with Ando, was how quickly he made decisions. Take for

こと。模型を安藤さんが見るなり、どんどん描き込みを入れるのです。「人が一生懸命つくった模型に落書きして……」と思ったのですが、でき上がってみると一つひとつの変更が非常に効果的なのです。特に3階の階段室の天井をバサッと斜めにカットする変更。階段室への光の入り方が格段によくなりました。それを一瞬で判断するのですから、すごいですね。

安藤さんは、「4×4の住宅」と同時に「ピノー現代美術館」など大規模なプロジェクトも平行して進めていました。何万m²もある建築に比べて、こちらは100m²ちょっと。「こんな小さな家で申し訳ない」と思ったものです（笑）。安藤事務所の打ち合わせ光景を見たのですが、スタッフみんながずらっと並んで、1人ずつ順番に図面を見せるわけです。安藤さんが「ここ納まってい

ないから描き直せ!」というと、スタッフがパッと出ていって描き直して、また列の後ろに並んでいる。安藤さんは、それぞれ異なる建物の図面を細かい部分まで確認して、すごいスピードで指示を与えていくのです。あれだけの仕事量をこなしながら高いクオリティを保ち続けるのは、並み大抵のことではありません。

建築家は、若くて仕事がない時期には小住宅にも取り組みますが、他の大きな仕事が増えてくると住宅から遠ざかってしまうのは、仕方のないことだと思います。でも安藤さんは、あれだけ大規模な建築を日本ばかりでなく海外でも設計しているにも関わらず、今も住宅に取り組んでいるのがすごいですよね。どんな規模の建築にも大変なエネルギーを使われていて、それだけでも大変なことだと思います。その上、1995年の震災後に

example the time I had a 1:20 scale model based on shop drawings made at my firm for a meeting at Ando's office. The moment he saw the model, Ando began to draw on it. At first, I was annoyed that he would scribble on something that had required such effort to make, but when he was finished, I saw that each change he made was quite effective. In particular, the way he cut the third-floor ceiling of the stairway at a diagonal greatly improved the introduction of light into the stairway. What was amazing was that he made the decision in an instant.

In addition to the 4 x 4 House, Ando was working then on large projects such as the François Pinault Foundation for Contemporary Art. The house was just over 100 square meters, whereas the large projects had floor areas of tens of thousands of square meters. I was sorry I was taking up his time with such a small house [laughing]. I saw a meeting conducted at Ando's office. His staff members lined up, and one after another they showed

him drawings. Ando would say, "This is not arranged correctly; redraw this." The staff member would immediately go out and, having corrected the drawing, stand again at the end of the line. Ando would check even the smallest details of these different drawings and give his instructions at great speed. It is no easy thing to continue to maintain a high standard of quality while managing such a heavy work load.

Architects take on small houses when they are young and have little work but inevitably accept fewer residential commissions as larger jobs begin to come in. The fact that Ando continues to design houses even though he is designing large buildings overseas as well as in Japan is amazing. He expends a great deal of energy, whatever the size of the project; his practice would be demanding by itself. However, he has also been active in planting trees with white flowers in devastated parts of Kobe as a leader of the Hyogo Green Network since the 1995 Hanshin-

は「ひょうごグリーンネットワーク」の旗ふり役となって、荒廃した神戸の街に白い花の咲く木を植える活動もしている。私は地元なのでよくわかりますが、今では立派な街路樹に育ってきています。また、「4×4の住宅」から見える瀬戸内海の島々では「瀬戸内オリーブ基金」による植樹活動も精力的に続けている。安藤さんは本当に建築が好きだからこそ、小さな住宅から都市や環境問題まで、建築を中心とする活動を幅広くやり続けられるのでしょうね。

安藤建築に住む喜び

住み始めてから3年が経ち、その間に結婚もしましたが、住み心地はとても快適です。各階4.75m四方のプランなので、でき上がるまでは「ちょっと狭いかな」と思っていました。でも実際の空間は想像以上の広がりがあり、狭さは感じません。開口の取り方や階高のコントロールが絶妙なんですよね。打ち放しコンクリートの壁も、心理的に冷たいとか重苦しい感じはまったくしません。日本人の感性にあったコンクリートの質感を、安藤さんが独自に追求してきた成果なのでしょうね。暑い寒いは覚悟していましたが、壁厚が約300mmあり、コンクリート躯体の熱容量が大きいためか、思ったほどの不快感はありません。

最初は階段の上下移動がしんどいなと思いましたが、すっかり慣れてしまいました。この建物に暮らしていると、ちょっとした不便は不便だと感じなくなるんです。瀬戸内海の美しい景色が視界いっぱいに飛び込んでくるリビング・キッチンなんて、うちでしか味わえませんから

Awaji Earthquake. Being a local, I am familiar with these activities; the planted saplings have grown now into fine trees lining streets. Ando is also promoting planting on islands in the Inland Sea (the sea over which the 4 x 4 House looks out) through the Setouchi Olive Foundation. No doubt he is able to continue his many activities, ranging from small houses to the city and environmental problems, because he truly loves architecture.

The Joy of Living in an Ando Building

I have been living in the house now for three years— I have married during that time — and it is extremely pleasant. Until the house was constructed, I thought it would be somewhat cramped because each floor is 4.75 meters square in plan. However, the space in reality is bigger than I had imagined and I do not think of it now as cramped. The way the openings are arranged and floor heights controlled is superb. The walls of exposed concrete do not seem cold or heavy at all, perhaps because Ando has sought to achieve a certain texture in concrete that appeals to the Japanese sensibility. I was resigned to it being hot or cold in the house, but, perhaps because the wall thickness is approximately 300 millimeters and the thermal capacity of the concrete building frame is large, I have not felt quite the discomfort I had anticipated.

I was worried at first about all the walking up and down the stairs I would have to do but have become accustomed to it. When one lives in this building, a little inconvenience no longer feels like an inconvenience. After all, few houses boast a living room and kitchen with such a spectacular view of the Inland Sea. All friends who come to visit are stunned.

Ando designed the fittings and the furniture such as tables and the kitchen. The dining table has drawers in

ね。遊びに来た友達も、「うわあ、すごい!」とみんな驚いています。

テーブルやキッチンなど、建具や家具まで安藤さんが設計してくれました。ダイニング・テーブルには引き出しがついていて、普段使いの食器が収納できます。そうした心配りが行き届いているためか、妻からも不満を聞いたことはありません。

学生時代に「住吉の長屋」を見たときは、特に住みたいとは思いませんでした。この家に暮らし始めた今では、「住吉」もすごく楽しい家だと思えます。私が階段の上り下りに慣れてしまったように、「住吉」のご夫婦も、「雨の日に傘を差して中庭を通らないとトイレに行けない」といった不便をつらいと感じていないのではないでしょうか。ちょっとした不便にはすぐに慣れてしまって、

中庭があることの豊かさを存分に楽しまれていると思います。あんな都市の真ん中にあっても、四季折々の光や風、天候の移り変わりを堪能できるのですからね。「住吉」やわが家のように小さな住宅でも、「小篠邸」のように大きな住宅でも共通する豊かさ——私たちの生の本質に関わるような豊かさを、安藤さんの住宅は与えてくれるのです。

「4×4の住宅」では「海とともに生活する豊かさ」があります。流行に左右されず、年月を経ても変わらない性質の豊かさです。それは私が最初に思い描いていた、いわゆるモダンで快適なといった価値観とはまったく異なる水準でしか計れない豊かさなのだと、この家に住んでつくづく思うのです。この家とともに、きっとこれからも夫婦でのびのびと楽しく暮らして行けると思います。

which I store the everyday tableware. My wife has never complained about the house, perhaps because of such thoughtful touches.

I did not particularly want to live in the Rowhouse in Sumiyoshi when I saw it as a student. Now that I have begun to live in this house, I believe living in "Sumiyoshi" might be enjoyable as well. Having to carry an umbrella to walk through the courtyard in the rain to reach the toilet is probably no more irksome for the couple living in "Sumiyoshi" than having to walk up and down the stairs is for me. One quickly becomes accustomed to a little inconvenience; the couple undoubtedly get a great deal of pleasure from the courtyard. After all, they can enjoy to the full the changing quality of the light and the breeze, from one season to the next or in different kinds of weather, even though the house is in the middle of the city. Ando's houses, whether small ones like the Rowhouse in Sumiyoshi or mine or large ones like the

Koshino House, are "opulent" in that they enable their occupants to savor the essence of life.

The 4 x 4 House is opulent in that it enables us to live at one with the sea. It is an opulence that is uninfluenced by fashion and does not change with the passing of time. Living in this house, I see that it is opulent but by standards entirely different from those associated with modernity and comfort. I am convinced that my wife and I will be able to continue to live naturally and pleasantly, together with this house.

六甲の集合住宅
Rokko Housing

1978-83 (phase I), 85-93 (phase II), 92-99 (phase III)
兵庫県神戸市———Kobe, Hyogo

六甲の集合住宅 I

Rokko Housing I

1978-83

敷地は、神戸六甲山の麓、覆いかぶさるように迫る、60度の勾配をもった南面する急斜面に位置する。敷地からは、大阪湾から神戸港にかけてを一望することができる。この立地条件を最大限活かした集合住宅形式として、われわれが提案したのは斜面形状に沿って埋め込まれたコンクリート・ラーメンによる段状の空間構成だった。

　全体は、5.8m×4.8mのユニットを基本単位とする、シンメトリーの構成を基調とする。そのシンメトリーの構成を自然の地形に馴染ませていく過程で生じた構成のズレを、意図的な余白の空間とした。各棟の隙間を巡る陰影深いこの余白の空間の連続が、各住戸への直接のアプローチとなるのと同時に、コミュニティを育むパブリックスペースの役割を果たす。

　斜面に沿ってズレながら積層する20の住戸は、いずれもさまざまな方向を向いた屋外テラスをもち、大きさも部屋構成もすべて異なる。全体としての一体感、統一感と、部分における多様性とを同時に満足させる集合の論理の発見を、ひとつの主題としていた。

　建物全外周を巡るドライエリアは、通風および断熱の効果をもたらす、自然の環境制御装置である。

The site is located on a south-facing 60-degree slope, as if spread across the foot of Mt. Rokko in Kobe. From the site, it is possible to have panoramic views extending from Osaka Bay to the port of Kobe. As a housing complex typology that makes maximum use of these site conditions, we proposed a tiered spatial composition that follows the shape of the slope by means of a buried concrete post-and-beam structure.

It is all based on a symmetrical composition with a standard unit measuring 5.8m by 4.8m. Compositional shifts are generated in the process of adjusting this symmetrical composition to the natural terrain, which are intended to produce marginal spaces. These continuous marginal spaces in the deeply shaded gaps surrounding each wing become direct approach routes to each unit, while simultaneously taking on the role of public spaces that foster community.

While shifting along the slope, the 20 layered units all have rooftop terraces that face in different directions, and they all differ in room composition and size. With an overall sense of identity, unity, and diversity in the parts, one theme was the discovery of a satisfying logic of assembly.

The dry area surrounding the entire perimeter of the building provides effective ventilation and insulation, as well as being a device to control the natural environment.

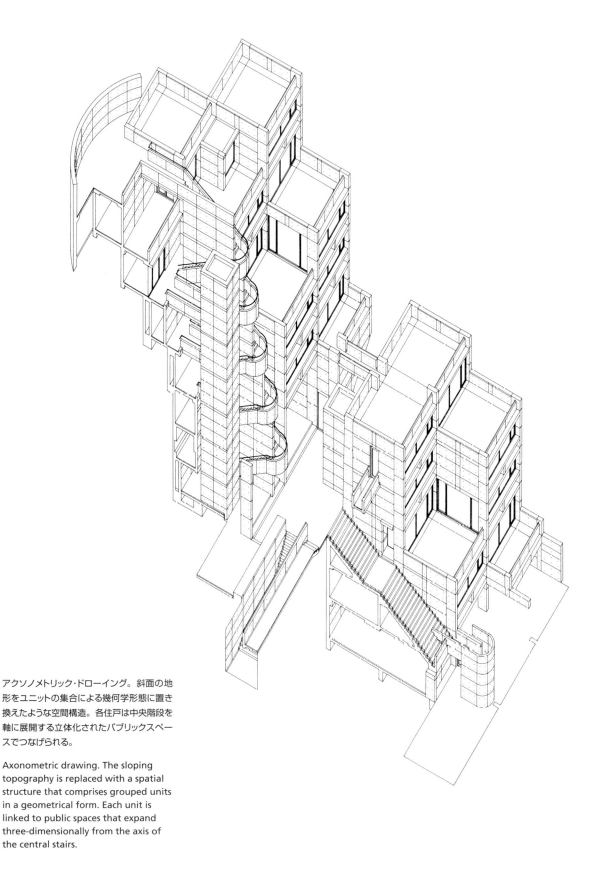

アクソノメトリック・ドローイング。斜面の地形をユニットの集合による幾何学形態に置き換えたような空間構造。各住戸は中央階段を軸に展開する立体化されたパブリックスペースでつなげられる。

Axonometric drawing. The sloping topography is replaced with a spatial structure that comprises grouped units in a geometrical form. Each unit is linked to public spaces that expand three-dimensionally from the axis of the central stairs.

自然と人工が対立しながら調和する風景。自然の中に
投げ出された幾何学は、自然との対比の中で自らの意
思を主張する。幾何学の線と出会うことで自然はその
存在をより際立たせる。

A harmonious scene of nature confronting
artifice. This geometry thrown down into nature
asserts its own will in the contrast with nature.
Nature itself becomes more conspicuous through
its encounter with geometrical lines.

ユニットの積層がつくる正面ファサード。微妙にずらされた構成のアシンメトリーが内部空間の奥行きとふくらみを期待させ、アプローチを演出する。

The front facade comprising an accumulation of units. The asymmetrical composition of subtle shifts anticipates the depth and swelling of the internal spaces, and creates approach routes.

上昇するにつれセットバックする階段。踊場を巡るたびに頭上に空を仰ぐ。
The stairs are set back as they ascend. The sky may be seen overhead each time a landing is traversed.

空に開かれた中央広場。住戸間の隙間を埋める緩衝地帯としてのパブリックスペース。
The central plaza is open to the sky. Public spaces are embedded as buffer areas in the gaps between units.

住戸の＜隙間＞に路地のように張り巡らされたパブリックスペース。光が交錯する陰影深い森のような空間が生まれている。

Public spaces stretch around the units in alley-like "gaps." The interplay of light produces spaces like a forest in deep shadow.

地質応力検討図。60度という急斜面に建設するため、70年代当時では珍しくコンピュータによる地盤解析を用いている。安藤が未知へのプロジェクトに挑戦した痕跡。

Geological stress diagram. In order to build on this steep slope of 60 degrees, the ground was analyzed by computer, which was unusual in the 1970s. This project shows traces of Ando challenging the unknown.

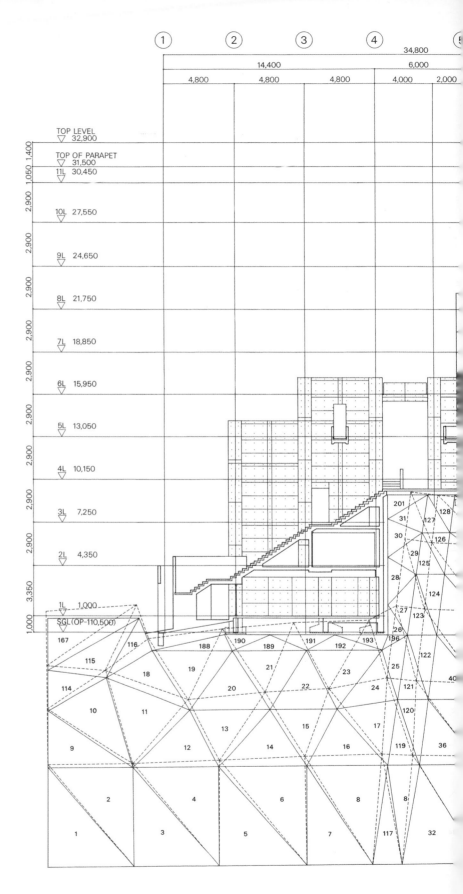

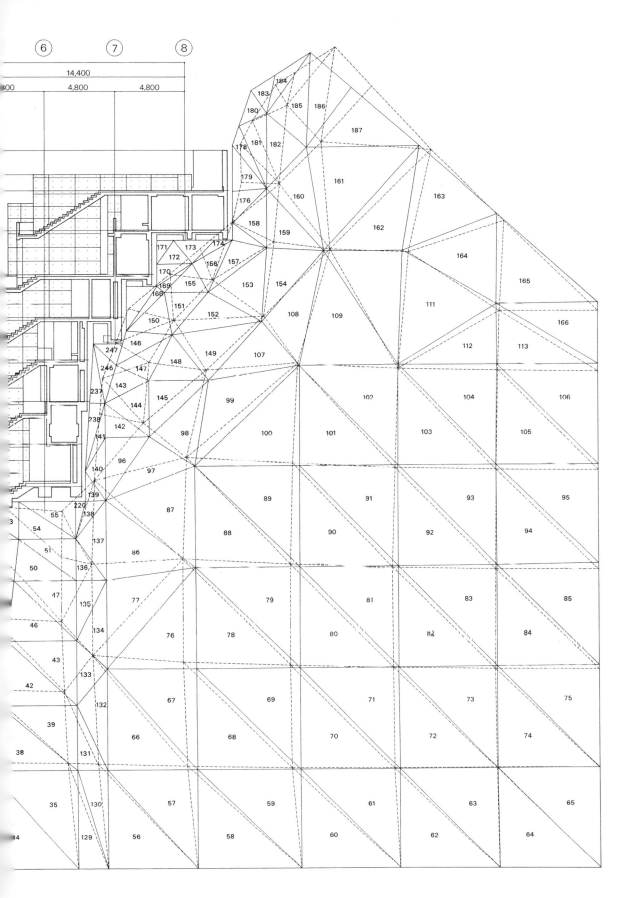

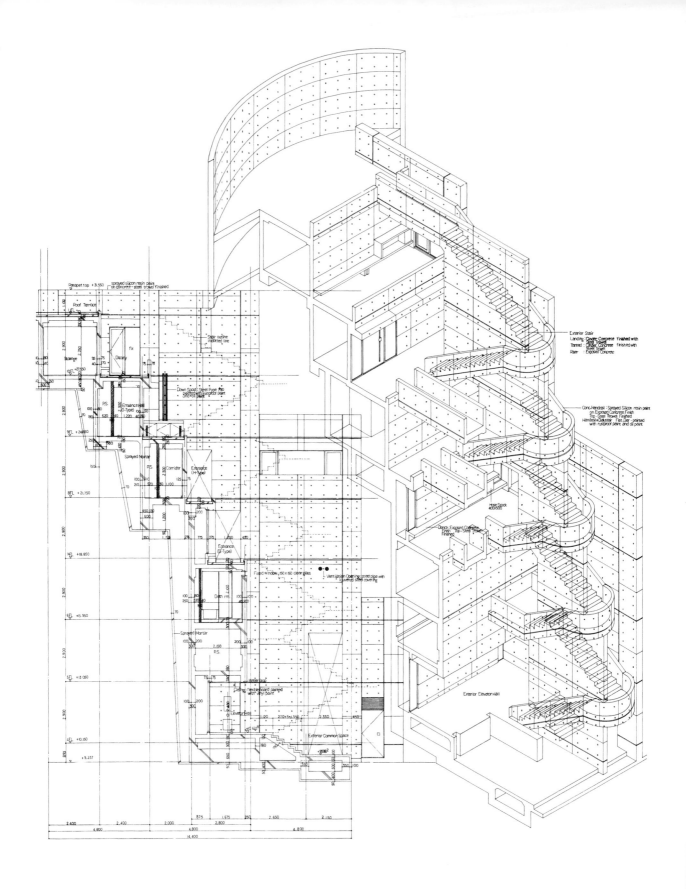

中央階段のアイソメトリック・ドローイング（左）とルーフ・プラン（下）。反復するリズムに微妙に変化を加えていく精緻なディテールの集積。

Isometric drawing of the central stair (left), and the roof plan (right). An accumulation of delicate details by incorporating slight changes in a repetitive rhythm.

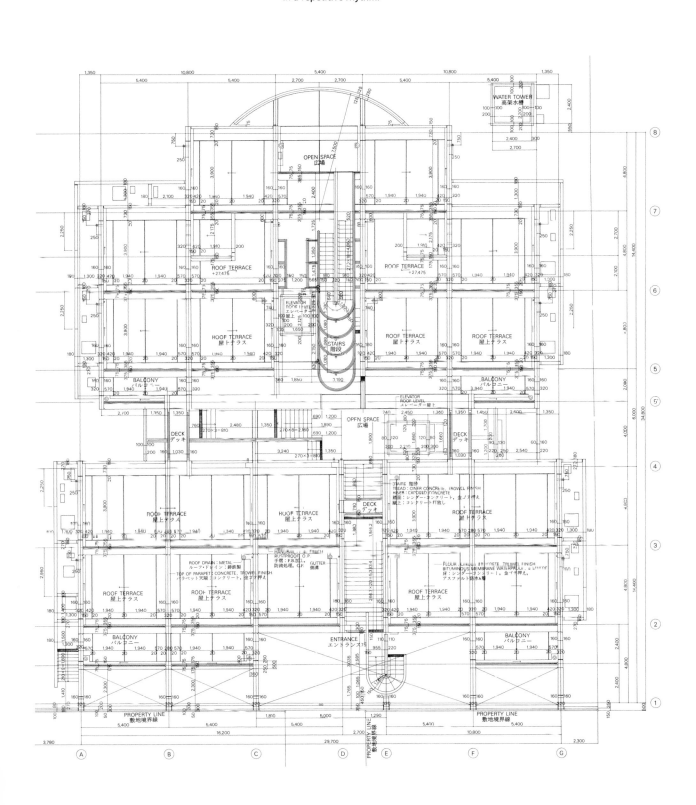

1983年の六甲の集合住宅Ⅰの完成に前後して、隣接する斜面地での六甲の集合住宅Ⅱの計画がスタートした。Ⅰ期が60度の斜面地約1,900m²に20戸の住居を配置したのに対し、Ⅱ期では同じく60度の斜面であるが、敷地面積は約3倍、延床面積は約4倍で50戸の住居をもつ。敷地いっぱいの建築で斜線制限等の法的規制が厳しく、形態が建物のコンセプトを明確に表現するに至らなかったⅠ期に対し、Ⅱ期では外的な要因に縛られることなく、建築的意図をそのままに表現することができた。

全体は、5.2m×5.2mの正方形グリッドを基本単位とするフレームを骨格にもつ。そのフレームをⅠ期同様、地形に埋め込んでいくことでズレを生じさせ、その余白の空間を軸に、変化に富んだ集合体をつくり出す。中心となるのは、各棟を東西に2分割する階段スペースである。建物の隙間を縫って走る余白の存在により、多様な方向性をもつ各住戸は、大きさ、プランとも多様なバリエーションをもつ。

Ⅱ期では、プログラムの上でも、パブリックスペースのさらなる充実が試みられている。中間の屋上広場の上部には、海の見える屋内プールが設けられているが、これは住人のほか、近隣住民への解放も想定して計画されたものだ。この主題は、続く六甲の集合住宅Ⅲにおいて、さらに大きく発展していく。

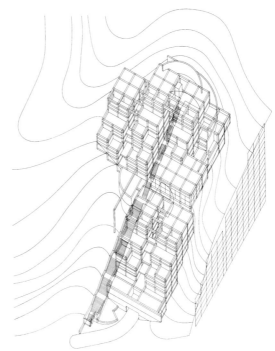

六甲の集合住宅Ⅱ
Rokko Housing Ⅱ
1985-93

In 1983, around the time that Rokko Housing I was completed, Rokko Housing II was begun on an adjacent slope. In contrast to phase I, which is an arrangement of 20 units on 1900m² of a 60-degree sloping site, phase II is also on a 60-degree slope, but contains 50 units on a site nearly three times larger, with a total floor area about four times larger. Phase I had severe setback lines and other legal restrictions on a building that fills the entire site, and so the form does not clearly express the concept of the building, but phase II I was not constrained by external factors and so the architectural intentions could be directly expressed.

Overall, there is a frame structure with a square grid that gives a standard unit measuring 5.2m by 5.2m. Like phase I, shifts were generated by burying this frame into the terrain, making an assemblage rich in variation along the axes of the marginal spaces. The central staircase space divides each wing into two parts, east and west. Due to the existence of marginal spaces threaded through gaps in the building, each unit has a varied directionality, as well as having variations in size and layout.

As well as the program, there were further attempts to enrich the public spaces in phase II.

An indoor pool with a view of the sea has been established above the intermediate rooftop plaza, but it was planned with the assumption that it would be open to people from the neighborhood as well as to the residents. This theme was further expanded in the following Rokko Housing III.

建築に軸線を与える中央階段。Ⅰ期より規模を拡大し
たⅡ期では、この中央階段を中心に、より充実したパ
ブリックスペースが展開する。

The central stair gives an axis line to the
architecture. Phase II is larger in scale than
phase I, and the public space is further enriched
around the central stair.

Ⅱ期からⅠ期を見る。ともにユニットの積層
による構成をとりながら、壁式ラーメンのⅠ期
に対し、Ⅱ期は通常のラーメン構造とすること
で、両者のスケール間の違いに応えている。

Looking at phase II from phase I.
Along with the composition of layered
units, as opposed to the wall-type
post-and-beam of phase I, phase II has
an ordinary post-and-beam structure,
a response to the difference in scale
between them.

建築に強固な幾何学の意志を刻むフレームの造形。

The frame is given form by the intention to
put a stable geometry in the architecture.

屋根のある中央プラザ。集合住宅の計画において、押し潰されがちなパブリックスペースが、ここでは建物の構成の核としてつくりこまれている。

The roofed central plaza. The public spaces that tend to become compressed in the planning of housing complexes are here made into the core of the building's composition.

ルーフトップにあるプラザ。
Plaza on the rooftop.

エントランスロビーより中央階段を見る。自然に囲まれた屋外空間が心地よさを生み出す。

Looking at the central stair from the entrance lobby. The outdoor spaces enclosed by nature give rise to a sense of comfort.

Ⅱ期ではプログラムも含め、更なるパブリックスペースの充実
が目標とされた。中央に位置する共用のプールはそのひとつ。

In phase II, the aim was to further enrich the public
spaces together with the program. The centrally located
communal pool is one outcome of this.

プールより屋上植栽越しに神戸の街並みと瀬戸内海を望む。
A view of the Kobe townscape and the Inland Sea from the pool, across the rooftop planting.

斜面の自然を受け止める中庭が設けられた住居内部。　Courtyards that capture the natural slope have been created in the residences.

各住戸は下のレベルの住戸の屋上をテラスとしてもつ。
5.2m グリッドを基本とする、ゆとりある住空間。

Each unit has a terrace that is the rooftop
of the unit on a lower level. These are generous
living spaces based on 5.2m grid.

大きな窓から斜面の自然を存分に取り込む住居。

The residences freely capture the natural slope with large windows.

II期完成時のI・II期全景。
斜面地の集合住宅というテーマの踏襲と発展。

Panoramic view of phase I and II, after phase II
had been completed. This is a continuing
development of the theme of a housing
complex on sloping ground.

Ⅰ・Ⅱ期の配置図。
周辺を含めた環境全体のスタディのためにⅡ期の図面には
常に隣接するⅠ期の形が描かれている。

Site plan of phases I and II. The drawing of phase II depicts
the constantly adjacent shape of phase I, in order to study the
whole environment including the surroundings.

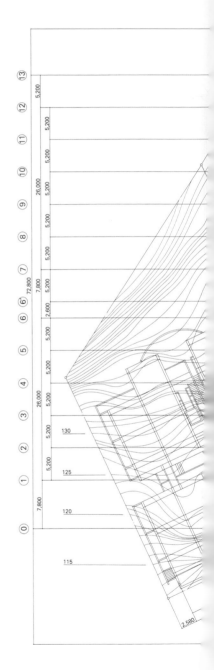

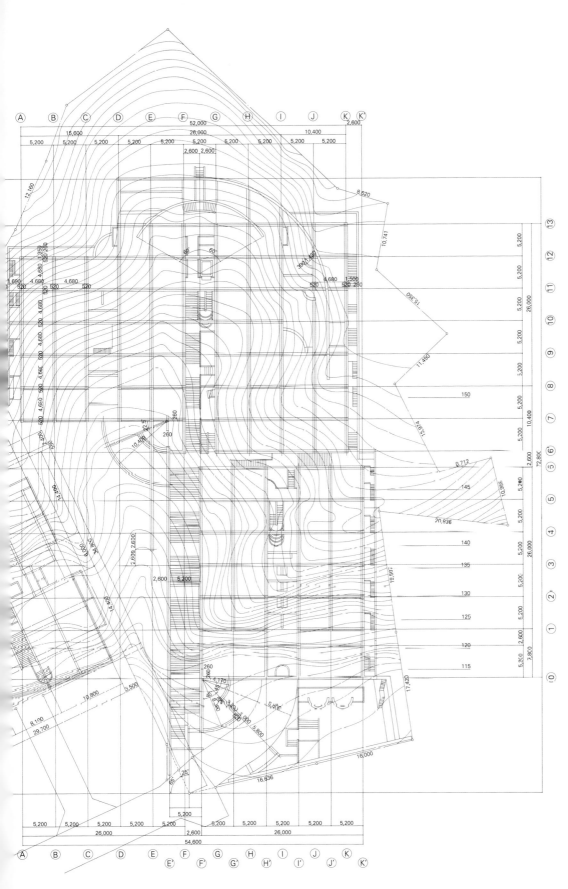

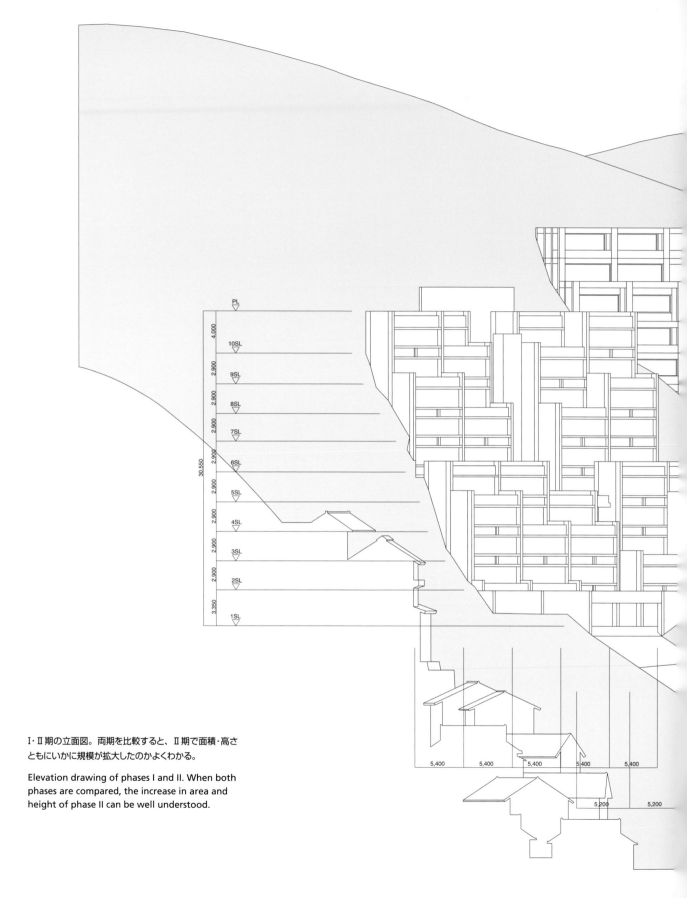

I・II期の立面図。両期を比較すると、II期で面積・高さ
ともにいかに規模が拡大したのかよくわかる。

Elevation drawing of phases I and II. When both
phases are compared, the increase in area and
height of phase II can be well understood.

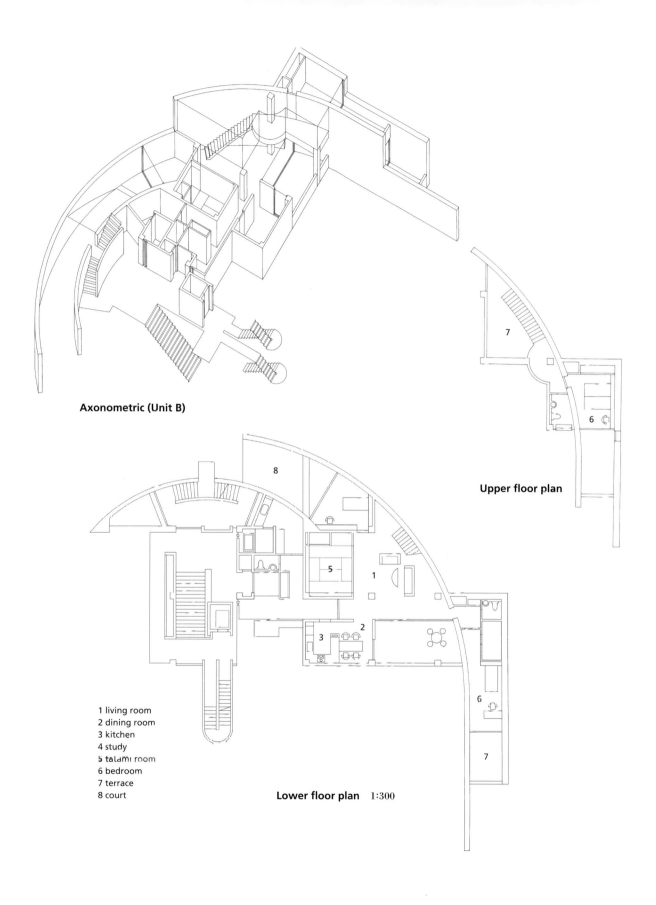

Axonometric (Unit B)

8

Upper floor plan

7

6

5

1

2

3

1 living room
2 dining room
3 kitchen
4 study
5 tatami room
6 bedroom
7 terrace
8 court

6

7

Lower floor plan   1:300

六甲の集合住宅Ⅱの完成時点で自主提案としてまとめていた六甲の集合住宅Ⅲの計画は、1995年の阪神淡路大震災の後、復興住宅という意味合いを加え、かたちを変えて実現することとなった。

　第Ⅲ期の構成は、高層棟、中層棟、低層棟に大きく分けられる。計画の基本となる考え方は、敷地の高低差に応じて多様な住戸平面を用意し、各住戸がそれぞれに異なる風景の中、固有の生活を営めるようにするなど、Ⅰ期、Ⅱ期を踏襲するものであったが、Ⅲ期では敷地条件も異なり、建設費、販売対象等の条件からすべての住戸の差異化を図ることはできなかった。それに代わり、今回、特に意識したのは、各棟に挟まるかたちで設けられた共用空間の充実である。第Ⅱ期の軸線を受けて、南北に展開する段状の動線と、それと交錯するように、東西に広がる緑地を設けた。軸線が交わる、澱み、溜まりとなる場所には広場的な設えを施し、全体として立体的な共用空間となるよう意図した。また、コートハウス形式をとる低層棟、中層棟の屋上庭園は、高層棟にとっての借景となっている。

　現在、隣接する斜面で六甲では4つ目となるプロジェクトの建設が進んでいる。

六甲の集合住宅 Ⅲ
Rokko Housing Ⅲ
1992-99

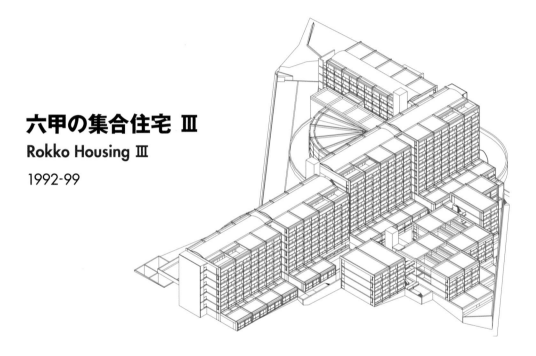

Planned as an independently organized proposal at the time Rokko Housing II was completed, Rokko Housing III gained the connotation of a revitalization housing project after the 1995 Hanshin-Awaji Earthquake, and it was implemented with an altered shape.

　The composition of phase III can be roughly divided into a high-rise wing, a mid-rise wing, and a low-rise wing. Following phase I and phase II, the basic layout idea was to prepare a variety of dwelling plans in response to the site's differences in elevation, and to allow each dwelling to maintain a distinct lifestyle within their differing sceneries. However, the site conditions were different for phase III, and aim of differentiating every unit was impossible in terms of construction costs and sales targets. Instead, this time there was a special awareness given to enriching the public spaces placed between the wings. Continuing the axis of phase II, a stepping north-south circulation route has been established, intersected by green tracts extending east-west. Plaza-like places have been installed where the axis is crossed, widened, or focused, with the intention of making an overall three-dimensional public space.

　Construction of a fourth project is currently underway on an adjacent slope of Mt. Rokko.

Ⅲ期完成時のⅠ・Ⅱ・Ⅲ期の全景。
Ⅲ期は高層棟・中層棟・低層棟による構成をとる。

Panoramic view of phases I, II and III
after phase III had been completed.
Phase III is composed of a high-rise
wing, a mid-rise wing and a low-rise wing.

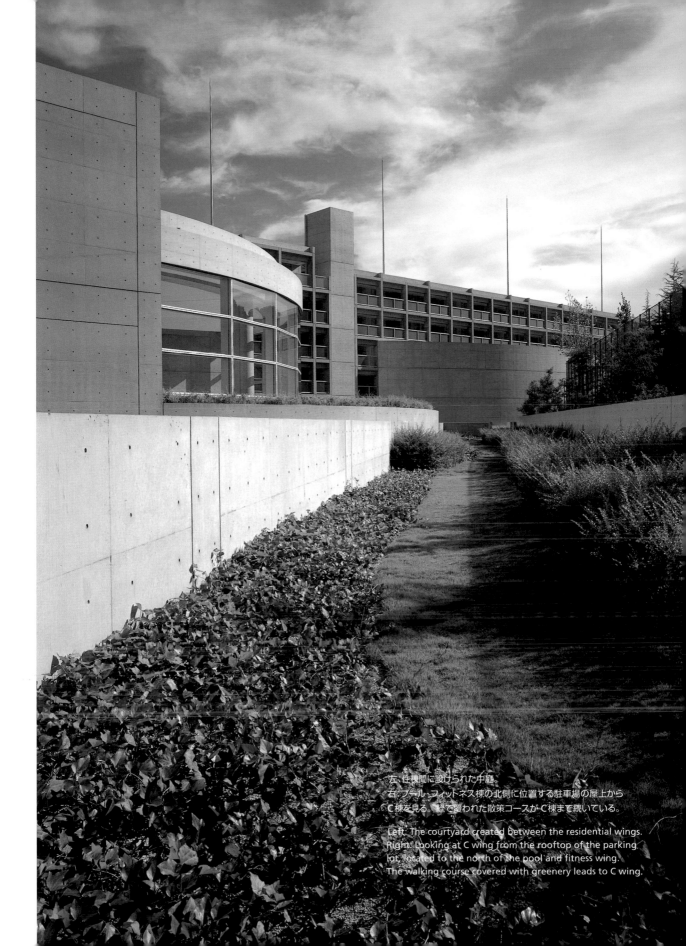

左、住棟間に設けられた中庭。
右、プール・フィットネス棟の北側に位置する駐車場の屋上から
C棟を見る。緑で覆われた散策コースがC棟まで続いている。

Left: The courtyard created between the residential wings.
Right: Looking at C wing from the rooftop of the parking
lot, located to the north of the pool and fitness wing.
The walking course covered with greenery leads to C wing.

D棟からD・B棟間の中庭を見下ろす。
中庭や各棟の屋上などに植栽が施されている。

Looking down from D wing at the courtyard
between D wing and B wing. Planting has
been placed in the courtyard and on the
rooftops of each wing.

左：フィットネス棟４階のプール。扇形の空間でⅡ期のヴォールト天井のイメージが踏襲されている。右：Ｄ棟のアーケード（共用廊下）から中庭越しにＣ棟を見る。

Left: Fourth-floor pool in the fitness wing.
The fan-shaped space follows the image of the vaulted
ceilings in phase II. Right: Looking across the courtyard
at C wing from the D wing arcade (shared corridor).

B棟最上階の住居。海まで続く市街を一望に見晴らせる高層のコートハウス。

A residence on the topmost floor of B wing. This is a high-rise court house that commands an unbroken view, from the urban area to the sea.

D棟屋上から西側を見る。左奥は神戸市街、右奥がC棟、右端がB棟。
中央はD棟のエレベーター・シャフト。

Looking at the west side from the D wing rooftop.
The Kobe townscape is at the distant left, C wing is
at the distant right, and B wing is on the right side.
The D wing elevator shaft is in the center.

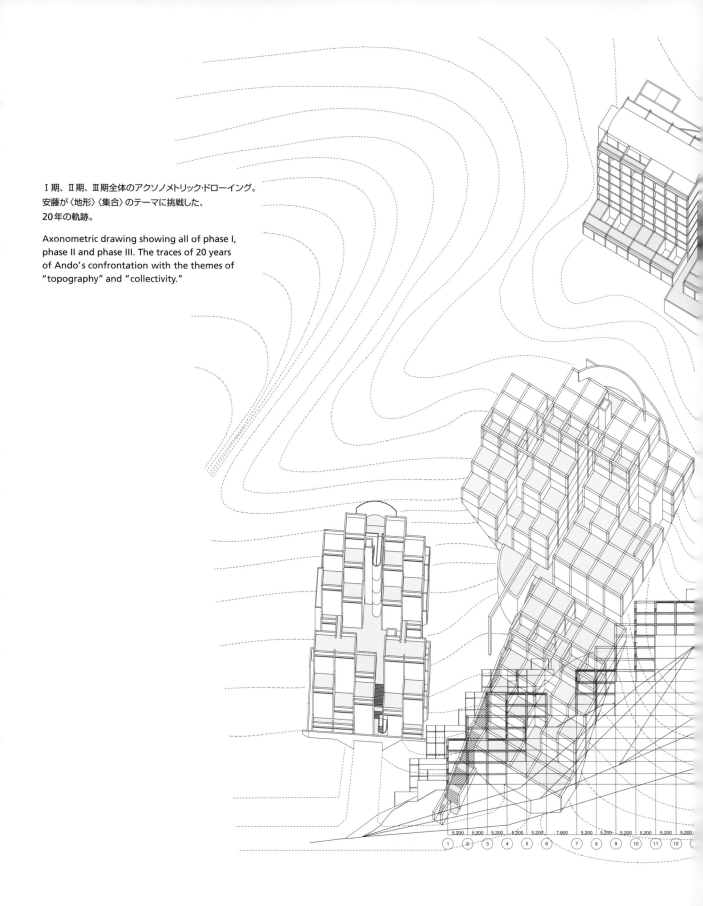

Ⅰ期、Ⅱ期、Ⅲ期全体のアクソノメトリック・ドローイング。
安藤が〈地形〉〈集合〉のテーマに挑戦した、
20年の軌跡。

Axonometric drawing showing all of phase I,
phase II and phase III. The traces of 20 years
of Ando's confrontation with the themes of
"topography" and "collectivity."

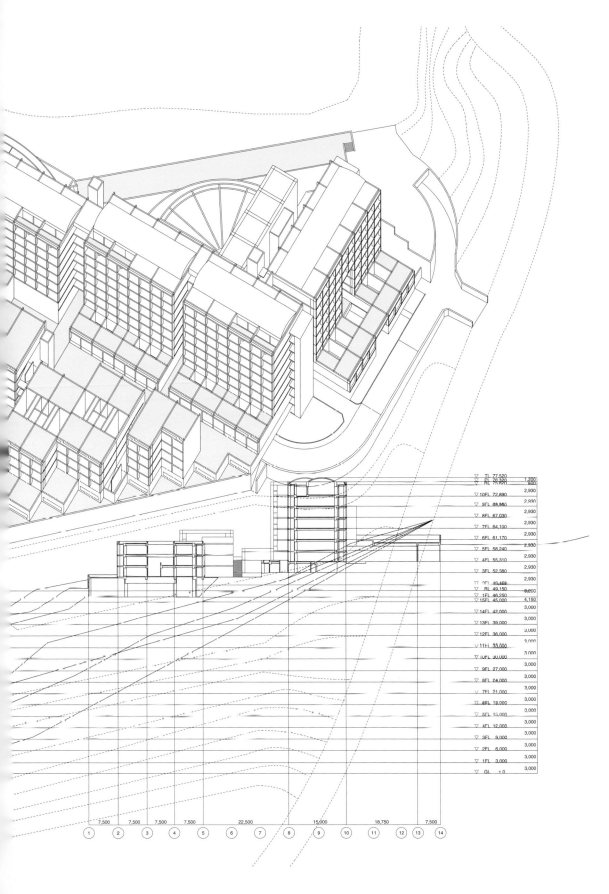

▽ TL 77.520
▽ RL 76.320   1.200
                     800
▽ 10FL 72.890   2,930
▽ 9FL 08.960   2,930
▽ 8FL 67.030   2,930
▽ 7FL 64.100   2,930
▽ 6FL 61.170   2,930
▽ 5FL 58.240   2,930
▽ 4FL 55.310   2,930
▽ 3FL 52.380   2,930
▽ 2FL 49.450   2,930
▽ RL 49.150   9,200
▽ 1FL 46.250
▽ 15FL 45.000   4,150
▽ 14FL 42.000   3,000
▽ 13FL 39.000   3,000
▽ 12FL 36.000   3,000
▽ 11FL 33.000   3,000
▽ 10FL 30.000   3,000
▽ 9FL 27.000   3,000
▽ 8FL 24.000   3,000
▽ 7FL 21.000   3,000
▽ 6FL 18.000   3,000
▽ 5FL 15.000   3,000
▽ 4FL 12.000   3,000
▽ 3FL 9.000   3,000
▽ 2FL 6.000   3,000
▽ 1FL 3.000   3,000
▽ GL ±0   3,000

7,500 7,500 7,500 7,500 22,500 15,000 18,750 7,500

① ② ③ ④ ⑤ ⑥ ⑦ ⑧ ⑨ ⑩ ⑪ ⑫ ⑬ ⑭

六甲の集合住宅──スケッチ
Sketches for Rokko Housing

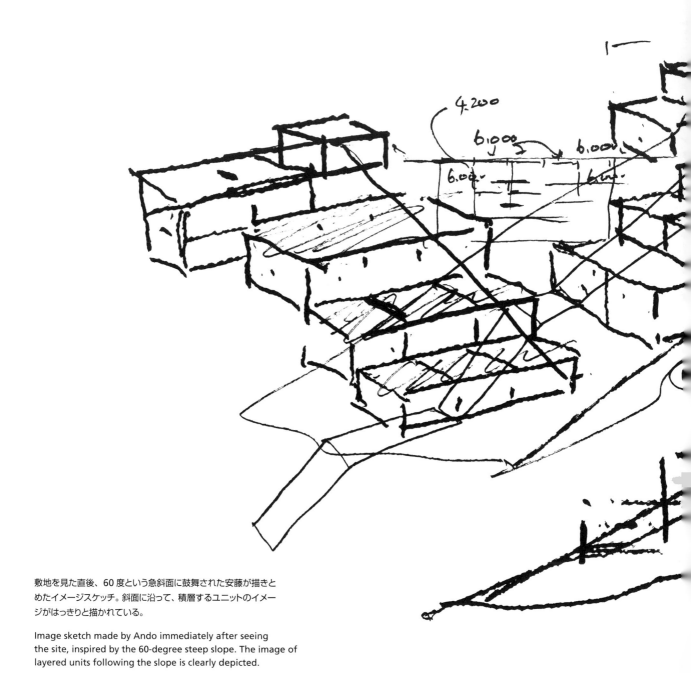

敷地を見た直後、60度という急斜面に鼓舞された安藤が描きとめたイメージスケッチ。斜面に沿って、積層するユニットのイメージがはっきりと描かれている。

Image sketch made by Ando immediately after seeing the site, inspired by the 60-degree steep slope. The image of layered units following the slope is clearly depicted.

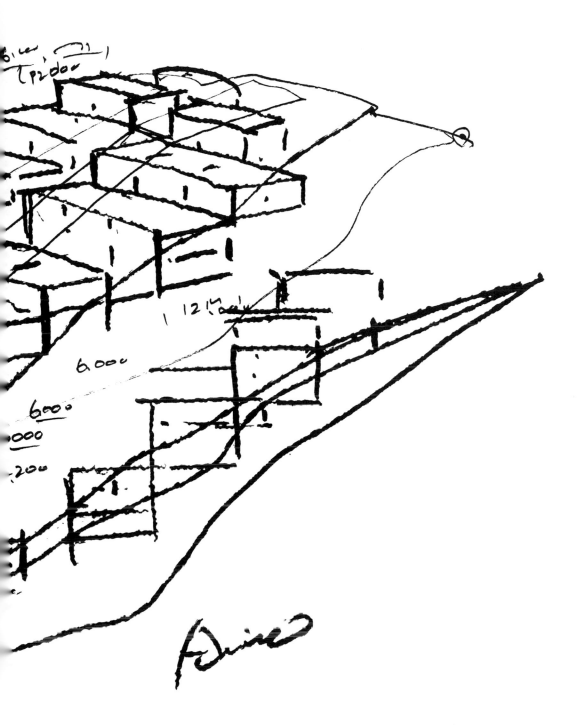

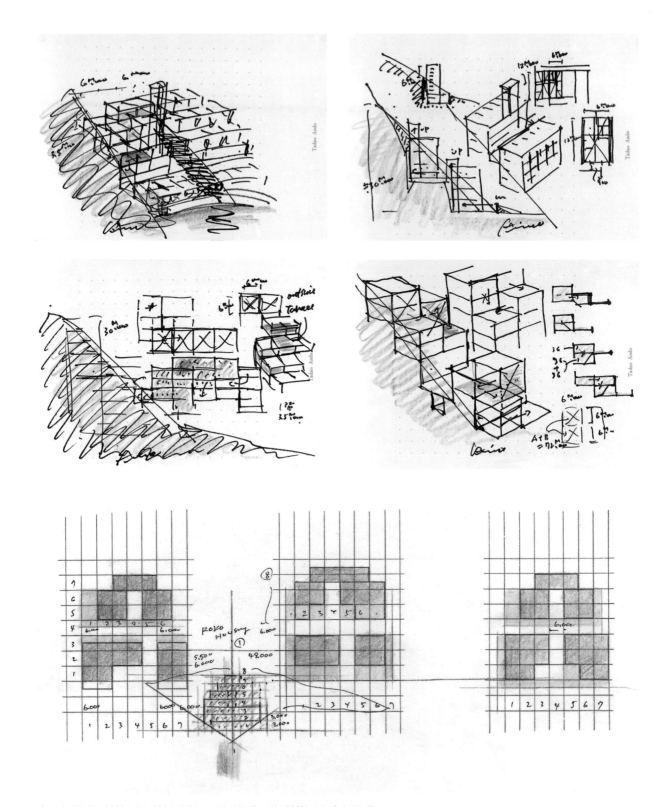

ブロックの構成。自然をいかに引き入れるか、ソリッドとヴォイドの関係をスタディしている。
Composition of the blocks. Studies of the relationships between solid and void with regard to how nature is introduced.

住棟に挟まれた余白の空間。公と私の緩衝地帯となる
立体化された路地。

Vacant spaces interposed between the residential
wings. These are three-dimensional alleys acting as
buffer areas between public and private.

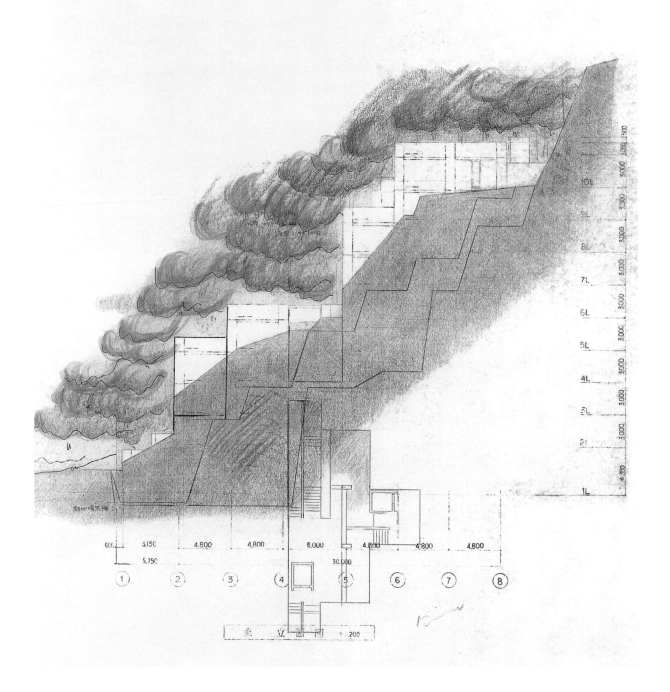

Ⅰ期の建設中に描かれた、Ⅱ期のイメージスケッチ。より大きなス
ケールで、斜面地集合住宅のさらなる発展形が模索されている。

Image sketch of phase II, drawn while phase I was under
construction. At a larger scale, groping for further
developments of the shape of a housing complex on
sloping ground.

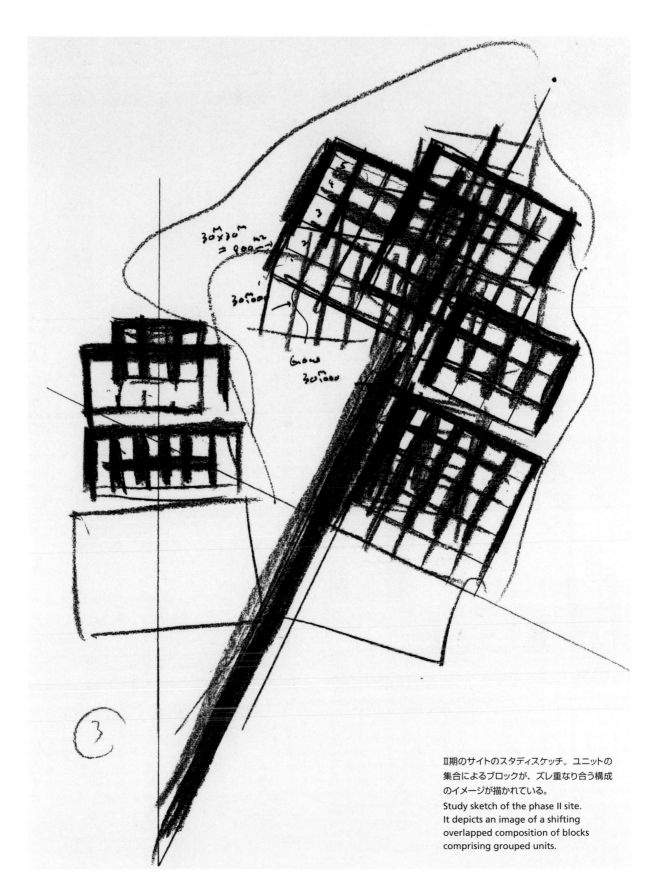

30×30m
□ 900m2

30,500

30,500

Ⅱ期のサイトのスタディスケッチ。ユニットの
集合によるブロックが、ズレ重なり合う構成
のイメージが描かれている。
Study sketch of the phase II site.
It depicts an image of a shifting
overlapped composition of blocks
comprising grouped units.

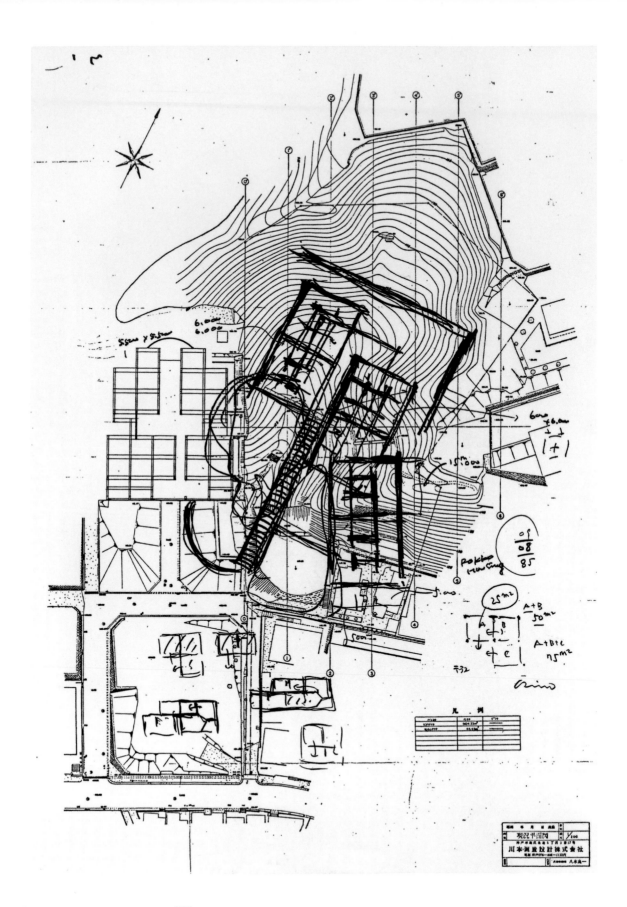

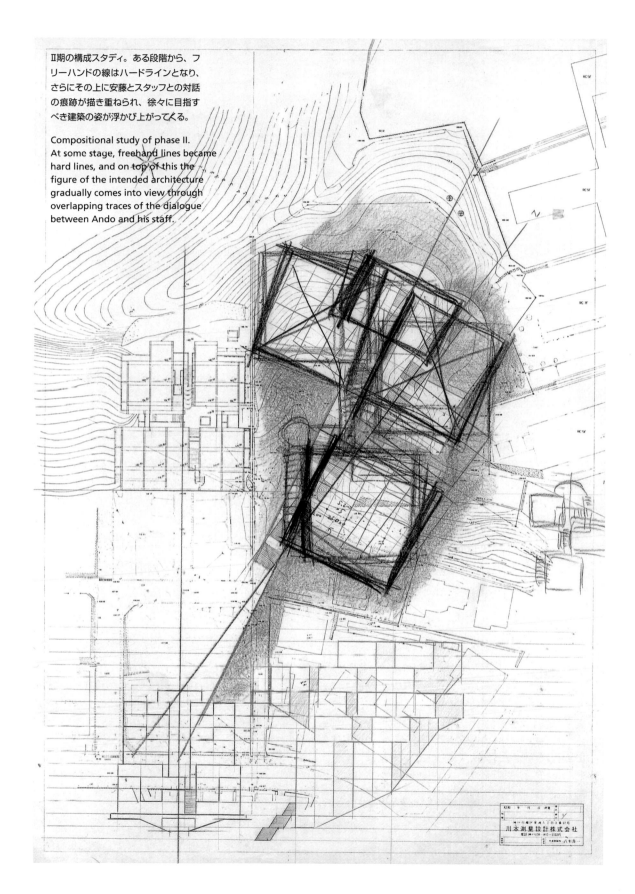

Ⅱ期の構成スタディ。ある段階から、フ
リーハンドの線はハードラインとなり、
さらにその上に安藤とスタッフとの対話
の痕跡が描き重ねられ、徐々に目指す
べき建築の姿が浮かび上がってくる。

Compositional study of phase II.
At some stage, freehand lines became
hard lines, and on top of this the
figure of the intended architecture
gradually comes into view through
overlapping traces of the dialogue
between Ando and his staff.

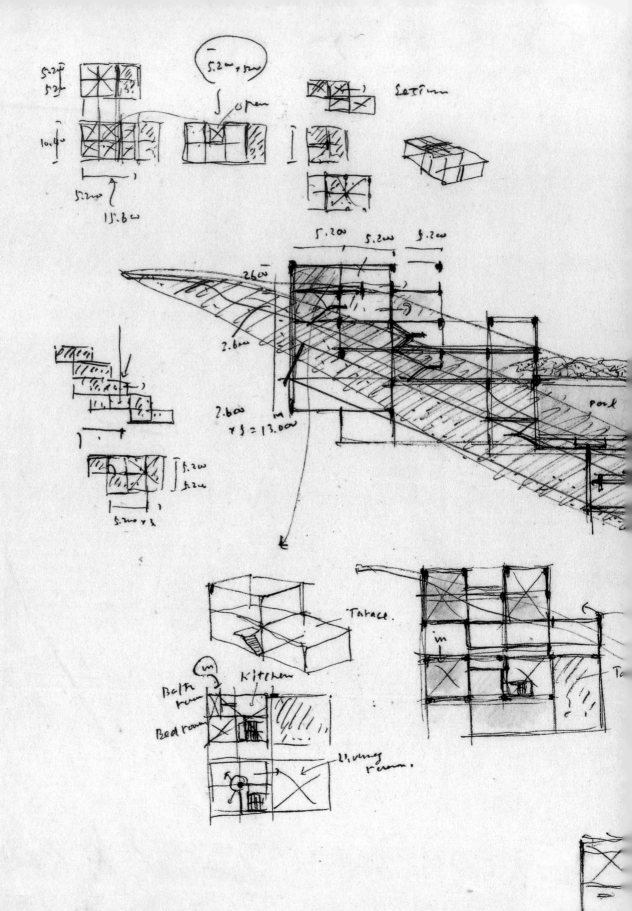

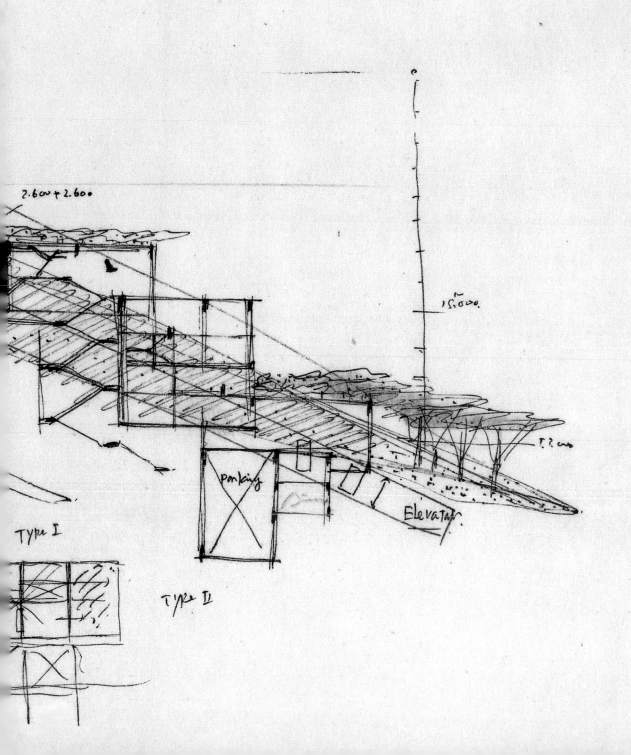

Ⅱ期の構成のスタディと同時に、Ⅰ期とⅡ期を
あわせた環境全体のイメージが描かれている。

Studies of the composition of phase II,
simultaneously depicting the image of
the entire environment fit to phase I and
phase II.

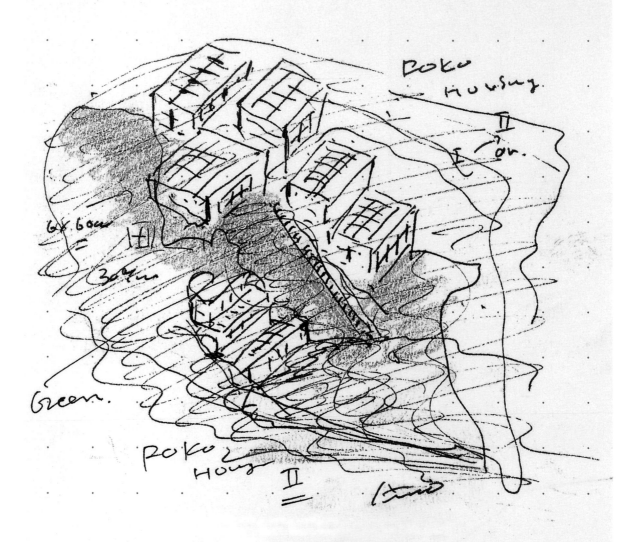

Tadao Ando

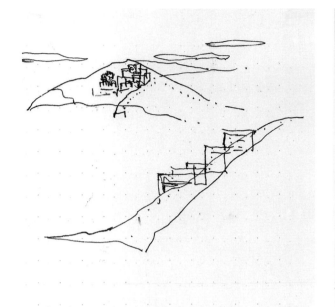

Tadao Ando

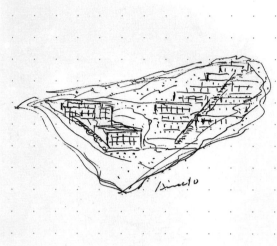

Tadao Ando

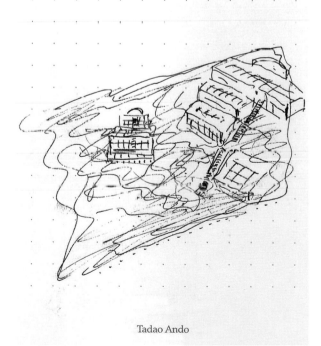

Tadao Ando

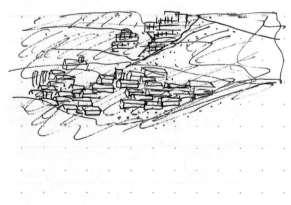

Tadao Ando

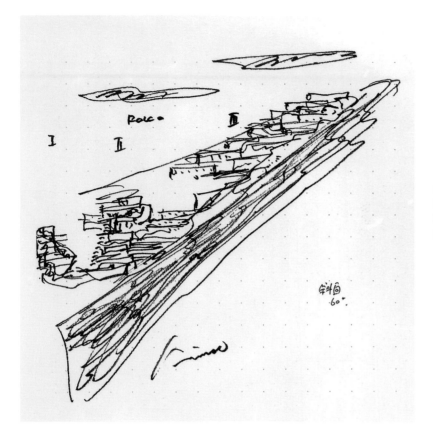

Ⅱ期の建設中に描かれたⅢ期のイメージスケッチ。依頼も受けないまま、安藤は自身の理想の風景を思い、そのイメージをスケッチに描き留めていく。

Image sketch of phase III, drawn when phase II was under construction. Without actually having been commissioned, Ando conceived his own ideal scene, and recorded this image in sketches.

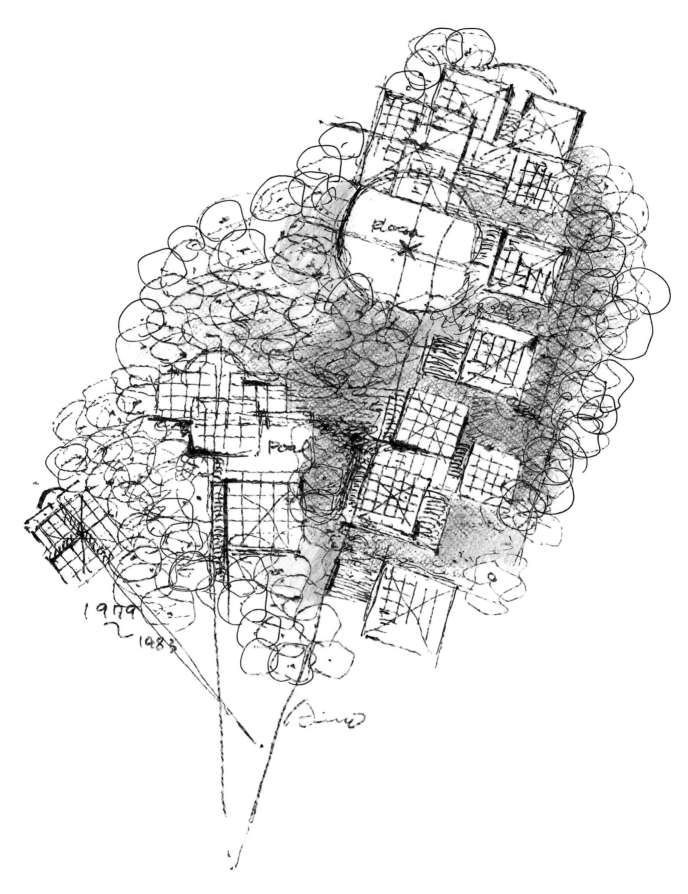

「切り分ける力」から
「通過する流れ」へ──安藤忠雄の住宅

越後島研一

光の教会　Church of the Light

序　「厳格な幾何学」と「純化された空間」

　安藤忠雄の作品は幾何学的だ。あらゆる輪郭は単純で鋭い。壁は開口がなく均質で、図形的な「純粋な面」に近い。線材も、柱と梁が同等な「均質格子」に近づく。外の芝生や水、空さえもが、切り取られた図形になってそこに参加する。全体も部分も、確かな物体でありながら、見慣れた現実とは違う、抽象的な存在感を誇るのだ。普通、「幾何学的」と称する建物が、実は表層的で味つけ的で、容易な部分でのみでの実現にすぎないことが、彼の作品を見ると痛感される。

　建築形態は機能を解決するためにあるので、表現の手段としては不自由だ。それを安藤ほどに可能なぎりぎりの地点まで純化した性格で覆い尽くすことは至難である。国際的な高い評価も、こうした誰にもほぼ同様な効果を与える、今日の世界共通語というべき建築美を徹底しえていることによる。30数年にわたって作風を変えず、むしろ評価を高めてきた理由も同様だ。

　しかし世界中どこにでも同じ建築を建てようとしているのではない。尋常ならざる幾何学の徹底は、独自性の片面にすぎない。確かに作品の内部では「厳格な幾何学立体の中にいる」と感じられる。しかしそうした器に盛られて、しばしば過激に純化された、1回限りの空間の魅力に出会うことが作品を訪れる楽しみなのだ。たとえば光の教会（1989）では、見る者の意識を厳しく限定する鋭い直方体の内側で、光の十字架の生々しい存在感と対する。近代建築が可能とした「主知的な建築美」の徹底と、われわれの深層にまで語りかける、全身的で原始的な「光との出会い」という両極が、高度に純化されつつ重なり合う。それが特定の宗教を超えた世界をも垣間見せる基本だ。個別の特殊事情を昇華することで、幅広い空間的魅力のエッセンスを原型的に示す。そこにおける幾何学を扱う自在さこそが、安藤の時代や場所を超えた創作を支えている。

「密集市街地」と「垂直の光」───出発点───

　彼の空間的発想を育んだのは、幼児から壮年まで住み続けた関西の長屋だ。「部屋のなかには昼間であってもほとんど光は届かない」（『光の教会─安藤忠雄の現場』建築資料研究社、2000年）、「住居は本来、暗いものであるという意識（が育てられた）」（『安藤忠雄─挑発する箱』丸善、1986年）という。そこには極小住宅に住む智恵が蓄えられていて、最初期の設計に活か

From "Power to Carve Out" to "Currents that Pass Through":

Houses by Tadao Ando

by Kenichi Echigojima

Introduction: "Severe Geometry" and "Purified Space"

Tadao Ando's works are geometric. His contours are all simple and sharp. His walls are of homogeneous quality without openings; they are close to being a graphic "pure plane." And his linear elements almost form "homogenous grids" with posts and beams as equal constituents. Even the outdoor elements of lawn, water, and sky participate in this geometric composition as cut-off pictorial forms. The whole as well as its parts, while they are all of concrete materials, emanate the abstract quality of presence that differs from our familiar reality. Seeing Ando's works, one is made to realize that other buildings popularly described as "geometric" are so only in a superficial and cosmetic sense, actualized only in facile parts.

Architectural forms are meant to solve functional problems; therefore they are inconvenient as a means of expression. It is impossibly difficult to characterize them as purified, as Ando does. His international reputation comes from the fact that he has thoroughly managed to realize such architectural beauty as a universal language that gives everyone almost the same sensation. And, for this reason, Ando has not changed his style for the past thirty-some years, while earning even a higher reputation.

Ando is not trying to build similar buildings all over the world, however. His exceptionally thorough geometry is only a part of his originality. Standing inside of his work, we are made aware of being "in a severe geometric three-dimensional form." But, what we really enjoy is a one and only encounter with an extremely purified space that is to be found inside that geometric container. Take the Church of Light (1989) for an example. Inside this sharp cuboid that severely constricts the viewer's consciousness, one is faced with the vivid presence of a cross of light. Here, while being highly distilled, two antitheses coexist ; thorough realization of "intellect-dominant architectural aesthetics," which modern architecture made possible, and a primordial whole body "encounter with light" that speaks to us at our depths. And, this is how we are given a glimpse of the World beyond any particular religion. It is a prototypical presentation of the essence of great spatial appeal through the sublimation of unique individual conditions. It is such full command of geometry that enables Ando's creation that goes beyond time and place.

"Dense Urban Space" and "Vertical Light"—the Point of Departure

It is the *nagaya* ("row house") in Kansai where he spent his childhood and lived throughout the prime of his manhood that nurtured Ando's way of spatial thinking. He wrote of such houses as a place where "almost no light reaches inside the room even during the daytime" (from *Hikari no kyokai: Ando Tadao no genba*, Tokyo: Kenchikushiryo Kenkyu-sha, 2000); there "my awareness that a house is essentially a dark place [was raised]" (from *Ando Tadao: Chohatsusuru hako*, Tokyo: Maruzen, 1986). Here we see how the architect kept the wisdom of living in a minimal house, which he later applied to his earliest designs. However, there was more to the original inspiration that Ando received from the nagaya: "One day [when I was fourteen years old], they

サヴォア邸　Villa Savoye

されることとなる。しかしそれ以上の発想の原点をこの長屋が与えた。

　「（14歳の）ある日2階を設けるため、屋根に穴が開けられた。その穴から暗い長屋の部屋に一筋、光が降りてくる。（中略）凄い、おもしろいなぁ」（前掲書『光の教会』）。自分の身体の延長のような、陰翳に満ちた場が、上空からの垂直の刺激で新たな生命を得る。このとき刻まれた記憶が、やがて「闇をひき裂く空間の力」へと理想化され、時代と交差し、創作の武器となってゆく。

　安藤は今や国際的に最大級の評価を得ているが、出発点においては、世界の動向を見据えて創作姿勢を定めたわけではない。むしろ逆だ。20代だった1960年代には、モダニズムが曲がり角を迎えていたことを意識してはいた。しかしそれを直接の発想基盤とはしなかった。「脱モダニズムというテーマが、自分の仕事の場となる大阪市街地の、いまだ在来工法の木造住宅が密集して建ち並ぶ風景と、あまりに遊離しているように感じた」「モダニズムを抱えたまま現代都市の矛盾と格闘していく。その方が当時の私にとっては余程リアリティがあった」（『建築手法』A.D.A. EDITA Tokyo、2005年）と回想する。世界的動向からは遠い、身近な環境への素直な実感から出発した。それが世界で通用するものとなったのは、そうした狭い発想契機を、普遍的な層まで掘り下げえたからだ。知りたいのはその具体的あり方である。本稿では、代表的な住宅作品を追うことで、身体感覚で直接に確認できる範囲から始まった創作が、幅広く、国際的な威力をもつに到るまでの要所を追う。

伝統の反対物───モダニズムを抱えて───

　まず注目すべきは上掲の「モダニズムを抱えたまま」の内容だ。確かに「幾何学の徹底」は近代建築のもっとも普遍的な側面を取り出したものだとみなせる。実際「純粋立体の美」の最高峰たるサヴォア邸を見て建築家を志したとも語る。しかし初期を特徴づける「コンクリートの閉鎖的な箱型」は、ル・コルビュジエに代表される「軽やかで開放的な箱型」からは遠い。

　振り返れば、彼が建築を志した時期までの日本建築では、サヴォア邸（1931）のような「厳格な直方体の美」は一般化していなかった。1930年代には西欧の「白い箱型」が直写されたが、早期に衰退し、伝統を基本に、各部を幾何学的に整えたような表現が一般化してゆく。その延長上に丹下健三もいた。国際的名作香川県庁舎（1958）も「過去に歩み寄った近代建築」だった。若き安藤は、この作品に感動しつつも、その直接に伝統を連想させる表現には不満を

香川県庁舎
Kagawa Prefectural
Government Office

made a hole in the roof in order to add the second floor [to the house]. Through that hole, there came down a single thread of light inside a dark nagaya room... How terrific, how interesting!" (from *Hikari no kyokai*). A memory of a shadow-rich space, which was like an extension of his own body, having gained a new life by virtue of vertical stimulus from the sky-this memory etched upon the architect would eventually be idealized as "the power of space that tears up the darkness." It would intersect with the times and become his creative weapon.

Now, Ando has gained the highest reputation internationally. At the starting point, however, he did not adopt his creative stance vis-à-vis the global trend. Quite the contrary. In the 1960s when he was in his twenties, Ando was aware of the fact that modernist architecture had come to a turning point, which he nevertheless did not make as the foundation of his ideas. As he recalls, "there seemed to be such a huge gap between the concept of 'post-modern' and the actual urban scenery full of traditionally built wooden houses in Osaka where I was working... Struggling with the contradictions of contemporary cities while holding onto modernism. That was far more real to me at that time" (from *kenchiku shuho*, Tokyo: A.D.A. Edita Tokyo, 2005). Thus Ando started with a straight sense of reality corresponding to his own familiar surroundings, far from the global trend. His work owes its global acceptance to the fact that Ando has managed to dig into his narrowly defined source of thinking down to a universal level of depth. What we want to know is how this was actually done. In the rest of this essay, by discussing his representative works in a chronological order, I will examine the crucial points in the development process of his creation; how it started from the architect's domain of direct physical sensibility and has reached an international realm of wide influence.

The Opposite of Tradition—Holding onto Modernism

First we must pay attention to what "holding onto modernism" means. Ando's "geometric thoroughness" can certainly be seen as the most universal aspect of modern architecture thus extracted. In fact, according to the architect, he was inspired to become an architect when he saw Villa Savoye (1931), the greatest achievement of "pure three-dimensional aesthetics." However, those "closed concrete boxes" that characterize his earlier career are far from the "light and open boxes" exemplified by Le Corbusier's designs.

We need to understand that, when Ando set his mind upon an architectural career, the "severely cuboidal aesthetics" of Villa Savoye had not been generally established in Japan. The "white box" of West European origin was directly copied in the 1930s and soon declined in Japan. What had become popular then was architectural expression based on tradition with individual details geometrically designed, along which line Kenzo Tange could be located. His famous Kagawa Prefectural Government Office (1958) was one example of "architecture that walked up to the past." While the building moved him, young Ando felt unsatisfied with its expressions that directly reminded him of tradition.

When Ando talked about "pursuing modernism a little further, picking up the pieces [that

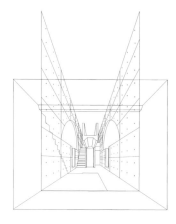

ツインウォール
Twin Wall

覚えた。

　だから「モダニズムをもう少し押し進め、落ちこぼれているものを拾い合わせながら、その中でできることはなにかを探る」（前掲書『挑発する箱』）とは、まずは身近な近代建築の修正を意識した発言だろう。柱梁が際立つ伝統的建築美と、それによって国際舞台に登場した日本的近代建築。この両者を支えていた「水平的で開放的な空間像」。これらすべてを否定する、つまり反対物といえるのが、安藤の、かつてないまでに幾何学的に純化された「閉鎖的な箱型」だったのだ。

　もうひとつ重要なのは、彼がル・コルビュジエを「闘う建築家」として評価している点だ。この巨匠は頑迷なアカデミズムと闘い、その武器が「白い箱型」だった。軽やかさを徹底することで、「重い箱型」という西欧の伝統を否定する。そうした正反対の性格を誇る武器を対抗させて闘う姿勢が、安藤以前の日本の近代建築には乏しかった。「闘った」とされる建築家でも、その武器たる作品は、慣れ親しんだ伝統を否定する反対物という意味では、概して不徹底だった。

切り分ける空間の力───ツインウォールの家（1973）───

　安藤は、劣悪な都市環境に対抗し、確かな壁で個人の空間を確保することを主張してデビューした。計画案ツインウォールの家（1973）が象徴的だ。壁に挟まれた細長い住居で「2枚の壁で構成されているというより、1枚の〈厚い壁〉に亀裂を創り出し、その内部に生活装置を組み込んだ」（『GA アーキテクト8 安藤忠雄』A.D.A. EDITA Tokyo、1987年）「壁をくり抜いてすみつく」（『SD』1982年6月号）と説明された。物体のかたまりを、空間の力が切り分け、隙間状の内部をつくる。幾何学が、亀裂的空間と重なり、上空から「切り分ける力」を呼び込み、それを満たす存在となる。14歳のときの「光の啓示」が建築家的な発想の枠を得たのだ。

　厳格な直方体状の空間は、それだけで混沌たる都市に確保された特別な場となりうる。しかし「切り裂く力」という空間のイメージが重なることで、より強く、密集地に積極的に棲みつく意志を反映できる。彼はこの時期、周囲に対する暴力的で攻撃的な感情に苛まれていた。それがここで建築家として根源的な「空間を生み出す力」へと昇華され、幾何学の鋳型と重なったのだ。

　そのまま実現するのは困難な3m×20mという異様な細長さも、重要な意味をもっていた。12年後の中山邸では、ほぼそのままの規模と形状で現れ、海外での最初の実現作シカゴの住

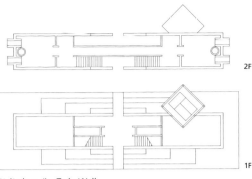

ツインウォール　Twin Wall

had] fallen behind, and searching for what one can do under the given situation" (from *Chohat-susuru hako*), he must have been thinking about revision of an architecture that was familiar to him. That is to say the architect intended to deny the traditional post-and-beam architectural aesthetics—and modern Japanese architecture that had entered the international stage by virtue of that aesthetics—and to negate "the image of horizontal and open space" itself that was behind the appreciation of Japanese architecture and its traditional aesthetics. Opposite of all this, what was established were Ando's "closed boxes," whose geometric purity was unprecedented.

Another important point is the fact that Ando has appreciated Le Corbusier as a "fighting architect." This master had to fight against stubborn academism, and the "white box" was his weapon. By pursuing lightness, he negated the Western tradition of the "heavy box." Before Ando, Japanese architects lacked such a belligerent attitude with which to fight others by adopting weapons with totally opposite characteristics. Even for those architects who we think were "fighters," their works were generally lukewarm as weapons to oppose and refute the familiar tradition.

The Carving Force of Space: Twin Wall (1973)

Ando launched his architectural career claiming to secure space for individuals by solid walls, standing up against poor urban environment. The Twin Wall plan (1973) is symbolic of this approach. It is described by the architect as a narrow house that is "more of a single 'thick wall' with a cleft made to house equipment for daily living, rather than being constituted by two walls" (from *GA Architect 8, Tadao Ando*, Tokyo: A.D.A. Edita Tokyo, 1987), and as a place where "one settles oneself by hollowing out a wall" (from "Kabe o kurinuite sumitsuku," *SD*, June 1982). A material mass is carved out by the power of space, which results in a crevice-like interior. The geometry overlaps with this crevice-like space, inviting in the "carving force" from the sky that fills the space. Here, the "revelation of light" that Ando received at age fourteen has acquired a framework for architectural thinking.

Severely cuboidal space by itself can be a special space secured within a chaotic city. When the spatial imagery of "carving force" is applied, however, it can reflect more strongly the dweller's will to choose to live in a built-up quarter. Around that period, Ando was tormented by his own violent and aggressive emotion against what was surrounding him. In this plan, such emotion was sublimated into his "power to generate space," which is essential for an architect, and found a geometric mold.

It was also important that the house be of an extraordinary elongated shape (3m x 20m) that should be difficult to be built as planned. The plan was realized twelve years later when Nakayama House was built with almost exactly the same size and shape; in the form of House in Chicago, Ando's first built work outside Japan, it reappeared about twice the size of the original, filling its given plot of ground. And hereafter, this fundamental "carving force" in its various formal manifestations would characterize the crucial moments along the architect's evolution. The

宅（1997）では、敷地いっぱいに引き伸ばされた約2倍の規模となって再現されることとなる。しかしそれ以上に、ここで基本たる「切り分ける力」はさまざまな異なるかたちをとって、後の展開の要所を特徴づけてゆく。まずは、極小規模の住吉の長屋において、もっとも過激に実現される。

亀裂としての住宅 ——— 住吉の長屋（1976）———

　住吉の長屋は高度に幾何学的だ。輪郭は鋭い直方体だし、街路側は、住居の壁というより、切り抜かれただけの「1枚の純粋な面」に近い。それ以上に、全体が機械的に3等分されている。機能に則すなら、各室や中庭の必要寸法で分割されるはずだ。ここでは幾何学的な整合性が先行している。大規模な、それも住宅以外であればともかく、極小住宅ではきわめて困難である。しかしそのために、幾何学的性格だけが支配する、動かし難い「輪郭の力」に到達しえている。こうした高度な鋳型に、強烈な「空間の力」が宿ることで、時代を超えた名作となったのだ。

　確かに意外に豊かな内部である。都市で忘れがちな自然との交感や、極小長屋が蓄積してきた伝統が、コンクリートの箱にふさわしく込められている。それらは時代を超えた意義をもつ特徴だ。しかしより重要なのは、各室を往来するための階段や通路を、屋外の中庭と兼用した点である。この「雨の日には傘をさして便所に行く」ことが安藤を有名にしたが、それ以上に稀有な名作たる理由なのだ。通常なら欠陥住宅というべきなのに、なぜか作品としての存在感は圧倒的だった。専門家は高く評価し、4年後には権威ある賞を受賞する。時を経るほどに1970年代を象徴する住宅とされ、さらには日本の近～現代の代表する名作のひとつとされるに到る。より大きな流れの中に置くほどに評価を高めてきたのだ。しかし長い間その適切な説明はなされてこなかった。意外なほどの空間の豊かさは、彼の他の作品にもあり、稀有な名作の意義としては弱い。あくまで「傘をさして便所に」という一点において、近代建築の一方の極に位置づけうるのだ。

　住吉の長屋は、丹下の香川県庁舎の階段室ほどの面積だ。にもかかわらず作品として、比肩しうる存在感をもつのは、ひとえに「空間の力」による。丹下が世界的な評価にまで高めた、1950年代日本建築の「開放的で水平的な広がり」は、慣れ親しんだ伝統をそのまま純化したものだった。その対極地点を、もっとも過激に提示したのが住吉の長屋なのだ。ツインウォールに集約されていた「切り分ける空間の力」は、ここでは日常機能を分断する地点にまで到り、

most radical of them was first realized as his minimalist Row House in Sumiyoshi.

A House as a Crevice: Row House in Sumiyoshi (1976)

Row House in Sumiyoshi is a highly geometric work. Its contours are sharply cuboidal, and the street facade is, rather than a house wall, close to being a "single pure plane" that has been simply cut out. Furthermore, the whole house is mechanically divided into three equal parts. If functional needs are followed, the house should be divided according to the necessary size of each room and a courtyard. Here, however, geometric coherency is given precedence, which is extremely difficult in the case of such minimalist houses, if less so in large-scale nonresidential buildings. And, this has allowed the design to reach the realm of unshakable "power of contours" where nothing but geometric characteristics reign. With such intense "power of space" lodging in this sophisticated mold, this house was born to become a timeless masterpiece.

The interior of the house is unexpectedly rich. Communication with nature, which tends to be forgotten inside a city, and the accumulated traditions of minimal nagaya living, which are of timeless significance, are appropriately invoked in this concrete box. More important is, however, the fact that the architect designed the stairway and paths that connect the rooms to share the space with an outdoor courtyard. As a result, the residents have to go to a toilet with an umbrella on a rainy day, which made Ando legendary. And, indeed, this has made the house one of the rarest masterpieces: While such a house would be usually deemed defective, its presence as a work of art was overwhelming. The experts gave it high opinion, and an award of great authority was given four years after its completion. The more time passes, the higher reputation it earns as a house that symbolizes the 1970s, and now it is regarded to be one of the representative works of modern and contemporary Japanese architecture. In short, this house has kept earning a higher reputation as it is put into a larger context. But, for a long time, there was no proper explanation for this phenomenon because a similarly surprising richness of space can be found in his other works, which gives a weaker reason for this house's position as the rarest of masterpieces. In fact, merely based on the fact that "the residents have to go to a bathroom with an umbrella," this work can be positioned at one extreme end of the modern architectural spectrum.

The area occupied by Row House in Sumiyoshi is about the same size as what a staircase occupies in the Kagawa Prefectural Government Office. Despite such a small scale, the house emanates a strong sense of presence comparable to that of Tange's building, which is due solely to the "power of space." The "horizontal and open space" of 1950s Japanese architecture, which Tange elevated to the level of global reputation, was derived by simply purifying the familiar tradition. Row House in Sumiyoshi has presented its antithesis in the most extreme manner. The "carving force of space," which was condensed in Twin Wall, has here reached the point where it carves out functions of daily living, which fills the entire house with extraordinary tension. Ando put a single house under his total control and with incomparable intensity by virtue of the carving effect brought down from the sky. This is what I mean when I speak of the house as the

落水荘　Fallingwater

全体に異様な緊張を漲らせている。一住居をこれ以上ない鮮烈さで、上空からもたらされる亀裂的な効果で支配し尽くした。それが丹下に到るまでの、周囲との親和を基盤とした空間像の対極という意味だ。こうした歴史的意義が、時代を経るほどに明瞭になった。密集地に直接に強引に棲みつくイメージが育んだ空間の可能性が、住宅の成立基盤を危うくする地点にまで徹底されたのだ。

負の飛躍───3大住宅の対極点───

　名作建築とはある時代に特有な空間を究めたものである。住宅は不利だ。人間の多面的な欲求に応える複雑さが、特別な性格だけを徹底するのを困難にする。快適さの感覚は保守的だから、ひとつの時代を鮮烈に集約し難くもある。しかし逆に、住吉の長屋のように、住宅が住宅ではなくなる境界にまで踏み込めば、決定的な存在感が得られることともなる。週末だけを過ごす別荘なら、雨が降る廊下も楽しめようが、疲れて帰宅して夜中に目覚めて便所に、と思うほどに、この住宅をひき裂いた力の苛烈さが見る者の心に刺さる。普通の日常生活を支える場ゆえに、ある特別な空間の力が、例外的な地点に到るまで究められたことを、圧倒的に印象づけるのだ。

　20世紀の3大住宅は各々が新しい可能性の極だった。ル・コルビュジエのサヴォア邸は「空中で完結する直方体の中に住む」、フランク・ロイド・ライトの落水荘（1939）は「ばらばらな断片の間に住む」、ミース・ファン・デル・ローエのファンズワース邸（1950）は「2枚の水平板の間に住む」ことを実現していた。「閉鎖的な箱の中に住む」という西欧の伝統を拒否した上で、代わりに発想された3種類の方向の各々を究めた。その意味で、近代建築の「新しさの構図」を明瞭にした名作たちだったのだ。

　ところでサヴォア邸と落水荘は週末住宅、ファンズワース邸は単身者用で、3棟とも敷地が広大だ。好条件のもと、新たな可能性をより高い地点にまで飛躍させた作品だった。その意味で、1950年代までのいわば巨匠時代における発想の特質が究められた3つの極というべき名作なのだ。

　住吉の長屋はこれらの対極に位置づけうる。「開放的で水平的な広がり」とは正反対の「垂直的な亀裂の効果」の極だからだが、それ以上に、3大住宅とは逆方向への飛躍の結果だからだ。当時でも最悪の条件を強いられた極限的な判断の場面での、ほとんどやむをえない決

ファンズワース邸　Fansworth House

antithesis of the space whose image, up to the time of Tange, had been founded on the concept of harmony with the surroundings. The more time passes, the clearer such historical significance has become. The spatial possibility that was developed by the image of willful dwelling in a dense urban area has been ultimately pursued to the point where the existential foundation of a house itself is threatened.

Negative Leap—The Opposite of the Three Masterpiece Houses

What we call an architectural masterpiece is a building that has achieved the space that is unique to a certain era. In that sense, residential architecture is handicapped as it cannot help becoming complicated in order to meet multifaceted human needs and cannot easily focus itself on a particular quality. Also, our sense of comfort is conservative, making it difficult to concentrate one particular era into a single house. On the other hand, once architecture reaches the realm where a house is no longer a house (as in the case of Row House in Sumiyoshi), it can achieve an indisputable sense of presence. One may very well enjoy a rain-drenched pathway if it is one's weekend house, but how about if one wakes up in the middle of the night to go to the bathroom, being tired after a long working day? With such a thought, I imagine how the powerful intensity that tore up the Sumiyoshi row house pierces through the mind of its viewer. Exactly because it is built as a place that supports someone's ordinary daily living, we are left with the overwhelming impression of the fact that a particular spatial power has been pursued to such an extraordinary degree.

The three 20th-century masterpiece houses, Le Corbusier's Villa Savoye (1931), Frank Lloyd Wright's Fallingwater (1939), and Mies van der Rohe's Farnsworth House (1950) each marked an ultimate pole of new architectural possibility. In Villa Savoye, "living in a cuboid that completes itself in midair" was realized, while in Fallingwater, it was "living among disparate pieces," and in Farnsworth House, "living between two horizontal planes." They all rejected the Western tradition of "living in a closed box," and pursed three different alternative directions. And it is in this sense that these were regarded to be masterworks that revealed the "new composition" of modern architecture.

Both Villa Savoye and Fallingwater are weekend houses while Farnsworth House is for a single resident, and all three houses are built on large lots. Under such favorable conditions, each of them pushed the new architectural possibilities even further. In this sense, these are the ultimate masterpieces in which one can see the ideas of a "maestro period" prior to the 1960s being ultimately pursued.

Row House in Sumiyoshi can be defined as an antipode of these masterpieces because it is an ultimate example of a "vertical crevice effect" instead of the exact opposite, "open and horizontal space." But a bigger reason is that it was a result of the leap to the opposite directions from the three masterworks. With the decision that was almost forced upon him under the worst conditions even at that time, the architect had to make the "negative leap" that, instead of expanding

断。理想へ向けて可能性を広げるのとは逆の、住宅の成立基盤を危うくする地点を露わにする「負の飛躍」だった。それゆえ西欧的な伝統の反対極たる3大住宅がつくる「新しさの構図」を逆照射しうる地点であり、しかし棄てたはずの伝統とは異なる、新しい意義をもつ極地点だったのだ。

　もともとサヴォア邸やファンズワース邸は、開放的で均質な場をさらに大地から浮上させて、「どこでも成立する空間」の性格を徹底していた。身近な実感に根差し、個々の現実との出会いを昇華する安藤は、劣悪な都市との闘いを避けて空中に理想を求めるのとは逆に、密集地を切り分け、そこだけの地面にへばりつく。1960年代は、大きくは、近代建築がもつ現実とは折り合い難い部分が強く意識され始めた時期だった。この意味で住吉の長屋は、近代建築を、批判的に継承してゆくために見返す、確かな原点ともなりえた。彼は狭い実感から出発したが、その発想の核には、時代に育まれた「ラディカルな否定精神」を据えていた。だから徹底した追求の極においては、大きな時代の流れと交差しえることとなった。それが「身体感覚から世界へ」という彼の過程における、最初の重要な通過点であり、また強力な創作的原点ともなったのだ。

引き裂かれる急斜面 ────六甲の集合住宅 (1983) ────

　住吉の長屋に集約された「切り分ける力としての空間」は、日本人が慣れ親しんできた伝統と、それと一体となって世界に進出した丹下的近代建築の反対物だった。加えて14歳のときの感動が、ある特殊な時代状況と出会って現実の力を得たものともみなせる。つまり、空間的発想を支える幾層もの要因が一同に会した、高度に強靭な創作契機だった。しかしそれはあくまで都市に建つ小住宅によって育まれたものだ。密集市街地では、上空から切り裂く空間の力が、僅かな人間的な場を確保する啓示となり、強力な創作的緊張を支えた。だから広大な敷地や大規模住宅では威力を削がれることともなる。それが「ポスト住吉の長屋」の課題だ。安藤は、建築家は住宅から始めて徐々にスケールを拡大せよという。小空間を基本に、身体感覚で「これで良し」と確認しつつ進むなら、まったく異なる状況でも同様な緊張を保ち続けるためにどうすればよいのか。

　注目すべきは、住吉の長屋の2年後に設計を開始した六甲の集合住宅だ。外観では「壁が両側から挟み込む」形状の単位が並ぶ。「都市に棲みつく強い意志をあらわす攻撃」（前掲書

its possibility toward ideals, gave us a glimpse of a point where the existential foundation of a house could be threatened. However, it was the point from which the "new composition" of modern architecture can be lit from the rear and which was of a new significance different from the tradition supposedly abandoned.

Both Villa Savoye and Farnsworth House thoroughly realized "the [universal] space that can exist anywhere" by creating an open and homogeneous space floating up off the earth. On the other hand, Ando, who is rooted in the awareness of his familiar surroundings and sublimates each of his encounters with reality, carves out the swarm and sticks to a uniquely given plot of ground instead of avoiding the fight against terrible cities to seek ideals in the air. It was in the 1960s that people largely started to become aware of a part of modern architecture that could not be compromised vis-à-vis reality. In this sense, Row House in Sumiyoshi could function as an original model that people could refer back to in order to inherit modern architecture critically. While Ando started with an awareness of his narrow reality, there was a "radical spirit of negation" at the core of his thinking. And therefore, his thinking, pursued thoroughly to its extreme, could intersect with the great current of the age. Thus, the Row House marked the first and significant point along the process of Ando's progress "from body sensation to the world" and stands as the powerful starting point of his creation.

A Steep Slope Torn Up: Rokko Housing (1983)

As we saw, the "space as carving force," which was distilled in Row House in Sumiyoshi, was the antithesis of the familiar Japanese tradition and of Tange's modern architecture that made inroads into the world together with that tradition. We can also say that it was the result of the fourteen-year-old Ando's experience of being impressed by light, which later took on a certain real power under the particular conditions of the times. In short, it was a highly strong moment of creation where multilayered elements of spatial thinking all converged. And, it was all developed by virtue of this small house built within a city. In such a densely built urban area, it was the spatial carving force from the sky that worked as a revelation to keep that little humane place and support the strong creative tension. However, such force is weakened on vast sites and in the case of large-scale housing, which is the "post-Sumiyoshi" issue. Ando says that architects should start with houses and gradually grow in terms of the scale of their works. Dealing with small-scale space, architects can proceed, confirming the validity of their decisions based on their physical sensations. But, what can they do to maintain similar tension in totally different circumstances?

Here, we should focus on the Rokko Housing that Ando started to design two years after the Row House in Sumiyoshi. Its exterior appearance is constituted of multiple units placed side by side, each of which is "sandwiched between walls on both sides." However, such standing walls, once described by Ando as "an assault expressing one's strong will to dwell in the city" (*Chohatsusuru hako*), have ended up losing their forceful carving tension with more than ten

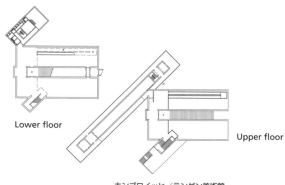

Lower floor

Upper floor

ホンブロイッヒ／ランゲン美術館
Langen Foundation / Hombroich Museum

『挑発する箱』）とされた壁が並立する姿も、自然を背景として10数個が反復されると、かつての強引に切り分ける緊張が希薄な表情となってしまう。しかしそれを補うのが、中央をずれつつ貫通する細長い亀裂だ。それ以上に全体が大きく急斜面を切り裂いた中に建つことだ。ツインウォールの発想を支えた「分厚い物体を切り分ける力」が、ここでは斜面を相手に壮大に蘇っている。こうして六甲では、部分から全体までを、3段階の亀裂的な空間の力が秩序づけ、支配している。

　この集合住宅は、当初は、斜面の前方の平坦部分に建てるよう依頼された。しかし、後に施工業者を探すのに苦労したほどの急傾斜地を、安藤は選んだ。そしてその傾いた大地の存在感は、「都市を垂直に切り裂く空間」のイメージを、そのまま「自然を切り裂きつつ通過する空間」へと、身体感覚を拡大させつつ、なめらかに実感的に転換してゆく恰好の舞台となった。

大地とともに引き裂かれる箱 ── 小篠邸（1981）──

　六甲に続いて設計が開始された小篠邸は、自然に恵まれた1000㎡を超える敷地に建つ。同様な敷地に建つ4年前の松本邸では、道路沿いに住宅を配し、手つかずの地面をできるだけ大きく残していた。小篠邸では、敷地を2分するように、中央に置いている。その上で、大地に沿った空間の流れを妨げるのではなく、むしろ新たな生命を与え、強調してみせているのだ。

　彼が基本とする閉鎖的な壁や箱は、水平方向の広がりを絶ち切る。だから都市では威力をもった。一方、壁が希薄な日本の伝統的建築は、空間の流れを吸収する柔らかい存在感を特徴とする。そうした伝統的な佇まいの感覚に慣れたわれわれは、自然の中に建つ閉鎖的な壁や箱には違和感を覚えやすい。小篠邸ではそれを、都市住宅と同様な閉鎖性を保ちつつ克服している。

　基本は2本の細長い箱だ。訪れた者は、まずそれらが挟む「幾何学的な隙間」を見通す。敷地の中央に建物を縦断させつつ、そうやって大地の起伏と流れを生き返らせる。壁や箱や、ましてや開口ではなく、隙間によって自然と対話しているのだ。しかし住宅を2分して外部を通過させるのは容易ではない。小篠邸では2つの箱をつなぐ廊下を半地下に置く。引き裂きつつ繋ぎ、そこに外部を呼び込む発想は、住吉の長屋と似るが、そのつくる空間が一変している。もともと半ば埋もれた住宅なので、大きくは「地面が切り分けられた」印象だ。その上で、不可分なはずの1棟の住居が2分され、「切り分けつつ水平方向に通過してゆく空間」を印象づける。

units repeated against the natural background. What compensates for this loss is the narrow cleft that runs in the middle of the building, slightly off center. Even a greater impact comes from the fact that the building was built on a site that had been created by extensively tearing up a steep incline. Here, the "force that carves up thick objects" that supported the Twin Wall concept has been revived on a grand scale. Thus in Rokko, the spatial power of crevice, working on three different levels, orders and controls the building, from its details to the whole.

Originally, Ando was asked to build on a flat plane in front of the slope. And yet, the architect chose the steep incline instead, which later made it difficult to find a contractor. It was this inclined earth that provided Ando an appropriate stage on which he could smoothly transform the image of the "space that vertically tears up a city" to that of the "space that passes through nature while tearing it up" with his own corporal sense being expanded.

A Box Torn Up Together with the Earth: Koshino House (1981)

Koshino House is built on a plot larger than 100 square meters with rich natural surroundings. Its design process started right after the Rokko Housing. In the case of Matsumoto House, which was completed four years earlier on a similar plot, the house was built along the street and left the ground untouched as much as possible. Here, however, the house is put in the middle of the site, dividing it into two, but it does not block the flow of space on the ground. Rather, it newly vitalizes and emphasizes that flow.

The closed walls and boxes, elemental units of Ando's architecture, sever the horizontal expansion of space, which was the reason why they had such power in the city. On the other hand, Japanese traditional architecture, with its weak and sparse walls, is characterized by its soft presence that absorbs the spatial flow. As we are accustomed to the atmosphere of such traditional settings, we tend to find something wrong with closed walls and boxes standing in the midst of nature. In Koshino House, Ando has overcome such feeling while maintaining the same closedness as in a house built in a city.

Koshino House basically consists of two slender boxes. A visitor to the house first sees through the "geometric gap" between them. This is how the architect revives the ups and downs and flows of the earth while placing a building in the middle of the site: he is talking to nature through this gap, and not via walls, boxes, or openings. However, it is not easy to divide a house into two parts and let the "outside" pierce it through. In Koshino House, Ando thus half-buried in the ground a passageway that connects the two boxes. While it resembles the Sumiyoshi row house in terms of the idea of bringing "outside" in, the resultant space is totally different. As the whole house is half-buried in the ground, it gives a general impression of "the earth carved out." On top of that, we find a house that is supposed to be indivisible divided into two. What impresses us here is the "space that passes along horizontally with the carving effect." The force that generated the Twin Wall in the dense urban zone has arrived at a "magnanimous carving manner" in this suburb.

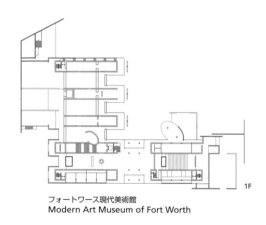

フォートワース現代美術館
Modern Art Museum of Fort Worth

密集市街地でツインウォールを生んだ力が、郊外において「伸びやかな切り分け方」に到った
のだ。

　安藤は小篠邸を「立体的な空間構成を意識した家」とし「空間をいかに立体的に構成する
か──素材をコンクリート打ち放し一本で勝負する私にとっては、それこそが一番楽しくもあり、
苦心するところ」(『ル・コルビュジエの勇気ある住宅』新潮社、2004年)と解説する。それは当初
は、都心の閉じた箱の内部に、亀裂的な吹き抜けを核とした空間の魅力を集約することだった
が、やがて広大な敷地を得て変化する。全体を複数の箱に分け、機能を立体的に再構成しつ
つ、その場にふさわしい自然との対話を、空間的に再現してゆくこととなったのだ。都市に「垂
直に切り込む空間の力」が、大地を切り分けて「幾何学を通過する流れ」という新たな生命を
得たとき、狭い身体感覚を基盤とした安藤の発想は一気に拡大した。その意味で小篠邸は、後
の多くの作品を予言する再出発点だった。たとえば13年後に設計を開始したホンブロイッヒ美
術館の企画展示棟は、小篠邸と似ている。この作品が、近年のフォートワース現代美術館や兵
庫県立美術館へとつながってゆくのだ。

幾何学を通過する空間 ───4×4の住宅 (2003) ───

　2棟の近年の重要な住宅を見よう。1999年に設計が開始された見えない家 (2004)では「よ
り本質的な空間の是非が問われる(中略)地中の建築」の実現として、「外から内部の様子は
ほとんどうかがい知ることが出来ない」「完全なプライバシー」(『a+u』2002年3月号)が目指さ
れた。しかし同時に、内部は孤立せず「周辺環境と常に呼応しあう」ことも重視した。これらは、
単純な矩形平面を大地に沈み込ませつつ、それを通り抜ける空間を確保することで可能となっ
ている。

　4×4の住宅は「空中の立方体」という明晰な「幾何学の美」を誇る。しかし内部では「立
方体の内側」という主知的な空間美より以上に、海を直接に独り占めする、原始的で本能的な
喜びに圧倒される。幾何学によって、この敷地でのみ可能な「空間の贅沢」が、極小住宅ででき
る最大限まで引き出されているのだ。海まで続く広い敷地だが、幅は狭く、周辺環境も良好
ではない。しかし両側をほぼ無窓としたため、左右に迫る隣地は内部では意識されない。背後
の道路は交通量が多く、線路も目前だが、それも内部では消える。立方体の背面は、ほぼ上半
分だけを開いているからだ。内部では悪条件を後退させ、背後は空、前面は海へ向かう効果

4F

兵庫県立美術館
Hyogo Prefectural Museum of Art

Ando himself described Koshino House as a "house where I was made to be aware of three-dimensional space composition" and explained that "what I enjoy most and suffer most is how to compose the space three-dimensionally, especially because my material weapon is nothing but bare concrete walls (from *Ru Korubyujie no yuki aru jutaku*, Tokyo: Shincho-sha, 2004). And, for him, this at first meant to concentrate the magnetism of a space generated by a crevice-like stairwell inside a closed box in the center of the city. Later, his approach changed when he was given opportunities to build on greater plots, and he started to spatially represent conversations with nature, appropriate in each case, by recomposing functions three-dimensionally. Thus, Ando's concepts narrowly based on his own physical sensation suddenly expanded when the "spatial power to vertically carve into the city" was revived as "the currents that pass through geometry." In this sense, Koshino House was a harbinger of many of his later works; for example, the special exhibition space for Hombroich Museum, which Ando started to design thirteen years later, resembles Koshino House, and this work will lead to his later museums in Fort Worth and Kobe.

The Space that Passes Through Geometry: 4x4 House

Now, let us take a look at two significant houses. With the Invisible House (2004), whose design process started in 1999, Ando sought to realize a house of "perfect privacy" whose "internal situation could be little observed or imagined from outside" as a manifestation of "the under ground architecture where more fundamental issues of space are asked" (from *a+u*, March 2002). And yet, he also took care to have the interior not isolated and "always breathe together with the surroundings," which was made possible by burring a simple rectangle in the ground and keeping a space that runs through it.

4x4 House exemplifies a clear "geometric aesthetics" as a "cube in the air." However, "inside the cube" triggers more than intellectual appreciation of spatial aesthetics; it overwhelms us with the primitive and instinctual joy of directly monopolizing the ocean. Through geometry, Ando has maximized "spatial luxury," which is possible only at this particular site, with the minimal house. Its large plot leads to the ocean, but it is narrow in width, and the surroundings are not that good either. However, with small window openings on both of the side walls, one can be unaware of the neighboring sites, which are very close on both sides. The busy traffic on the backside and the train track in front also disappear once one is inside the house. This is because the only the upper half of the backside of the cube is opened. The house lets any undesirable conditions retire from the awareness of its residents and emphasizes the effect of the sky through the backside opening and the sea through the front. It is as if the house functions as a "tube," purifying the surrounding conditions into the "space that passes through a cube."

It is reported that the client of this house, when he saw the its design, felt that it "lacks typical Ando-ness." But, the starting point of Ando's thinking is to be found here in a condensed form. Certainly his works are unique, but they are far from what is normally called "the world of

だけを際立たせる。いわば「筒」の効果によって、周囲の状況を「立方体を通過する空間」へと純化しているのだ。

　施主はこの案を見て「安藤らしさが乏しい」と感じたというが、ここには彼の発想の原点が集約されている。確かに彼の作品は独自だが、普通にいう「個性的な世界」からは遠い。むしろ個人の狭い感覚的こだわりは徹底して排され、そのつど可能な極を、ぎりぎりに削ぎ落として示す。「純粋な幾何学」そのものでも「その場所の魅力の強調」でもなく、双方がもっとも純化したあり方で高め合う地点を探す中に、作者の存在は解消されてしまうという境地さえ垣間見えてくる。形態の純化と、場所の可能性の純化が重なるという意味で、幾何学は目的かつ手段なのである。そうした意味での「自在さ」が、裸になってこの住宅に集約されているのだ。

　しかし彼は、白紙の状態から「幾何学」だけを武器に空間を発想するのではない。少数の磨き抜かれた「幾何学と空間が重なった原型」によって敷地と語り合うのだ。それが単に「幾何学的」という以上の独自性をつくってきた。たとえば近年の美術館作品で目立つ、空中へ水面へと通過してゆく「開放的な筒型」が、極小の立方体と重なって4×4の住宅が生まれた。住吉の長屋で確認された原点が、小篠邸での拡大を経て、「筒」となり、浮上してここまで到達したのだ。

むすび　住宅が語るもの

　安藤はまず過密都市との闘いを通して、その狭い範囲での独自性を異例な極にまで到達させ、強固な創作の原点を得た。次いでそこからさまざまな異なる可能性をも取り込んで、独自性を自在に操ってゆく。身近なリアリティに根差し、それを保ちつつ、まったく異なる条件下でも応用できるものと化してゆく。それが「身体感覚から国際舞台へ」という過程に見える流れだ。

　数十年にわたって第一線で活躍する建築家は少ない。高度な作品を目指すほどに個人が可能とする発想の範囲は限られてくるからだ。ル・コルビュジエをはじめとして、長持ちした人々の多くは、作風を変えながら時代の動向に応じて行った。安藤が稀有なのは、30年以上の建築家生命を誇るという以上に、発想の基本を守りつつ、時代や規模や機能や敷地等の、巨大な変化に対応してきたことだ。そうしたやり方は、初期から今に到るまでの、住宅設計の持続によって可能となってきた。短期間で小規模の試みを実現する中で、さまざまな条件を超えた原点を確認しつつ、自在に操れる実践的な武器を磨いたのだ。だから住宅群は、本稿で見た「亀裂から筒型へ」という過程に代表されるような、彼の創作姿勢のもっとも具体的な流れを教えてくれる。

individuality." Rather, any narrow obsession with individual sensibility is thoroughly eliminated, and, in every case, possibilities are presented in the leanest manner. His works are not about "pure geometry" itself, nor "emphasis on the appeal of the site." They are an attempt to find a place where both of these can strengthen each other in the most purified way; a place where we can get a glimpse of the state in which the author's presence becomes null. Thus, geometry is both a goal and a means in the sense that purified forms and purified possibilities of a place can overlap each other. Such "freedom" is nakedly condensed in this house.

It is not that Ando conceive his space from tabula rasa with "geometry" as his only weapon. He communicates with sites via small number of sophisticated "prototypes in which geometry and space overlap," which made his architecture unique more than just "geometric." This 4x4 House was born when "open tubes," which pass in the air and through the water as seen in his recent museum buildings, overlaps with a minimal cube. The architect's starting point that was confirmed in Row House of Sumiyoshi has traveled this far to turn up here as a "tube," after expanding through the Koshino House.

Conclusion: What House Can Tell

Ando has established his creative origins, developing his narrow-bound originality to an extraordinary extreme through his fights against the dense city. Subsequently, he freely manipulated that originality by adopting various possibilities. Rooted in his familiar reality, he has managed to keep his originality while adapting it to totally different conditions. This is how we see his evolution "from the level of physical sensation to the global stage."

There are not many architects who remain active on the top level for decades. The higher level of works an architect purses, the more his or her domain of possible ideas can get limited. Such long-lived architects as Le Corbusier adapted themselves to world trends by changing their styles. What makes Ando rare is not only the fact that he's been active as an architect more than thirty years but the fact that he has responded to the great changes of the world in terms of times, scales, functions, and sites while preserving the basics of his thinking. This was possible as he kept designing houses from the beginning up to now. By realizing each of his small-scale experiments in a short period of time, Ando could verify his origins while overcoming various conditions, and he developed his practical weapons that are freely available to him. Studying his houses as we did in this essay, we can thus trace how the architect's creative stance has been developing, i.e. "from a crevice to a tube."

作品年表

1969-2008

Chronological Table of Projects

1969-72

1971
スワン商会ビル（小林邸）
"Swan" Kobayashi House

1973

冨島邸
Tomishima House

ゲリラ（加藤邸）
"Guerilla" Kato House

1974

立見邸
Tatsumi House

平岡邸
Hiraoka House

芝田邸
Shibata House

内田邸
Uchida House

宇野邸
Uno House

専用住宅／共同住宅／茶室
House, Housing and Tea House

海外作品
Outside Japan

商業建築／公共建築
Inside Japan

未完プロジェクト
Unbuild Project

完成作品は竣工年、未完プロジェクトは
設計開始年に従って配置しています。

1969
JR 大阪駅前プロジェクト
JR Osaka Station Area
Reconstruction Project

ポートアイランドプロジェクト
Port Island Project

1975

双生観（山口邸）
"Soseikan"
Yamaguchi House

高橋邸
Takahashi House

松村邸
Matsumura House

四軒長屋
Tenement House
with Four Flats

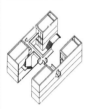

ツインウォール
Twin Wall

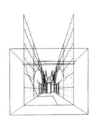

1976

住吉の長屋（東邸）
"Row House in Sumiyoshi"
Azuma House

貫入（平林邸）
"Interpenetration"
Hirabayashi House

番匠邸
Bansho House

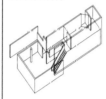

帝塚山タワープラザ
Tezukayama Tower Plaza

岡本ハウジング
Okamoto Housing Project

ローズガーデン
Rose Garden

北野アレイ
Kitano Alley

アートギャラリー
コンプレックス
Art Gallery Complex

甲東アレイ II
Koto Alley II

1977

領壁の家（松本邸）
"Wall House"
Matsumoto House

帝塚山の家（真鍋邸）
"Tezukayama House"
Manabe House

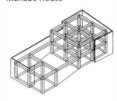

1978

大楠邸
Okusu House

ガラスブロックの家（石原邸）
"Glass Block House"
Ishihara House

甲東アレイ
Koto Alley

Sunny Garden
Sunny Garden

1979

ガラスブロックウォール
（堀内邸）
"Glass Block Wall"
Horiuchi House

片山ハウス
Katayama Building

大西邸
Onishi House

上田邸
Ueda House

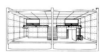

松谷邸
Matsutani House

1980

松本邸
Matsumoto House

福邸
Fuku House

北野アイビーコート
Kitano Ivy Court

大淀のアトリエ(1期)
Atelier in Oyodo (Phase I)

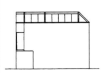

STEP
STEP

中之島プロジェクトI
(大阪市役所)
Nakanoshima Project I
(Osaka City Hall)

STEP II
STEP II

1981

番匠邸増築
Bansho House Addition

小篠邸
Koshino House

児島の共同住宅(佐藤邸)
"Kojima Housing"
Sato House

泉邸
Izumi House

リンズギャラリー
Rin's Gallery

ファッション・ライブ・シアター
Fashion Live Theater

1982

大淀のアトリエ(2期)
Atelier in Oyodo (Phase II)

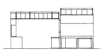

石井邸
Ishii House

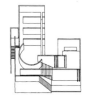

双生観の茶室(山口邸増築)
"Tea House for Soseikan"
Yamaguchi House Addition

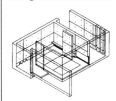

赤羽邸
Akabane House

九条の町屋(井筒邸)
"Town House in Kujo"
Izutsu House

ドールズハウス
Doll's House

サンプレイス
Sun Place

1983

梅宮邸
Umemiya House

六甲の集合住宅I
Rokko Housing I

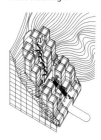

金子邸
Kaneko House

茂木邸
Motegi House

ビギ・アトリエ
BIGI Atelier

1984

植条邸
Uejo House

小篠邸増築
Koshino House Addition

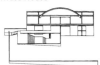

岩佐邸
Iwasa House

畑邸
Hata House

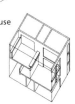

南林邸
Minamibayashi House

太田邸
Ota House

フェスティバル
Festival

TIME'S I
Time's I

心斎橋 TO
Shinsaibashi TO

MELROSE
MELROSE

1985

中山邸
Nakayama House

大淀の茶室（ベニヤの茶室）
Tea House in Oyodo
(Veneer Tea House)

服部邸ゲストハウス
Guest House
for Hattori House

吉本邸
Yoshimoto House

青葉台アトリエ
Aobadai Atelier

青山 TO
Aoyama TO

アトリエ・ヨシエ・イナバ
Atelier Yoshie Inaba

モン・プティ・シュ
Mon-petit-chou

ジュンポートアイランドビル
Jun Portisland Building

渋谷プロジェクト
Shibuya Project

1986

孫邸
Son House

大淀のアトリエ（3期）
Atelier in Oyodo (Phase Ⅲ)

細工谷の家（野口邸）
"Town House in Saikudani"
Noguchi House

佐々木邸
Sasaki House

TS ビル
TS Building

沖辺邸
Okibe House

城戸崎邸
Kidosaki House

大淀の茶室（ブロックの茶室）
Tea House in Oyodo
(Block Tea House)

六甲の教会
Chapel on Mt. Rokko

リランズ・ゲイト
Riran's Gate

北野 TO
Kitano TO

太陽セメント本社ビル
Taiyo Cement
Headquarters Building

OXY 北野
OXY Kitano

BIGI 3rd
BIGI 3rd

TK ビル
TK Building

ゲストハウス
OLD/NEW 六甲
Guest House
Old/New Rokko

福原病院
Fukuhara Clinic

渋谷神社総合開発計画
Shibuya Shrine
Redevelopment Project

1987

田中山荘
Tanaka Atelier

Ⅰ 計画
Ⅰ Project

神宮前のアトリエ
Atelier, Jingumae

天王寺博覧会テーマ館
Main Pavilion
for Tennoji Fair

OXY 鰻谷
OXY Unagidani

伊豆プロジェクト
Izu Project

水の劇場
Theater on the Water

六甲山バンケットホール
Banquet Hall on Mt. Rokko

1988

小倉邸
Ogura House

吉田邸
Yoshida House

B-Lock 神楽岡
B-Lock, Kaguraoka

大淀の茶室（テントの茶室）
Tea House in Oyodo
(Tent Tea House)

Ⅰ ハウス
Ⅰ House

唐座
Karaza

GALLERIA [akka]
GALLERIA [akka]

水の教会
Church on the Water

中之島プロジェクトⅡ
（アーバン・エッグ＋地層空間）
Nakanoshima Project Ⅱ
(Urban Egg + Space Strata)

伊藤ギャラリー
Ito Gallery

1989

城尾邸
Shiroo House

横浜ハウジング
Yokohama Housing

光の教会
Church of the Light

モロゾフ P&P スタジオ
Morozoff P&P Studio

兵庫県立こどもの館
Children's Museum, Hyogo

COLLEZIONE
COLLEZIONE

夏川記念館
Natsukawa Memorial Hall

ライカ本社ビル
Raika Headquarters
Building

矢尾クリニック
Yao Clinic

1990

松谷邸増築
Matsutani House Addition

岩佐邸増築
Iwasa House Addition

伊東邸
Ito House

ストックホルム
現代美術館・建築美術館
国際設計競技案
The Modern Art Museum
and Architecture Museum,
Stockholm, International
Design Competition

B-Lock 北山
B-Lock Kitayama

国際花と緑の博覧会
「名画の庭」
Garden of Fine Art,
Expo'90 / Osaka

十文字美信設仮設劇場
Temporary Theater for
Bishin Jumonji,
Photographer

S ビル
S Building

JR 京都駅改築設計競技案
The Reconstruction of
JR Kyoto Station,
International Design
Competition

1991

大淀のアトリエⅡ
Atelier in Oyodo Ⅱ

石河邸
Ishiko House

佐用ハウジング
Sayoh Housing

ミノルタセミナーハウス
Minolta Seminar House

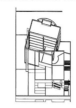

姫路文学館
Museum of Literature,
Himeji

ロックフィールド
静岡ファクトリー
Rock Field Shizuoka Factory

播磨ヘリポート
Harima Heliport

真言宗本福寺水御堂
Water Temple

TIME'S Ⅱ
TIME'S Ⅱ

甲南大学
スチューデントサークル
プロジェクト
Konan University
Student Circle Project

奈良市民ホール
国際設計競技案
Nara Convention Hall
International Design
Competition

1992

宮下邸
Miyashita House

1992年セビリア万国博覧会
日本館
Japan Pavilion
Expo'92 / Sevilla

シカゴ美術館
屏風ギャラリー
Gallery for Japanese Screen,
the Art Institute of Chicago

大手前女子大学
アートセンター
Otemae Art Center

熊本県立装飾古墳館
Forest of Tombs Museum,
Kumamoto

ベネッセハウス ミュージアム
Benesse House
Museum / Naoshima

姫路市立星の子館
Children's Seminar House,
Himeji

1993

ギャラリー野田
Gallery Noda

YKK 津田沼寮
YKK Seminar House

六甲の集合住宅Ⅱ
Rokko Housing Ⅱ

李邸
Lee House

ヴィトラセミナーハウス
Vitra Seminar House

兵庫県立看護大学
College of Nursing,
Art and Science, Hyogo

垂水の教会
Church in Tarumi

六甲アイランドプロジェクト
Rokko Island Project

1994

日本橋の家（金森邸）
"House in Nipponbashi"
Kanamori House

テートギャラリー
現代美術館国際設計競技案
Tate Gallery of Modern Art,
International Design
Competition

大阪府立近つ飛鳥博物館
Chikatsu-Asuka
Historical Museum, Osaka

京都府立陶板名画の庭
Garden of Fine Art, Kyoto

兵庫県立木の殿堂
Museum of Wood

サントリーミュージアム
＋マーメイド広場
Suntory Museum + Plaza

紀陽銀行堺ビル
Kiyo Bank, Sakai Building

マックスレイ本社ビル
Maxray Headquarters
Building

鹿児島大学稲盛会館
Inamori Auditorium

成羽町美術館
Nariwa Museum

1995

大淀のアトリエ・アネックス
Atelier in Oyodo Annex

海の集合住宅プロジェクト
Seaside Housing Project

丘の集合住宅プロジェクト
Hilltop Housing Project

ユネスコ瞑想空間
Meditation Space, UNESCO

ローマ司教区教会
国際設計競技案
Vicariato di Roma,
International Competition
for the Church of
the Year 2000

播磨高原東小学校
Harima Kogen
Higashi Primary School

綾部工業団地交流プラザ
Ayabe Community Center

市立五條文化博物館
Museum of Gojo Culture

ベネッセハウス オーバル／
Benesse House Oval /
Naoshima

大山崎山荘美術館
Oyamazaki Villa Museum

宇ノ気町立金津小学校
Kanatsu Primary School,
Unoke

長良川国際会議場
Nagaragawa
Convention Center

大谷地下劇場計画
The Theater in the Rock, Oya

1996

白井邸
Shirai House

ギャラリー小さい芽（澤田邸）
"Gallery Chiisaime"
Sawada House

平野区の町屋（能見邸）
"Town House in Hirano"
Nomi House

マンハッタンのペントハウス
Penthouse in Manhattan

スタジオ・
カール・ラガーフェルド
Studio Karl Lagerfeld

上海釜山航路
フェリーターミナル
Shanghai Pusan
Ferry Terminal

姫路文学館南館
Museum of Literature II,
Himeji

1997

青木の集合住宅
Ohgi Housing

八木邸
Yagi House

シカゴの住宅
House in Chicago

モンテンルパ
社会復帰センター
Muntilupa
Resocialization Center

ライン世界文化博物館
The Museum of
World Cultures
on the River Rhine

播磨高原東中学校
Harima Kogen Higashi
Junior High School

小海高原美術館
Koumi Kogen Museum

越知町立
横倉山自然の森博物館—
横倉山・牧野富太郎展示室
The Yokogurayama
Natural Forest Museum,
Ochi

TOTO セミナーハウス
TOTO Seminar House

1998

ネパール了供病院
Shiddhartha Children
and Women Hospital

渡辺淳一文学館
Junichi Watanabe
Memorial Hall

ダイコク電機本部ビル
Daikoku Denki
Headquarters Building

織田廣喜ミュージアム
Daylight Museum

朝日新聞岡山支局
Asahi News Paper
Okayama Bureau

エリエール松山ゲストハウス
Elleair Matsuyama
Guesthouse

1999

六甲の集合住宅Ⅲ
Rokko Housing Ⅲ

ネルソン・アトキンス美術館
国際設計競技案
Nelson Atkins Museum,
International
Design Competition

レイナ・ソフィア美術館
国際設計競技案
Museo Nacional Centro de
Arte Reina Sofia,
International
Design Competition

パリ原始博物館
国際設計競技案
Musée du Quai Branly,
International
Design Competition

アントワープ市立博物館
国際設計競技案
Museum Aan de Stroom,
Antwerp, International
Design Competition

セントポール寺院聖台
デザインコンペティション
A New Font for St. Paul's
Cathedral, International
Design Competition

光の教会／日曜学校
Church of the Light,
Sunday School

南寺（直島・家プロジェクト）
Minami Dera (Art House
Project in Naoshima)

西宮市貝類館
Shell Museum
of Nishinomiya City

淡路夢舞台
Awaji-Yumebutai
(Awaji Island Project)

2000

ダラスの住宅
House in Dallas

FABRICA
（ベネトンアートスクール）
FABRICA
(Benetton Communication
Research Center)

カルダー美術館
Calder Museum

BOSCH セミナーハウス
国際設計競技案
BOSCH Sminar House,
International
Design Competition

セント・ジョーンズ・
セミナーハウス
St. John's Abbey
Seminar House

ロックフィールド
静岡ファクトリー
（Ⅱ期増築＋ランドスケープ）
Rock Field Shizuoka
Factory Study Center

南岳山光明寺
Komyo-ji Temple

ミュぜふくおかカメラ館
Fukuoka Camera Museum

新潟市立豊栄図書館
Toyosaka City Library

2001

神宮前の集合住宅
Jingumae Housing

4×4の住宅（東京）
4x4 House (Tokyo)

ピューリッツァー美術館
Pulitzer Foundation
for the Arts

アルマーニ・テアトロ
Armani / Teatro

グラウンド・ゼロ
プロジェクト
Ground Zero Project

ピノー現代美術館
François Pinault Foundation
for Contemporary Art

クラーク美術館
Clark Art Institute
Expansion Project

大阪府立狭山池博物館
Sayamaike Historical
Museum, Osaka

神戸市水際広場
Kobe Waterfront Plaza

兵庫県立美術館
Hyogo Prefectural
Museum of Art

国際芸術センター青森
Aomori Contemporary
Art Center

司馬遼太郎記念館
Shiba Ryotaro
Memorial Museum

宝塚温泉
Takarazuka Onsen (Spa)

四国村ギャラリー
Shikokumura Gallery

2002

マンチェスター市ピカデリー公園
Piccadilly Gardens
Regeneration, Manchester

フォートワース現代美術館
Modern Art Museum
of Fort Worth

灘浜ガーデンバーデン
Nadahama Garden Baden

国際子ども図書館
The International Library
of Children's Literature

アウディジャパン本社ビル
Audi Japan Headquarters

西田幾太郎記念哲学館
Nishida Kitaro Museum
of Philosophy

コキュオフィスビル
COCUE Office Building

アサヒビール神奈川工場
ゲストハウス
Guesthouse,
Asahi Kanagawa Brewery

尾道市立美術館
Onomichi City Museum
of Art

加賀市立錦城中学校
Kinjo Junior High School,
Kaga

2003

4×4の住宅
4x4 House

西麻布の集合住宅
Nishiazabu Housing

マリブの住宅
House in Malibu

一戸南小学校
Minami Primary School,
Ichinohe

野間自由幼稚園
Noma Kindergarten

ロックフィールド
玉川ファクトリー
Rock Field
Tamagawa Factory

2004

見えない家
Invisible House

仙川プロジェクトⅠ
Sengawa Project Ⅰ

仙川プロジェクトⅢ
Sengawa Project Ⅲ

ゴールデン・ゲート・
ブリッジの住宅
Golden Gate Bridge House

ホンブロイッヒ／ランゲン
美術館
Langen Foundation /
Hombroich

ICED TIME TUNNEL /
The Snow Show 2004
ICED TIME TUNNEL /
The Snow Show 2004

加子母村ふれあい
コミュニティセンター
Kashimo-mura
Community Center

地中美術館
Chichu Art Museum /
Naoshima

県立ぐんま昆虫の森
昆虫観察館
Gunma Insect World
Insect Observation Hall

絵本美術館
まどのそとのそのまたむこう
Iwaki Museum of
Picture Books for Children

仙川プロジェクトⅡ
Sengawa Project Ⅱ

2005

高槻の住宅
House in Takatsuki

テアトリーノ
Teatrino

ロックフィールド
神戸ヘッドオフィス／
神戸ファクトリー
Rock Field
Kobe Headquarters /
Kobe Factory

hhstyle.com/casa
hhstyle.com/casa

2006

滋賀の住宅
House in Shiga

表参道ヒルズ
（同潤会青山アパート建替計画）
Omotesando Hills
(Omotesando
Regeneration
Project)

パラッツォ・グラッシ
Palazzo Grassi Renovation

アブダビ海洋博物館
Abu Dhabi Maritime
Museum

さくら広場
Sakura Hiroba

さくら広場（門真）
Sakura Hiroba (Kadoma)

ベネッセハウス
＜ビーチ＞＜パーク＞
Benesse House / Beach,
Park

坂の上の雲ミュージアム
Saka no Ue no Kumo
Museum

2007

仙川プロジェクトV
Sengawa Project V

深井邸
Fukai House

回遊式住宅
Walk-around House

21_21デザインサイト
21_21 Design Sight

竜王駅
Ryuo Station (JR-Line)

仙川プロジェクトIV
Sengawa Project IV

曹洞宗太岳院
Taigakuin Temple

2008 竣工予定

仙川プロジェクトVI
Sengawa Project VI

東急東横線渋谷駅
Shibuya Station (Tokyu Toyoko Line)

東京大学情報学環・福武ホール
Fukutake Hall, the University of Tokyo

作品データ［掲載順］ Projects Data

見えない家
Invisible House

①イタリア トレヴィゾ／ Treviso, Italy
②住宅／ House
③1999.6-2001.12
④2002.2-04.5
⑤30,600m²
⑦1,350m²（住宅本棟／ main house）、
　100m²（ゲート守衛棟／ guard house）
⑧地下2階 地上1階（住宅本棟）、
　地上1階（ゲート守衛棟）／
　2 basement 1 story (main house)、
　1 story (guard house)
⑨鉄筋コンクリート造／ Reinforced Concrete
⑩『GA Houses』63 83、『a+u』2002.3、
　『新建築』2005.3

シカゴの住宅
House in Chicago

①アメリカ合衆国 イリノイ州 シカゴ／ Chicago,
　Illinois,U.S.A.
②住宅／ House
③1992.5-94.12
④1993.12-97.12
⑤1,395m²
⑥403m²
⑦835m²
⑧地下1階 地上3階／ 1 basement 3 stories
⑨鉄筋コンクリート造／ Reinforced Concrete
⑩『GA Houses』45 57、
　『a+u』1998.11 2002.3

マンハッタンのペントハウス
Penthouse in Manhattan

①アメリカ合衆国 ニューヨーク州 ニューヨーク／
　New York, New York, U.S.A.
②住宅／ House
③1996-
⑦712m²
⑨鉄筋コンクリート造＋鉄骨造／
　Reinforced Concrete+Steel Frame
⑩『GA Houses』59、『SD』2000.10、
　『a+u』2002.3

谷間の家
Crevice House in Manhattan

①アメリカ合衆国 ニューヨーク州 ニューヨーク／
　New York, New York, U.S.A.
②住宅＋ギャラリー／ House & Gallery
③2006.9-
⑦317m²
⑨鉄筋コンクリート造／ Reinforced Concrete

マリブの住宅
House in Malibu

①アメリカ合衆国 カリフォルニア州 マリブ／
　Malibu, California, U.S.A.
②住宅／ House
③2003-
⑥20.5m²
⑦411.9m²
⑨鉄筋コンクリート造＋鉄骨造／
　Reinforced Concrete+Steel Frame
⑩『GA Houses』80

ゴールデン・ゲート・ブリッジの住宅
Golden Gate Bridge House

①アメリカ合衆国 カリフォルニア州 サンフランシスコ
　／ San Francisco, California, U.S.A.
②住宅／ House
③2004-
⑥1,200m²
⑦1,050m²
⑨鉄筋コンクリート造／ Reinforced Concrete
⑩『GA Houses』86

住吉の長屋（東邸）
"Row House in Sumiyoshi" Azuma House

①大阪府大阪市／ Osaka, Osaka
②住宅／ House
③1975.1-75.8
④1975.10-76.2
⑤57.3m²
⑥33.7m²
⑦64.7m²
⑧地上2階／ 2 stories
⑨鉄筋コンクリート造／ Reinforced Concrete
⑩『新建築』1977.2、『建築文化』1977.2
　1980.2、『都市住宅』1977.2 1984.7、
　『GA Houses』4、『SD』1981.6

冨島邸
Tomishima House

①大阪府大阪市／ Osaka, Osaka
②住宅／ House
③1971.1-71.11
④1972.2-73.2
⑤55.2m²
⑥36.2m²
⑦72.4m²
⑧地上2階／ 2 stories
⑨鉄筋コンクリート造／ Reinforced Concrete
⑩『都市住宅』1973.7、『SD』1981.6

大淀のアトリエ II
Atelier in Oyodo II

①大阪府大阪市／ Osaka, Osaka
②アトリエ／ Atelier
③1989.6-90.5
④1990.6-91.4
⑤115.6m²
⑥91.7m²
⑦451.7m²
⑧地下1階 地上5階／ 1 basement 5 stories
⑨鉄筋コンクリート造／ Reinforced Concrete

大淀のアトリエ・アネックス
Atelier in Oyodo Annex

①大阪府大阪市／ Osaka, Osaka
②アトリエ／ Atelier
③1994.1-94.4
④1994.4-95.3
⑤182.8m²
⑥104.3m²
⑦247.4m²
⑧地下1階 地上3階／ 1 basement 3 stories
⑨鉄筋コンクリート造／ Reinforced Concrete
⑩『住宅特集』1997.12

小篠邸
Koshino House

①兵庫県芦屋市／ Ashiya, Hyogo
②住宅／ House
③1979.9-80.4
④1980.7-81.3
⑤1,141m²
⑥224m²
⑦231.4m²
⑧地上2階／ 2 stories
⑨鉄筋コンクリート造／ Reinforced Concrete
⑩『新建築』1981.6、『SD』1981.6、
　『都市住宅』1985.11、『GA Houses』14

小篠邸増築
Koshino House Addition

①兵庫県芦屋市／ Ashiya, Hyogo
②アトリエ／ Atelier
③1983.1-83.6
④1983.11-84.3
⑤1,141m²
⑥52.7m²
⑦52.7m²
⑧地上1階／ 1 story
⑨鉄筋コンクリート造／ Reinforced Concrete
⑩『住宅特集』1985夏

小篠邸ゲストハウス
Guest House for Koshino House

①兵庫県芦屋市／Ashiya, Hyogo
②住宅／House
③2004.10-05.5
④2005.6-06.5
⑤1,141.2m²
⑥125.4m²
⑦250.8m²
⑧地上2階／2 stories
⑨鉄筋コンクリート造／Reinforced Concrete
⑩『GA Houses』94

中山邸
Nakayama House

①奈良県奈良市／Nara, Nara
②住宅／House
③1983.6-84.7
④1984.10-85.4
⑤263.3m²
⑥69.1m²
⑦103.7m²
⑧地上2階／2 stories
⑨鉄筋コンクリート造／Reinforced Concrete
⑩『GA Houses』20、『住宅特集』1985夏

城戸崎邸
Kidosaki House

①東京都世田谷区／Setagaya-ku, Tokyo
②住宅／House
③1982.10-85.10
④1985.10-86.10
⑤610.9m²
⑥351.5m²
⑦556.1m²
⑧地上3階／3 stories
⑨鉄筋コンクリート造／Reinforced Concrete
⑩『住宅特集』1987.10、『建築文化』1987.10
　1988.5、『SD』1989.9

李邸
Lee House

①千葉県船橋市／Funabashi, Chiba
②住宅／House
③1991.7-92.6
④1992.7-93.7
⑤484.1m²
⑥174.8m²
⑦264.8m²
⑧地上3階／3 stories
⑨鉄筋コンクリート造／Reinforced Concrete

平野区の町屋（能見邸）
"Town House in Hirano" Nomi House

①大阪府大阪市／Osaka, Osaka
②住宅／House
③1995.2-95.12
④1996.1-96.8
⑤120.5m²
⑥72.1m²
⑦92.1m²
⑧地上2階／2 stories
⑨鉄筋コンクリート造／Reinforced Concrete
⑩『住宅特集』1997.12、『GA Houses』48、
　『GA Japan』27

滋賀の住宅
House in Shiga

①滋賀県大津市／Otsu, Shiga
②住宅／House
③2004.1-05.5
④2005.8-06.5
⑤598.5m²
⑥225.5m²
⑦312.5m²
⑧地上2階／2 stories
⑨鉄筋コンクリート造／Reinforced Concrete

4×4の住宅
4x4 House

①兵庫県神戸市／Kobe, Hyogo
②住宅／House
③2001.4-02.4
④2002.8-03.3
⑤65.4m²
⑥22.6m²
⑦117.8m²
⑧地下1階 地上4階／1 basement 4 stories
⑨鉄筋コンクリート造／Reinforced Concrete
⑩『GA Houses』74、『住宅特集』2003.6、
　『GA Japan』62

六甲の集合住宅I
Rokko Housing I

①兵庫県神戸市／Kobe, Hyogo
②共同住宅／Housing
③1978.10-81.10
④1981.10-83.5
⑤1,852m²
⑥668m²
⑦1,779m²
⑧地上10階／10 stories
⑨鉄筋コンクリート造／Reinforced Concrete
⑩掲載誌／『SD』1982.12 1989.9、
　『新建築』1983.10、『建築文化』1983.10

六甲の集合住宅II
Rokko Housing II

①兵庫県神戸市／Kobe, Hyogo
②共同住宅／Housing
③1985.8-87.4
④1989.10-93.5
⑤5,998.1m²
⑥2,964.7m²
⑦9,043.6m²
⑧地上14階／14 stories
⑨鉄筋コンクリート造／Reinforced Concrete
⑩『住宅特集』1987.5、『建築文化』1987.10、
　『SD』1989.9、『新建築』1991.9 1993.10、
　『GA Houses』39、『GA Japan』5

六甲の集合住宅III
Rokko Housing III

①兵庫県神戸市／Kobe, Hyogo
②共同住宅／Housing
③1992.9-97.10
④1997.11-99.2
⑤11,717.2m²
⑥6,544.5m²
⑦24,221.5m²
⑧地上11階／11 stories
⑨鉄筋コンクリート造／Reinforced Concrete
⑩『SD』1992.6、『新建築』1995.10
　1999.9、『GA Japan』40

凡例／legend

①所在／location
②用途／principal use
③設計期間／design period
④施工期間／construction period
⑤敷地面積／site area
⑥建築面積／built area
⑦延床面積／total floor area
⑧規模／scale in building
⑨主体構造／structure
⑩掲載誌

略歴 Profiles
安藤忠雄 Tadao Ando

略歴	1941	● 大阪に生まれる
	1962-69	● 独学で建築を学ぶ
	1969	● 安藤忠雄建築研究所を設立
受賞	1979	●「住吉の長屋」で昭和54年度日本建築学会賞
	1985	● フィンランド建築家協会から、国際的な建築賞 アルヴァ・アアルト賞（第5回）
	1989	● 1989年度フランス建築アカデミー大賞（ゴールドメダル）
	1993	● 日本芸術院賞
	1995	● 1995年度プリツカー賞
	1996	● 高松宮殿下記念世界文化賞
	2002	● 2002年度アメリカ建築家協会（AIA）ゴールドメダル
		● ローマ大学名誉博士号
		● 同済大学（上海）名誉教授
		● 京都賞
	2003	● 文化功労者
	2005	● 国際建築家連合（UIA）ゴールドメダル
名誉会員	2002	● イギリス ロイヤルアカデミー オブ アーツ名誉会員
教職	1987	● イェール大学客員教授
	1988	● コロンビア大学客員教授
	1990	● ハーバード大学客員教授
	1997-	● 東京大学教授
	2003-	● 東京大学名誉教授
	2005	● 東京大学特別栄誉教授
		● カリフォルニア大学バークレー校客員教授
主な作品	1983	● 六甲の集合住宅Ⅰ（兵庫 神戸）
	1989	● 光の教会（大阪 茨木）
	1992	● ベネッセハウス ミュージアム（香川 直島）
	1993	● 六甲の集合住宅Ⅱ（兵庫 神戸）
	1994	● 大阪府立近つ飛鳥博物館（大阪 河南）
	1995	● ベネッセハウス オーバル（香川 直島）
	1999	● 六甲の集合住宅Ⅲ（兵庫 神戸）
	2000	● 淡路夢舞台（兵庫 東浦）
		● 南岳山光明寺（愛媛 西条）
		● FABRICA（ベネトンアートスクール）（イタリア トレヴィソ）
	2001	● ピューリッツァー美術館（アメリカ セントルイス）
		● アルマーニ・テアトロ（イタリア ミラノ）
		● 大阪府立狭山池博物館（大阪 大阪狭山）
	2002	● 兵庫県立美術館（兵庫 神戸）
		● 国際子ども図書館（東京 台東）
		● フォートワース現代美術館（アメリカ フォートワース）
	2003	● 4×4の住宅（兵庫 神戸）
	2004	● 地中美術館（香川 直島）
		● ホンブロイッヒ／ランゲン美術館（ドイツ ノイス）
	2006	● 同潤会青山アパート建替計画（表参道ヒルズ）（東京 渋谷）
		● パラッツォ・グラッシ再生計画（イタリア ヴェネツィア）

Profile

1941	● Born in Osaka, Japan
1962-69	● Self-educated in architecture
1969	● Established Tadao Ando Architect & Associates

Awards

1979	● Annual Prize, Architectural Institute of Japan "Row House in Sumiyoshi"
1985	● The 5th Alvar Aalto Medal, The Finnish Association of Architects, Finland
1989	● Gold Medal of Architecture, Académie d'Architecture (French Academy of Architecture), France
1993	● Japan Art Academy Prize, Japan
1995	● The Pritzker Architecture Prize, U.S.A.
1996	● The 8th Premium Imperiale
2002	● Gold Medal of the American Institute of Architects, U.S.A.
	● Honorary Degree, Università Degli Studi di Roma, Italy
	● Honorary Degree, Tongji University, Shanghai, China
	● The Kyoto Prizes, Japan
2003	● Person of Cultural Merit, Japan
2005	● Gold Medal of Union Internationale des Architectes

Affiliations

2002	● Honorary Academician, The Royal Academy of Arts in London

Academic Activities

1987	● Visiting Professor, Yale University
1988	● Visiting Professor, Columbia University
1990	● Visiting Professor, Harvard University
1997-	● Professor, The University of Tokyo
2003-	● Emeritus Professor, The University of Tokyo
2005	● Special University Professor Emeritus, The University of Tokyo
	● Regent Professor, University of California, Berkeley

Representative Works

1983	● Rokko Housing I, Kobe, Hyogo
1989	● Church of the Light, Ibaraki, Osaka
1992	● Benesse House Museum, Naoshima, Kagawa
1993	● Rokko Housing II, Kobe, Hyogo
1994	● Chikatsu-Asuka Historical Museum, Kanan, Osaka
1995	● Benesse House Oval, Naoshima, Kagawa
1999	● Rokko Housing III, Kobe, Hyogo
2000	● Awaji-Yumebutai (Awaji Island Project), Higashiura, Hyogo
	● Komyo-ji Temple, Saijo, Ehime
	● FABRICA (Benetton Communications Research Center), Treviso, Italy
2001	● Pulitzer Foundation for the Arts, St. Louis, U.S.A.
	● ARMANI / TEATRO, Milan, Italy
	● Sayamaike Historical Museum, Osaka-Sayama, Osaka
2002	● Hyogo Prefectural Museum of Art, Kobe, Hyogo
	● The International Library of Children's Literature, Taito, Tokyo
	● Modern Art Museum of Fort Worth, Fort Worth, U.S.A.
2003	● 4×4 House, Kobe, Hyogo
2004	● Chichu Art Museum / Naoshima, Naoshima, Kagawa
	● Langen Foundation / Hombroich Museum, Neuss, Germany
2006	● Omotesando Hills (Omotesando Regeneration Project), Shibuya, Tokyo
	● Palazzo Grassi Renovation, Venice, Italy

クレジット　Credits

安藤忠雄の建築 1

Tadao Ando 1
Houses & Housing

2007年3月30日　初版　第1刷発行
2019年7月30日　初版　第5刷発行

著者-------------安藤忠雄

発行者-----------伊藤剛士

発行所----------TOTO出版
（TOTO株式会社）

〒107-0062　東京都港区南青山1-24-3
TOTO乃木坂ビル2F
[営業] tel：03(3402)7138
　　　　fax：03(3402)7187
[編集] tel：03(3497)1010
URL：https://jp.toto.com/publishing

デザイン----------太田徹也

プリンティング
ディレクション-------高栁 昇

印刷・製本-------株式会社東京印書館